WHITE
BANNERS

SUNY series in Medieval Middle East History
Jere Bacharach, Editor

WHITE BANNERS

Contention in 'Abbāsid Syria, 750–880

PAUL M. COBB

State University of New York Press

Published by
State University of New York Press, Albany

Printed in the United States of America

For information, address State University of New York Press, 90 State Street, Suite 700, Albany, N.Y. 12207

Production by Diane Ganeles
Marketing by Michael Campochiaro

Library of Congress Cataloging-in-Publication Data

Cobb, Paul M., 1967–
White banners : contention in ʿAbbāsid Syria, 750–880 / Paul M. Cobb.
p. cm. — (SUNY series in medieval Middle East history)
Includes bibliography ( ) and indexes.
ISBN 0-7914-4879-7 (alk. paper)—ISBN 0-7914-4880-0 (pbk. : alk. paper)
1. Syria—History—750-1260. 2. Abbasids. I. Title. II. Series.

DS97.3 .C63 2001
956.91'02-dc21 00-030080

10 9 8 7 6 5 4 3 2 1

For my parents

Contents

Acknowledgments

The last task of writing a book is the happiest of all: thanking (without implicating) the many people and institutions who were instrumental in its shaping. This book began as a University of Chicago dissertation. In light of the substantial changes wrought on it to produce the present work, that dissertation should now be considered superseded. In it, I acknowledged a long list of people for their help on that phase of this project, and many of them helped to bring this phase to fruition too. From the very beginning to the very end my committee members, Fred M. Donner, Wadād al-Qāḍī, and Walter E. Kaegi, have provided priceless critical advice and encouragement. Fred Donner was an exceptional teacher and mentor: a master of enjoining the right and forbidding the wrong, that burden of believers, rebels, and graduate advisers. Also at Chicago, help and inspiration at critical junctures came from Paul Wheatley, Donald Whitcomb, and John Woods. Even after I had left the nest, the faculty and staff of the Oriental Institute and of the Center for Middle Eastern Studies have been generous with their time and expertise. Particular thanks go to Charles Jones of the Research Archives of the Oriental Institute, and to Bruce Craig of the Middle East department of the Joseph Regenstein Library. Mr. Muhannad Salhi of that department provided eleventh-hour bibliographical help. This study could hardly have been conceived anywhere but at Chicago. If it still betrays its origins, I will be gratified.

I would like to thank Jere Bacharach for so meaningfully encouraging the study and writing of medieval Islamic history by editing this series. SUNY Press and its editors Zina Lawrence, Michael Rinella, and Diane Ganeles have been models of patience and skill. The map of 'Abbāsid Syria was prepared by Ms. Ingrid Villa-Real Alonso of the Department of Art, Art History and Design at the University of Notre Dame, and, along with the indices, was generously funded by Notre Dame's Institute for the Study of the Liberal Arts. Permission to produce the cover illustration of the ivory figure from early Islamic Humeima was kindly granted by the site's excavator, John Oleson of the University of Victoria.

My international scholarly debts are hard to repay. I would like to thank Prof. Iḥsān 'Abbās of the University of Jordan for being willing to give up a peaceful afternoon to discuss my project and the perils of Ibn 'Asākir. In Damascus, Najda al-Khammāsh, Stefan Leder, and Bernadette Martel-Thoumain provided me with hospitality and essential tips. The Institut Français des Études Arabes in Damascus was an intellectual—and (briefly) physical—home during my stay. The Institut's librarian, M. Olivier Dubois, was a valuable help in finding my way. The efficient staff of the Maktabat al-Asad in Damascus were paragons of openness and understanding.

Others provided citations, alerts, and ready responses to queries, among them: Jere Bacharach, Michael Bonner, C. E. Bosworth, Lawrence Conrad, Amikam Elad, Peter Golden, Matthew Gordon, Alexandrine Guérin, and the daunting intellectual collective called H-Mideast-Medieval. James Lindsay, an expert on all things 'Asākirid, encouraged another young fool to attempt to tackle the goldmine that is the TMD. Patricia Crone generously shared her notes on Syrian careers with me and shaped this book in innumerable ways.

This book was begun while I was employed in the Department of History at Wake Forest University, where the William C. Archie Fund provided financial assistance at an early stage. I would like to thank my colleagues at Wake Forest for recognizing the value of Middle Eastern history. I am fortunate that my current colleagues in the Department of History and at the Medieval Institute of the University of Notre Dame are equally enlightened and supportive. A cavalcade of fabulous students at Smith College, Wake Forest, and Notre Dame have smiled and nodded through many of the ideas in this book, and so deserve no small thanks.

I was fortunate enough to have many friends and relatives for support along the way. Among them are Sharon Albert, Golfo Alexopoulos, Sandra Campbell, Elvira, Alex, Lucy and Angus Donner, Don-John Dugas, Benjamin Fortna, Robert and Roseanne Harteker, Nat Herold, John Iskander, Peter Kapper, Marion Katz, Kate Lang, Eric Nakajima, Monica Sanning, Warren Schultz, Mark Stein, Jake Viebrock, Terry Wilfong, John Williams, Peter Wissoker, and Sara Wolper. In Syria, I would still be in IFEAD's library without the intervention of Katia Boudoyan, Iyad Charchar, Rebecca Foote, Franck Fries, and especially Charif Kiwan, the most politic notable I know. John Meloy and Clare Leader provided unparalleled hospitality and good cheer in Egypt, Chicago, and all points in between: I highly recommend them. My family—all of it—has been supportive of me from the beginning. My parents, Justin and Patricia Cobb, opened my first book for me and have continued to support my dubious endeavors. I have dedicated this book to them.

Finally, pride of place in this long list belongs to L. M. Harteker, my prime contender, who walked this project into daylight in Hyde Park, Northampton, Winston-Salem, and South Bend, and who destroyed it and showed me how to rebuild it. If there is any good history or any good writing in this book, it is hers.

A Note on Transliteration, Place Names, and Dates

I have employed the system of the transliteration of Arabic used in the *International Journal of Middle East Studies*. For the details of this system, I refer the curious reader to the chart provided in the back of any issue of that journal. My only innovation is that, for the sake of clarity, I have not indicated elision (thus, *bi-ism-Allāh,* not *bi'smi'llāh* or the like). In the rare cases where I have transliterated from other languages, I have followed the systems employed by the Library of Congress. Since this study is intended largely for Islamicists, when I have cited sources in Syriac or Greek I have also (when possible) cited the translations of these works into modern European languages. In such cases, the original text citation and the translation citation are separated by a slash.

Place names have been transliterated according to the same system. The exceptions are those places that are familiar to readers by other equivalents, and also some that aren't, but should be (e.g., Mecca, not Makka; Samarra, not Samārrā'). Likewise, I have chosen to use the conventional term "Syria" throughout this book to designate the 'Abbāsid province of al-Shām, despite the confusion it could produce with the contemporary nation state of the Arab Republic of Syria. "Syria," as used in this book, refers to geographic Syria, a region embracing the entire area south of the Taurus Mountains between the eastern shore of the Mediterranean and the Euphrates, a region currently including the states of Syria, Lebanon, Jordan, and the lands controlled by Israel and the Palestinian Authority.

The *ajnād* (or subdistricts) of early Islamic Syria are a special case. Because the names of these districts are often identical with the names of their capital cities, it is difficult to tell in the original sources where events are precisely localized. Usually, only context can tell. Where this context exists, I have distinguished between district and capital city by rendering the latter by their common English equivalents (e.g., Homs is the capital of the district of Ḥimṣ, Damascus of Dimashq, and Qinnasrin, for a time, of Qinnasrīn). To avoid confusion with modern nation states, the districts of al-Urdunn and Filastīn have been rendered as such and not as "Jordan" or "Palestine." I have used "b." and "bt." throughout to indicate *ibn* and *bint* (son/daughter of) in Arabic personal names.

Following common practice, I have rendered dates according to the Muslim calendar (AH or *Anno Hegirae*) and the Common Era (CE), separated by a slash. Thus, 132/750 is the year 132 of the Muslim calendar and the year 750 of the Common Era.

Abbreviations

'Abbās, *Bilād al-shām*	'Abbās, Iḥsān. *Ta'rīkh bilād al-shām fī al-'aṣr al-'abbāsī, 132-255 H / 750–870 M.* Amman: Lajnat ta'rīkh bilād al-shām, 1993.
Agapius, *'Unwān*	Agapius [Maḥbūb] of Manbij. *Kitāb al-'unwān. Part II.* Edited by A. Vasiliev in *Patrologia Orientalis* 8 (1911): 399–550.
Azdī, *Mawṣil*	al-Azdī, Muḥammad b. Yazīd. *Ta'rīkh al-mawṣil.* Edited by 'Alī Ḥabība. Cairo: al-Majlis al-a'lā li-al-shu'ūn al-islāmiyya, 1967.
'Aẓīmī, *Ḥalab*	al-'Aẓīmī, Muḥammad b. 'Alī. *Ta'rīkh ḥalab.* Edited by Ibrāhīm Za'rūr. Damascus: n.p., 1984.
Balādhurī, *Ansāb*	al-Balādhurī, Aḥmad b. Yaḥyā b. Jābir. *Ansāb al-ashrāf.* Volume III. Edited by 'Abd al-'Azīz al-Dūrī. Wiesbaden: Franz Steiner, 1978. Volume IV/1. Edited by Iḥsān 'Abbās. Wiesbaden: Franz Steiner, 1979.
Balādhurī, *Ansāb* MS	MS Istanbul, Süleymaniye Kütüphanesi (Reisülkuttap Mustafa Efendi) 597 (vol. I) and 598 (vol. II).
Balādhurī, *Futūḥ*	al-Balādhurī, Aḥmad b. Yaḥyā b. Jābir. *Kitāb futūḥ al-buldān.* Edited by M. J. de Goeje. Leiden: E. J. Brill, 1866.
BSOAS	*Bulletin of the School of Oriental and African Studies.*

BṬ	Ibn al-'Adīm, Kamāl al-Dīn 'Umar. *Bughyat al-ṭalab min ta'rīkh ḥalab.* Edited by Suhayl Zakkār. 11 vols. Damascus: n.p., 1988.
Crone, *Slaves*	Crone, Patricia. *Slaves on Horses. The Evolution of the Islamic Polity.* Cambridge: Cambridge University Press, 1980.
CSCO	*Corpus Scriptorum Christianorum Orientalium.*
EAC	Kennedy, Hugh. *The Early Abbasid Caliphate.* London and Sydney: Croom Helm, 1981.
EI2	*Encyclopaedia of Islam, New Edition.* Leiden: E. J. Brill, 1958–.
FHA	*Fragmenta Historicorum Arabicorum.* Edited by M. J. de Goeje. 2 vols. Leiden: E. J. Brill, 1869.
Ibn al-Athīr, *Kāmil*	Ibn al-Athīr, 'Izz al-Dīn 'Alī. *al-Kāmil fī al-ta'rīkh.* Edited by C. J. Tornberg. 13 vols. Beirut: Dār ṣādir and Dār bayrūt, 1965–67.
Ibn al-Faqīh, *Mukhtaṣar*	Ibn al-Faqīh al-Hamadhānī. *Mukhtaṣar kitāb al-buldān.* Edited by M. J. de Goeje. Leiden: E. J. Brill, 1885.
Ibn Taghribirdī, *Nujūm*	Ibn Taghribirdī, Abū al-Maḥāsin Yūsuf. *al-Nujūm al-ẓāhira fī mulūk miṣr wa-al-qāhira.* 16 vols. Cairo: Dār al-kutub al-miṣriyya, 1963–72.
JAOS	*Journal of the American Oriental Society.*
JESHO	*Journal of the Economic and Social History of the Orient.*
Khalīfa, *Ta'rīkh*	Khalīfa b. Khayyāṭ al-'Uṣfurī. *al-Ta'rīkh.* Edited by Akram Ḍiyā' al-'Umarī. 2 vols. Najaf: Maṭba'at al-ādāb, 1967.
Kindī, *Wulāt*	al-Kindī, Abū 'Umar Muḥammad b. Yūsuf. *Kitāb al-wulāt wa-kitāb al-quḍāt.* Edited by Reuven Guest. Gibb Memorial Series no. 19. Leiden: E. J. Brill, 1912.
Maqdisī, *Bad'*	al-Maqdisī, Muṭahhir b. Ṭāhir. *Kitāb al-bad' wa-*

	al-ta'rīkh. Edited by Clément Huart. 6 vols. Paris: Ernest Laroux, 1899–1919.
Mas'ūdī, *Murūj*	al-Mas'ūdī, 'Alī b. al-Ḥusayn. *Murūj al-dhahab wa-ma'ādin al-jawhar*. Edited by Charles Pellat. 7 vols. Beirut: al-jāmi'a al-lubnāniyya, 1965–1979.
Michael the Syrian	Michael the Syrian. *Chronique de Michel le Syrien*. Edited by J.-B. Chabot. 4 vols. Paris: Academie des Inscriptions et Belles-Lettres, 1924.
MTMD	Ibn Manẓūr, Jamāl al-Dīn Muḥammad. *Mukhtaṣar ta'rīkh dimashq li-ibn 'asākir*. Edited by 'Abd al-Ḥamīd Murād. 29 vols. Damascus: Dār al-fikr, 1984–1996.
Raba'ī, *Faḍā'il*	al-Raba'ī, 'Alī b. Muḥammad. *Faḍā'il al-shām wa-dimashq*. Edited by Ṣalāḥ al-Dīn al-Munajjid. Damascus: Maṭba'at al-taraqqī, 1950.
Ṣafadī, *Umarā'*	al-Ṣafadī, Khalīl b. Aybak. *Kitāb umarā' dimashq fī al-islām*. Edited by Ṣalāḥ al-Dīn al-Munajjid. Damascus: al-Majma' al-'ilmī al-'arabī, 1955.
SI	*Studia Islamica*.
Ṭabarī	al-Ṭabarī, Muḥammad b. Jarīr. *Ta'rīkh al-rusul wa-al-mulūk*. Edited by M. J. de Goeje et al. 3 series. Leiden: E. J. Brill, 1879–1901.
Ṭabarī, *History*	al-Ṭabarī, Muḥammad b. Jarīr. *The History of al-Ṭabarī*. General editor Ehsan Yarshater. 39 vols. Albany: State University of New York Press, 1985–1999.
Theophanes, *Chronographia*	Theophanes Confessor. *Theophanis chronographia*. Edited by Carolus de Boor. Leipzig: B. G. Teubner, 1883.
TMD	Ibn 'Asākir, Abū al-Qāsim 'Alī. *Ta'rīkh madīnat dimashq*. Edited by 'Umar al-'Amrāwī. 70 vols. Beirut: Dār al-fikr, 1995–98.

Ya'qūbī, *Buldān*	al-Ya'qūbī, Aḥmad b. Abī Ya'qūb. *Kitāb al-buldān.* Edited by M. J. de Goeje. Leiden: E. J. Brill, 1892.
Ya'qūbī, *Ta'rīkh*	al-Ya'qūbī, Aḥmad b. Abī Ya'qūb. *Ta'rīkh al-ya'qūbī.* Edited by M. T. Houtsma. 2 vols. Leiden: E. J. Brill, 1883.
ZDMG	*Zeitschrift der deutschen morgenländischen Gesellschaft.*
ZḤ	Ibn al-'Adīm, Kamāl al-Dīn 'Umar. *Zubdat al-ḥalab min ta'rīkh ḥalab.* Edited by Sāmī al-Dahhān. 3 vols. Damascus: Institut Français de Damas, 1951–68.

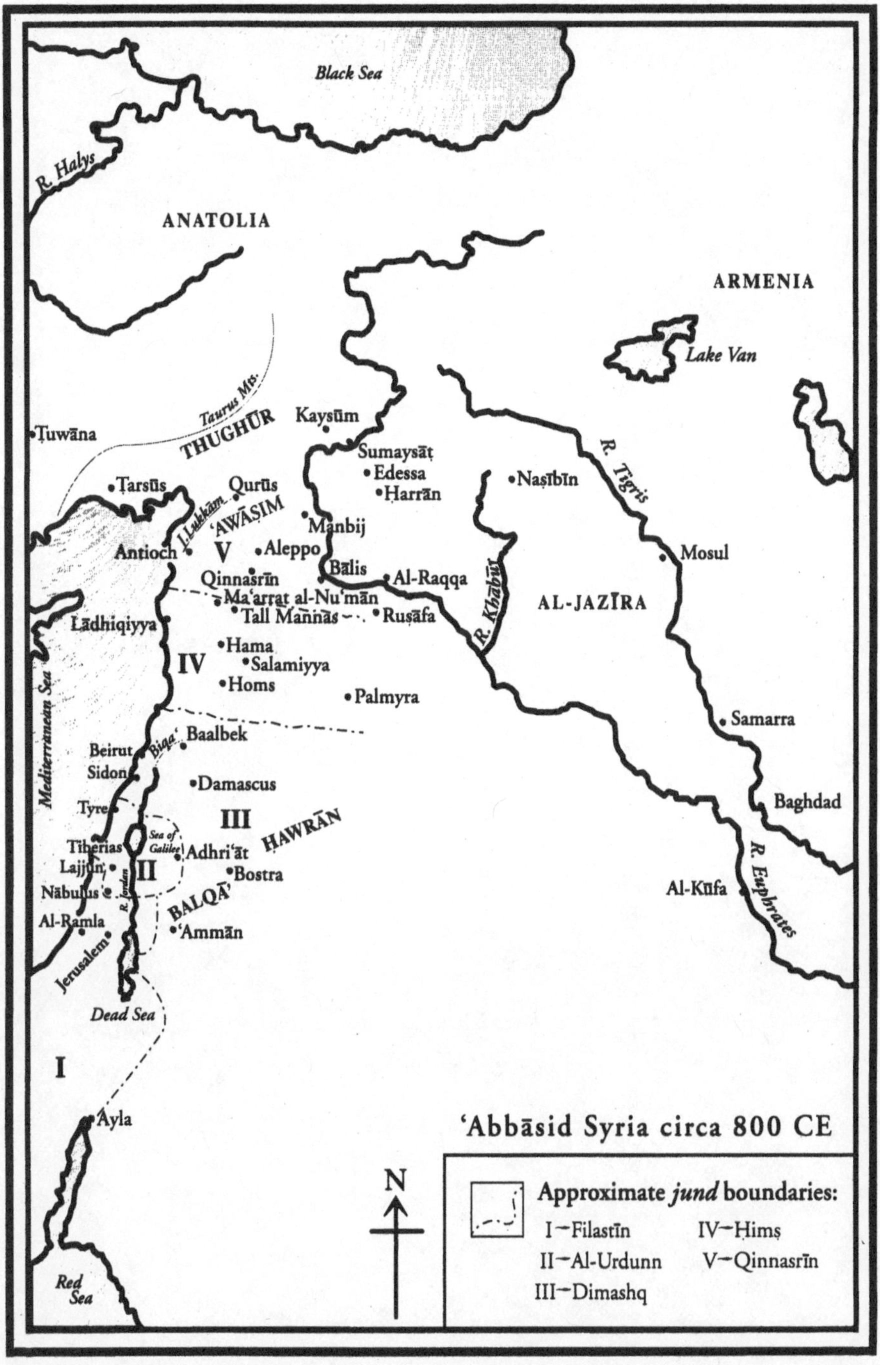

Black Sea
R. Halys
ANATOLIA
ARMENIA
Lake Van
Taurus Mts.
Ṭuwāna
THUGHŪR
Kaysūm
Sumaysāṭ
Edessa
Ḥarrān
Naṣībīn
R. Tigris
Ṭarsūs
Qurūs
J. Lukkām
'AWĀṢIM
Manbij
Antioch
V
Aleppo
Bālis
Al-Raqqa
Mosul
Qinnasrīn
Ma'arrat al-Nu'mān
Tall Mannas
Ruṣāfa
R. Khābūr
AL-JAZĪRA
Lādhiqiyya
Hama
Salamiyya
IV
Homs
Palmyra
Mediterranean Sea
Samarra
Biqā'
Baalbek
Beirut
Sidon
Damascus
Tyre
III
HAWRĀN
Baghdad
Sea of Galilee
Tiberias
Adhri'āt
Lajjūn
II
Bostra
R. Jordan
Nābulus
BALQĀ'
R. Euphrates
Al-Kūfa
Al-Ramla
'Ammān
Jerusalem
Dead Sea
I
Ayla
Red Sea
N
'Abbāsid Syria circa 800 CE
Approximate *jund* boundaries:
I—Filasṭīn
IV—Ḥimṣ
II—Al-Urdunn
V—Qinnasrīn
III—Dimashq

CHAPTER ONE

Introduction

> Damascus is . . . a symbol. One might call it a bunch of symbols. It is a symbol of the permanent physical conditions that run throughout history.
>
> Hilaire Belloc, *Places,* 1942

Early Islamic Syria: An Overview

In the last stages of the Muslim conquests of the Near East, the Byzantine emperor Heraclius paused during his retreat into Anatolia. Before abandoning Syria forever to the Muslims, he turned backward and called out, "Farewell Syria! What a good land this is for the enemy!"[1] The story is legend, but the sentiments are valid: it *was* a good land. Syria, or *al-Shām,* as the Arab conquerers called it, was a relatively wealthy and populous region of the medieval Middle East. Part of its wealth was a consequence of its climatic complexity. In this one province, a traveler arriving by the Mediterranean sea could cross through verdant coastal plains, forested foothills, snow-capped mountains, thickly settled river valleys, and rugged steppe. To this climatic complexity should be added the almost universal ethnic and confessional diversity of the early Islamic oikumene. Syria's populace included Aramaeans, Greeks, and Persians as well as Arabs, and religious communities including Muslims, Jews, and Christians of various stripes. Historically, Syria's geographic and demographic diversity had made it a challenge for the regimes that successively governed it. Yet because of its great strategic, economic, and fiscal potential, Syria could also greatly reward those governments that found the right approach to ruling it.[2]

From almost the beginning of Islamic history, Syria and its populace were central to the development of the early Islamic state. Over the course of the Islamic conquests of the 630s, Syria became one of the first regions to be removed from the control of the Byzantine Empire and made subject to the emergent Islamic caliphate centered in Medina in western Arabia. Shortly after the conquest of Syria, Mu'āwiya b. Abī Sufyān was named governor of the new province, and his name has resonated in the history of Syria ever since. When the Islamic community was divided during the First Civil War (or *fitna*), it was through his control of Syria and his close ties with the troops so recently settled there that Mu'āwiya was able to contest the political claims of his rival 'Alī b. Abī Ṭālib at the battle of Ṣiffīn (37/657), and, by 41/661, to make a successful bid for the caliphate himself. In so doing, Mu'āwiya became the first caliph of what would become Islam's first dynasty, the Umayyads. Mu'āwiya's own clan, the Sufyānids, only retained power until the Second Civil War beginning in 64/683. However, another Umayyad clan, the Marwānids, emerged victorious from that conflict, and the Umayyad dynasty as a whole ruled until 132/750.

By the end of Islam's first century, the influence of the Umayyad dynasty extended over an expanding domain that was home to one of the most creative and complex civilizations in world history, a domain that would eventually stretch from Spain to the steppes of Central Asia. And at the heart of this vast caliphate stood the metropolitan province of Syria. As long as the Umayyad dynasty remained in power, the Syrian capital of Damascus and its environs were the frequent residences of caliphs from both the Sufyānid and Marwānid clans. The Umayyad caliphs, however, were not fixed to a court in Damascus, but frequently relocated to other urban and rural residences throughout Syria. In these peripatetic courts were forged the foundations of the cosmopolitan cultural order that so distinguished the Islamic world from its contemporaries.

Wherever there were courts, there were elite groups to serve them. Some of these Umayyad elites were former Byzantine and Sasanian officials who had recast themselves to serve new masters. Others were Umayyad kinsmen, whose private estates dotted the countryside. Still others were leaders of the Arab tribes that had migrated to Syria even before the Islamic conquests, and who formed the backbone of the Umayyad army and the mainstay of the dynasty itself.

All of these elite groups depended for their survival upon the patronage and wealth that the caliph and his officials might offer. Occasionally, Umayyad elites competed with one another over access to this patronage. This was especially true of the Umayyad tribal armies. Given their reliance on the Syrian troops (along with those of the Jazīra, or northern Iraq), Umayyad caliphs and the men who served them became very adroit in exploiting the rivalries between the two main tribal factions in Syria, Qays (or Muḍar) and Yaman. In the course of the Umayyad period, Muslim soldiers from both factions experienced both the pleasures and pains resulting from their closeness to the Umayyad court. Even outside the military, many humbler Syrians profited from their proximity to the sources of power and privilege to a degree unknown to the population of any other province.

In 100/718, few would have predicted that all this would soon change. However, in 132/750, change it did. In that year, the last Umayyad caliph, Marwān II, was defeated in battle at the river Zāb in Iraq and finally killed in Egypt as he fled his enemies. In the midst of the Umayyad succession struggle known as the Third Civil War, Marwān himself had come to power as a usurper and, as caliph, he had faced opposition on almost every front. The forces that finally defeated Marwān and toppled the Umayyad dynasty were the armies of an underground movement that was bent on placing control of the Muslim community in the hands of the family of the Prophet Muḥammad. The ʿAbbāsid clan of the Banū Hāshim provided the leadership for this movement, encouraging its first public stirrings in the eastern province of Khurāsān. Even before Marwān's death, the ʿAbbāsids had installed one of their own as caliph. Yet, the ʿAbbāsid victory of 132/750 did not merely topple Marwān and implant an ʿAbbāsid, al-Saffāḥ, as caliph. These events had wide-ranging effects on the caliphate, that were, for lack of a better term, revolutionary.

Nowhere was the impact of the ʿAbbāsid revolution felt as it was in Syria. With the almost complete eradication of the Umayyad ruling house and the transfer of the seat of caliphal power to Iraq, the ʿAbbāsid revolution severed the Syrians' connection with the center of power and threw into question their fate as a privileged elite. What future would the former beneficiaries of the Umayyad regime have under ʿAbbāsid rule? Under the Umayyads, Damascus had been the hub of the caliphate. Under the ʿAbbāsids, Damascus continued to be an important regional center and the home of provincial governors, but Baghdad, founded in 145/762 by the caliph al-Manṣūr, became the new center of the Islamic world. In his conception of the new city, al-Manṣūr allotted space for the Khurāsānī troops that had brought the ʿAbbāsids to power, but the Syro-Jazīran troops of the former Umayyad army were not invited to participate in the *translatio imperii*. Syria still provided troops as well as revenues to the emerging ʿAbbāsid state. Yet for the caliphs themselves, Syria was most important as the home of the holy city of Jerusalem and, above all, of the Byzantine-Muslim frontier in the north. ʿAbbāsid caliphs and commanders invested increasingly large amounts of resources and energy into the frontier, a process that culminated in the reign of al-Rashīd (r. 170/786 to 193/809).

Indeed, Syria and the frontier played a crucial role in the Fourth Civil War that followed the death of al-Rashīd by providing military support for al-Rashīd's son and successor al-Amīn against al-Amīn's rival and brother, al-Ma'mūn. The Fourth Civil War was a period of great instability for the ʿAbbāsid caliphate, and amid the conflict, Syria was effectively left to govern itself. With al-Ma'mūn's victory in 198/813, however, ʿAbbāsid authority was reimposed. ʿAbbāsid officials once again levied Syria's taxes, ʿAbbāsid commanders resumed the frontier campaigns, and ʿAbbāsid caliphs once again controlled the province from Baghdad. As many caliphs had done before him, al-Ma'mūn even toured Syria on his way to Jerusalem and the holy cities of Mecca and Medina. It all seemed very familiar. Yet, in many ways, Syria—and the rest of the caliphate—would never be the same again.

For al-Ma'mūn's victory also meant a new order in Baghdad, an order that would, in time, subtly alter Syria's relationship to the center. Al-Maʿmūn's religious policy divided the Muslim religious elites (*ʿulamā'*) of Syria as it did in other provinces, but serious political changes did not occur until later. Al-Ma'mūn's successor, al-Muʿtaṣim, recruited new contingents of Turkish freedmen or *ghilmān* for his army. In 221/836, he founded a new ʿAbbāsid capital in which to house them just north of Baghdad at Samarra. Henceforth, many of these Samarran recruits rose to positions of great influence in both center and province. In 244/858, when the caliph al-Mutawakkil resided in Damascus during a frontier campaign, it was one of his last gestures of command over his Turkish troops.

Indeed, the influence of the Turkish community of Samarra would come to threaten the authority of the caliph himself. As commanders in the caliphal army, bureaucrats in the administration, and advisers in the caliph's palace, Turks from Samarra gained a dominant role in the affairs of the capital. But the duties of many of the high-ranking *ghilmān* also included governing the provinces, Syria among them. As provincial officials, Samarra's new men learned the ropes of provincial government, and provincial rebellion, too. In 254/868, as 'Abbāsid central authority faltered throughout the caliphate, the ambitious Turkish soldier Aḥmad b. Ṭūlūn acquired the governorship of the key province of Egypt and ruled it as a virtually autonomous ruler. By 266/880, he had added most of Syria to his Egyptian domains. With the exception of a brief interlude in the early tenth century, the era of direct 'Abbāsid control in Syria had come to an end.[3]

Contentious Syrians

Although Syria was a good land, for the 'Abbāsid caliphs in Baghdad and Samarra, it was also a land that was not easy to govern. Natural disasters, logistical complexities, and Byzantine incursions were only a few of the potential headaches that Syria raised in the palace-complexes of 'Abbāsid Iraq. But if the early Islamic sources tell us anything, it is that the chief obstacle that the 'Abbāsid government faced was the contentious population of Syria itself. Throughout the period of direct 'Abbāsid rule (132/750 to 266/880), Syrians of different social backgrounds engaged in a wide range of activities that the central government in Iraq viewed as threats to its interests. The most spectacular of these activities occured when Syrians rebelled against the 'Abbāsids in support of an Umayyad claimant, a process that the medieval texts often (but not always) referred to as "going white" (*tabyīḍ*): donning white clothes or raising the white banners of revolt in opposition to 'Abbāsid black. But Syrians could also offer revolts, rebellions, factional fighting, urban uprisings, and peasant jacqueries to make claims that had nothing to do with the Umayyad legacy. Syrian contention is a veritable leitmotiv of early Islamic history, one that chroniclers and commentators duly reported.

Take, for example, this account, in which a Syrian asks the caliph al-Ma'mūn (d. 218/833) to favor the Syrian troops as he does his own troops from Khurāsān. The caliph replies by enumerating the troublesome qualities of each of Syria's tribal factions:

> O brother from the people of Syria, you have reproached me in strong terms! By God, I have never made [the tribal faction of] Qays dismount from the backs of their horses [that is, dismissed them from service] except at times when I saw that there was not a single dirhem left in the public treasury. As for Yaman, I have never liked them, nor they me. As for Quḍā'a, their chiefs live in expectation of the Sufyānī and his appearance, so that they might join his party. As for Rabī'a, they have been angry with God ever since He sent His Prophet from [the rival faction of] Muḍar, and there have never been two of them rising in rebellion without one of them being a Khārijite. Now get out, may God wreak [evil] on you![4]

This account is only one example of the wide-ranging and multifaceted commentary that 'Abbāsid contemporaries throughout the period produced on Syrian contentiousness.[5] Yet, despite the breadth of this commentary, no one has ever thoroughly investigated the full range of Syrian unrest over the whole period of direct 'Abbāsid rule. In light of the prominence that 'Abbāsid-era commentary on Syria grants to such contention, the question begs to be asked: Why did Syrians so frequently rebel against 'Abbāsid rule?

When discussing rebellion, the medieval authors of our sources used a variety of overlapping terms to refer to incidents of unrest in Syria, including *fitna* (outbreak of discord, "civil war"), *'aṣabiyya* (tribal factionalism) and simply *wathba* (assault) or *khurūj* (rebellion). Despite their varied names and their varied causes,[6] all these rebellious activities share certain features that permit them to be studied under the general rubric of "contention." As the focus of study here, contention is the episodic making of claims that bear on other people's interests, a claim-making that, in the context of early Islamic Syria, almost always involved violence. As such, Syrian contention is distinct from both collective action, which need not be contentious (e.g., festivals, religious gatherings, labor) and from nonviolent or continuous claim-making activites (e.g., the day-to-day functioning of patronage networks, the voicing of complaints in a governor's or caliph's *maẓālim*).[7] Moreover, contention comes in many forms. Any given culture will tend to express contention in a number of set ways, or *repertoires*. As such, contention tends to be fairly conservative and resistant to significant innovation, with every earlier act of contention setting a precedent for future contention and influencing its subsequent forms, issues, and even outcomes.[8]

The historical study of contention in this sense traces its genealogy back to the work of Charles Tilly and his students. For the most part, Tilly has been interested in how repertoires of European contention in the eighteenth and nineteenth centuries suddenly changed, a process that he links to new configurations of capital and state power, including the rapid pace of state-making and—most especially—the rise of industry.[9] Although more and more new work is being done on non-European contention,[10] most historical study of contention has followed Tilly's lead, and has focused with varying degrees of scale and precision on European societies on the eve of modernity. The present study is intended as a contribution to the study of contention outside the privileged space of early modern and modern Europe.[11]

Although some earlier studies have examined individual early Islamic Syrian revolts, none have examined the violent claim-making of Syrians in its full breadth. This gap in scholarship on Syria is mainly due to the nature of the medieval sources that were available to previous generations of scholars. Generally, these traditional sources have little to say about Syria or Syrian contention. However, newly available local-historical sources from Syria now make a thorough study of Syrian contention possible. Foremost among these new Syrian sources is the rich and seemingly inexhaustible *Ta'rīkh madīnat dimashq,* or "History of Damascus" by Ibn 'Asākir (d. 571/1175).[12]

Although these Syrian sources are later compilations, they are especially precious because they have preserved citations from much earlier sources, many of which no longer survive in the original. Nevertheless, these sources are not "documentary" reflections of contention, but literary retellings, each providing its own unique interpretive challenges. While some historians might wish to avoid sources like these, for medieval Syria, they are all that we have to work with. I approach these literary sources from what one discussion of Arabic historiography has called the "minimum" position: I am inclined to view much in these sources with suspicion, but I nonetheless feel that with careful scrutiny they can yield significant results.[13] The present study, therefore, is the first to make use of the welter of new information emerging from sources like Ibn

'Asākir and the first to examine the full range of Syrian contention in any detail.

This, then, is a study of medieval politics—politics in the sense of the differential deployment of power in society, and "power" in the context of early Islamic society most often meant the right to armed coercion. As it happens, the medieval sources are well-suited to the study of power in this sense. The social terminology that they used readily divided society into those elites who had some access to caliphal patronage or military resources (the governors or *umarā'*; the tribal notables or *ashrāf*), and those nonelites who did not (the urban masses known by various names; the rural peasantry or *fallāḥūn*). For this reason, I have striven to maintain the social distinctions that they observed.

Other ways of dividing up Syrian society exist, of course. Relative wealth, social status, social function, access to the means of production—all of these figure implicitly or explicitly in older studies of Syria and Islamic society. For those readers seeking a clear-cut division of society into strata or classes, the terminology used in this study will seem to be based upon a frustrating mix of function (e.g., governors, peasants) and social status (e.g., tribal *ashrāf*). However, in a society where combined ties of lineage, loyalty, and patronage frequently overruled any presumed horizontal ties of corporate identity or "class" (or whatever), this terminology at least has the advantage of being authentic.[14]

In addition, this terminology highlights how different segments of Syrian society tended to use different repertoires of contention and not others, and I have structured the work accordingly. In general, I have analyzed the various incidents of Syrian contention by grouping them according to the terminology that the medieval Arabic sources used to designate the actors who were most active in making claims. Thus, chapter three discusses the provincial governors and military unrest; chapter four the remnants of the Umayyad nobility and anti-'Abbāsid sentiment; chapter five the *ashrāf* and their role in tribal factionalism; and chapter six the political activity of nonelites: the collective violence of urban crowds and the coping strategies of the rural poor. The structure of this study thus reflects my primary focus on *people*—on the actors of Syrian contention—and not on some larger narrative of Islamic or 'Abbāsid political history.

Between the fall of the Umayyads in 132/750 and the Ṭūlūnid conquest of Syria in 264/877, generations of Syrians with different social origins made violent claims on the central government, the local government, and on one another. Why? My reading of the variety of relevant sources—Arabic, non-Arabic, and the rich Syrian local-historical traditions—shows that the shape and frequency of Syrian contention in the 'Abbāsid period varied with its actors and their place in the social order. Provincial governors, the highest-ranking members of local society, used military revolt to engage in the dynastic politics of the 'Abbāsid court. Occasionally, some remaining members of the Umayyad family took advantage of Syrian factionalism. Aided by vague but pervasive notions of Umayyad legitimacy they sought to build up their own constituencies as genuine alternatives to 'Abbāsid rule. Syria's local notables, the *ashrāf,* engaged in factional conflict to ensure an equitable (or at least favorable) distribution of the government's privileges. The lower strata of Syria's urban and rural populations rebelled primarily to uphold customary notions of political order though they also took up arms as bandits simply as a way of coping with adversity.

Although it cannot be said that there is one cause for the high incidence of contention in 'Abbāsid Syria, this study does trace Syrian contention to a common historical background: Syria's new role as a province in the 'Abbāsid state and its incorporation into the 'Abbāsid system of provincial government. In this system, the caliphal government in Baghdad or Samarra worked out a relationship with Syrian society that diffused power throughout society and created a milieu in which contention was an inherent facet of provincial life. This relationship between government and rebellion, then, should form the starting point for any discussion of Syrian contention.

CHAPTER TWO

Who Will Act Equitably Between the People?: The Dynamic of Provincial Power in Syria

In 132/750, when the 'Abbāsids absorbed Syria as a new province of their new caliphate, they employed a system of provincial government common to many states before and after them, one that relied more on the give-and-take of center and province than on the direct coercion of the populace. What made the 'Abbāsid government in Syria unique, however, was how it responded to its two main local challenges. First, the administrative and geographical complexity of the province of Syria multiplied the difficulties that any governor would face. Second, these local complexities obliged the 'Abbāsid governors to rely upon the cooperation of Syria's *ashrāf,* former imperial elites that had their own ambitions to pursue. To surmount these two challenges, the 'Abbāsids used a flexible system of provincial government that was inherently unstable, with an ever-present potential to encourage contention.

Administrative Geography in "the Syrias"

Unlike other provinces such as Egypt and al-Jazīra, which were more or less monocephalous, the 'Abbāsid province of Syria was a composite province, subdivided into five military-administrative districts (*jund,* pl. *ajnād*). These were, from south to north: Filasṭīn, al-Urdunn, Dimashq, Ḥimṣ, and Qinnasrīn, with their capitals at the cities of al-Ramla, Tiberias, Damascus, Homs, and

Qinnasrin respectively.[1] Contemporaries recognized the composite nature of the province, and often used the term *al-shāmāt,* "the Syrias," to refer to the *ajnād* taken together.[2] The *ajnād* had been in place at least since the time of the early Umayyads, who drew their troops from the Muslim population settled in Syria and al-Jazīra.[3] A governor-general oversaw the province as a whole, while subgovernors controlled each *jund* separately.[4] In addition to the five *ajnād,* a further subdistrict was added in 170/785, when the caliph al-Rashīd separated the entire Byzantine-Muslim frontier region of northern Syria, al-Jazīra, and southern Anatolia into a new administrative district called al-'Awāṣim, with its capital at Manbij.[5]

Sources usually refer to the governors of this region as being in charge of *al-'awāṣim wa-al-thughūr,* but it is unclear whether the *thughūr,* or front-line frontier region, formed a distinct adminstrative unit as such. Indeed, the fluctuating boundaries of the *ajnād* over the course of the early Islamic period suggest that they were seen less as static districts but more as abstract sources of revenue and manpower. As such, the boundaries of the *ajnād* do not determine the jurisdiction of its governor or the homes of its troops: it is the other way around.

In addition to these districts, the sources occasionally mention a governor in charge of "the coasts (*al-sawāḥil*)," which refers to the leadership of the fleet responsible for policing the Syrian coastal cities and for conducting naval warfare in the eastern Mediterranean (*ghazw al-baḥr*).[6] Because the main shipyards were located at Tyre, the revenues accruing to the governorate of the coastal regions were grouped with those of al-Urdunn.[7] Not infrequently, the same person held the governorate of both regions.[8]

To the logistical challenge of governing a large province composed of different subdistricts, each *jund* contributed its own share of local socio-economic variations. In the south, the *jund* of Filasṭīn occupied an important place on transit-trade and pilgrimage routes to Africa and the Arabian peninsula. Filasṭīn in general, and Jerusalem in particular, were common destinations for Muslim and non-Muslim pilgrims alike. Moreover, the capital of Filasṭīn, al-Ramla, was the crucial stop on the route from north Africa and Egypt to Iraq. This route was important for the flow of travel and commerce between the western and central Islamic lands. But, for the 'Abbāsid government, the route was vital because it bore the caravans from the western provinces carrying the tax revenues and tribute bound for the capital at Baghdad or Samarra.

From Filasṭīn, Syria's main road passed northward through the *jund* of al-Urdunn and the other Syrian *ajnād* to the north. Southern Syria was traditionally considered the heartland of Arab tribes who belonged to the tribal confederation known as Yaman, but the reality was more complex. Yamanī tribes certainly prevailed in al-Urdunn, especially in the vicinity of the capital of Tiberias, where the tribe of Ash'ar predominated,[9] but Filasṭīn was home to a mixture of tribes, including some from the rival confederation of Qays.[10]

In contrast to these two southern regions, the *jund* of Dimashq was an especially lucrative district. Part of the *jund's* relative wealth was due to geography: located centrally in Syria, the *jund* was dominated by its capital city, Damascus. In the 'Abbāsid period, as in the past, Damascus was the major urban center of central Syria, in the heart of a fertile agricultural region including the surrounding orchards and farms of the Ghūṭa. But the district's administrative peculiarities, a heritage of Umayyad practice, further increased its revenues, for the fiscal jurisdiction of Dimashq also extended to the subordinate region of al-Balqā' that ran south along the east bank of the Jordan River. As a result, Dimashq was the largest *jund*, being roughly the size of the *ajnād* of Ḥimṣ, Filasṭīn, and al-Urdunn combined.[11] The tribal makeup of the population of the *jund* of Dimashq was predominantly Yamanī but also included a significant minority of Qaysī tribes.[12] In the western part of the district, the Lebanon mountain range interposed itself between the cities of the interior and those of the coast, and extended north into the *jund* of Ḥimṣ.

Ḥimṣ and Qinnasrīn, the adjoining district to the north, shared many basic similarities, but they also differed in important ways. Unlike the more "civilian" *ajnād* of southern Syria, Ḥimṣ and Qinnasrīn possessed a more militarized character. "If you want the proper residence for the caliphs, then choose Damascus; but if you want strife and the Holy War, then choose Ḥimṣ" was the advice that one late Umayyad Syrian *ḥadīth* offered.[13] This militarized atmosphere in Ḥimṣ and Qinnasrīn was due to their proximity to the districts of al-'Awāṣim and the *thughūr,* the Byzantine-Muslim frontier proper, which extended north from Qinnasrīn into the Taurus range and southern Anatolia. Despite their shared character, however, Ḥimṣ differed from Qinnasrīn in that it was dominated by Yamanī tribes,[14] while Qinnasrīn, with al-Jazīra across the Euphrates, was traditionally the preserve of Qaysī tribes.[15]

The geographic and economic diversity of the subdistricts of

Syria directly affected the amount of land-tax (*kharāj*) that they could produce. Estimates of the revenues for the *ajnād* of Syria in the reign of al-Rashīd (170-93/786-809) give some impression of the relative wealth of these regions: Filasṭīn provided 320,000 *dīnārs* to the central fisc; al-Urdunn, 96,000; Dimashq, 420,000; Ḥimṣ, 320,000; Qinnasrīn, 490,000.[16] These figures reflect not only the extent of cultivation, but also the density of settlement within a given region. Thus, the *jund* of Qinnasrīn, which benefited from comparative fertility (especially around Aleppo) and a high density of settlement, generated the most revenues from Syria at this period.[17] Revenue figures are lacking for the 'Awāṣim and the *thughūr* because, until the reign of al-Mutawakkil (232-247/847-861), the 'Awāṣim and the *thughūr* were exempt from *kharāj*, providing only the canonical tithe (*'ushr*). This money went toward upkeep of the local infrastructure and payment of troops rather than to the central fisc.

The Dynamic of Provincial Power

Consistent and stable administration of the five different *ajnād* of Syria proved to be a serious challenge to the 'Abbāsid government. The central government responded by employing a flexible system of provincial administration that, in principle, differed little from Umayyad practice.[18] Both dynasties used a system of provincial rule in which the actual institutions of provincial government were keenly responsive to local conditions. In practice, this meant that 'Abbāsid governors pursued the goals of the central government in cooperation with local political and administrative traditions. This system was crucial in enabling the central government to maintain control of provinces that were often very different. Ironically, it was the system's attentiveness to the ebb and flow of power in the province that was both its source of strength and its primary flaw.

The linchpin in the system of provincial government was, of course, the provincial governor (*wālī* or *amīr*). Alongside the governors, one occasionally finds officials in charge of extracting revenue (*ṣāḥib al-kharāj* or *'āmil*), who were also, like the governors, appointed by the caliph. But quite often the office of governor was combined with that of the financial official.[19] In fact, the governor's control over vast sums of revenue was one of the main attractions of the position: whatever stipend a governor might receive from the center would inevitably be supplemented (justly or not) by money raised locally, regardless of the revenues required by the central fisc. Although such practices were common, an overgreedy governor could become a terrible burden on the subject population. A Christian chronicler writing in the Jazīra during the 220s/840s described the practices of such governors in almost apocalyptic tones:

> More than at any other period of Arab rule, calamities are multiplied upon the people at the present time because of the cupidity of the governors. For each one takes for himself [revenues] that he adds on top of the taxes, and he adds to it and augments it as much as he likes. They appoint and set up special officials for each category [of tax] so that they consume and devour the poor folk coming and going.[20]

But, as the chronicler implies, abuse of this scale was exceptional. In addition to revenue extraction, provincial governors had other tasks to occupy them. They led prayers in the congregational mosque, led troops in campaigns,[21] and maintained order.[22] A whole range of activities followed from these principal duties. Governors were supposed to oversee the swift execution of the law, maintain the security of the populace,[23] and adjudicate occasional disputes.[24] They kept the roads safe and passable,[25] oversaw the construction and maintenance of public works,[26] and generally acted as the local agents of caliphal interests. Some governors were renowned for their achievements in these areas. Yaḥyā b. Da'ūd al-Khursī, governor of Egypt for al-Mahdī, was lauded for maintaining civic order and preventing petty theft. Amājūr al-Turkī, governor of Dimashq from 256-264/870-878, was particularly respected for "keeping the roads safe" and quashing banditry.[27] To accomplish his duties, the governor usually had at his disposal a number of lesser officials: regional tax agents,[28] caliphal troops, perhaps supplemented by local militias (*shurṭa* / pl. *shuraṭ*), scribes (*kātib*/pl. *kuttāb*), and, often, a judge (*qāḍī*/pl. *quḍāt*).[29]

However much such a group of bureaucrats and soldiers would have seemed like an occupying force,[30] especially in the former Umayyad heartland, governors did not maintain order simply through brute coercion.[31] The logistical realities of governing a far-flung caliphate made it necessary for the central government to work out different governing arrangements for different provinces. This meant that, in order to rule effectively, provincial governors had to acknowledge a variety of local political and administrative traditions. In a caliphate composed of a number of very diverse provinces, a more rigid system would be doomed to failure. As Hugh Kennedy has shown, the caliphs could not govern north Africa in the same way that they governed Khurāsān.[32]

In a complex province like Syria, perhaps more than in any other province of the caliphate, it was imperative that governors be cognizant of the local political scene. With its five different *ajnād*, each with its own share of local economic and administrative peculiarities and each governed by separate officials, the province of Syria posed a particular challenge for the 'Abbāsid administration. If the caliphs could not govern north Africa in the same manner in which they governed Khurāsān, then neither could they govern Qinnasrīn as if it were al-Urdunn.

To become familiar with local conditions, provincial governors required a certain amount of time to learn the ropes. However, terms of office in the 'Abbāsid period were fairly short for governors, often no more than a year. Such a rapid turnover of officials ensured the creation of a body of experienced, "professional" governors but also discouraged the governors from establishing strong local ties and networks of loyalty that might threaten central authority. It also meant that governors rarely had the time to become intimately familiar with local affairs. As a result, the official body of troops and administrators that assisted the governor were not enough to ensure that he could govern efficiently. Provincial governors could only accomplish their tasks effectively by cooperating with local power elites: families of *ashrāf* or prominent tribal chiefs who were already familiar with the region's political traditions.

The resulting system of government was thus a relatively ad hoc arrangement that was not based on centrally directed formal institutions of coercion or authority, or on a tributary relationship between the center and a semiautonomous local ruler. Rather, the system of provincial government employed in 'Abbāsid Syria rested upon the mediation of provincial interests with those of the center, articulated along lines of kinship and patronage. In such an arrangement, the diplomatic use of largesse, family ties, and the cooperation of local elites was as much a standard tool of the governor's trade as was the army.[33]

Yet the role of intermediary that many Syrian *ashrāf* took was a new feature of Syrian politics, itself a product of the 'Abbāsid revolution. In Marwānid times, the *ashrāf* who governed the subdistricts of Syria were military men, soldiers and commanders who owed their status as Syria's tribal-factional elite to their place in the Umayyad government. With the collapse of that government, however, members of Syria's fallen sharifian families of the early 'Abbāsid period found their status as a military elite ever more circumscribed as mere provincial troops. More and more of Syria's *ashrāf* found themselves blocked out of caliphal service and cast only as notables, local elites whose status now rested on the classical qualities of *ḥasab wa-nasab* (wealth and lineage) and who were distinguished by their lack of any formal, routinized connection with the 'Abbāsid government. No longer imperial elites yet not quite ordinary subjects, the Qaysī and Yamanī *ashrāf* of 'Abbāsid Syria and their factional followings competed furiously for the few formal positions of influence that were offered to them. For the 'Abbāsid provincial governors, such violent concern for status and position made the *ashrāf* of Syria both pliable and dangerous interlocutors. For despite the 'Abbāsid system's success as a solution to the problems of provincial government in Syria, its attention to local detail—its very flexibility and the source of its success—was also a key generator of contention.[34]

The reason for this paradox lies in the dynamic of provincial power that surrounded the relationship between the governor and the local *ashrāf*. Ideally, this relationship was a symbiotic one: to maintain central authority, the governors needed the *ashrāf* with their independent sources of power or prestige in local society; in turn, the status that *ashrāf* thus gained from their access to central authority enabled them to maintain their positions in the dog-eat-dog world of urban politics.[35] When the system worked, it was flexible enough that local elites could manipulate it for their own interests,[36] while simultaneously aiding an anxious central government by keeping the governor dependent upon their assistance, and thereby curtailing his authority and preventing it from becoming seditiously absolute.

But the system did not always work. The provincial governor's position in the dynamic of power between center and province has been described as "unenviable,"[37] and it surely cannot have been a simple job for a conscientious governor to maintain himself. On the one hand, the governor had to impose government policy on the province and above all collect the necessary revenues. But if this was done without regard to local interests, he could lose his post, if not more. Prolonged local rebellions and complaints about overtaxation or negligence usually ended with the central government sacking the governor and confiscating his wealth. That was exactly what happened to ʻAbd Allāh b. Sulaymān al-Hāshimī, al-Manṣūr's governor of al-Balqā'. ʻAbd Allāh was lucky, however: he went on to govern Yemen for al-Mahdī. Occasionally, less fortunate governors ended their tenure by being imprisoned, tortured, or executed.[38]

On the other hand, in order to collect the necessary revenues, the governor had to cooperate with local interests, above all the *ashrāf*. But here also there was danger: the center viewed with suspicion any warm relationship between governor and locals, particularly one that emerged in a wealthy province; too often, these kinds of relationships were preludes to open acts of sedition.[39] They could also drag the governor and his troops into costly and destabilizing provincial conflicts. Although the central government may well have wished their governors to remain above these sorts of intrigues, governors who successfully rose above local politics were rare. Most of them took the expedient of manipulating provincial political tensions, despite the risk. In ʻAbbāsid Syria, where local politics were usually based on tribal factionalism, this meant that most governors had to engage the loyalties of the *ashrāf* of either of the rival Qaysī and Yamanī factions. Thus, al-Rashīd's governor of Dimashq, Ibrāhīm b. Muḥammad al-Mahdī, was renowned for his scrupulous attention to factional balance. He could boast that he was the only governor of Dimashq who had never merited a factional nickname from the populace.[40]

The nature of provincial government is summed up in an account about the sacking of ʻAbd al-Wahhāb b. Ibrāhīm, al-Manṣūr's governor of Filasṭīn. Like many governors of the time, he was a relative of the caliph. However, ʻAbd al-Wahhāb was so ruthless in his extraction of revenue from the populace that al-Manṣūr sent agents out to investigate the situation. As the story goes, when the agents returned to the caliph, one of them pulled out a plucked bird as a graphic example of the state in which ʻAbd al-Wahhāb had left the *jund*.[41] Worse still, ʻAbd al-Wahhāb was accused of having a man killed in an act of factional partisanship, a clear breach of the neutrality that a servant of the state should ideally have maintained.[42] Having removed ʻAbd al-Wahhāb from office, al-Manṣūr upbraded him in a final reprimand: "You bastard! So, you have killed the Ghassānī and shown favoritism toward one group over another? If you had abandoned your religion, you would at least have been acting indiscriminately. Instead, you have shown favoritism: who, then, will act equitably between the people?"[43] Although ʻAbd al-Wahhāb's financial predations were clearly a source of concern, they were not the direct cause of his removal from office.

Rather, al-Manṣūr reserved his ire for another charge, that ʿAbd al-Wahhāb might be playing favorites (*taʿaṣṣub*) among local politicos instead of remaining neutral. The principle at stake was not so much the justice of the man's death, as it was the destruction of local political equilibrium, concepts that are both contained in the Arabic verb (*ʿadala*) that the author of this account placed in al-Manṣūr's mouth.

The provincial governor was thus at the center of an unstable relationship, precariously poised between the twin pitfalls of rebellion and tyranny. The balancing act that ʿAbd al-Wahhāb never mastered was a fourway routine, in which the governor juggled provincial and central interests on one side and jostled to remain aloof of local political conflicts on the other. With a central component as unstable as this, the early ʿAbbāsid system of provincial government was a system that had the potential for rebellion already built into it. For if some governors were tempted to tip the balance in the favor of the central government, others tipped it in favor of themselves.

CHAPTER THREE

A Good Reputation and Supporting Hands: Provincial Governors and Provincial Rebellion

Given the instability inherent in the 'Abbāsid caliphate's system of provincial government, there were clear limits to the central authority of Baghdad and Samarra. On one side, logistical and pragmatic concerns prevented the caliphal government from ruling its provinces with an iron fist. On the other, too much of the velvet glove of provincial autonomy would lead to fiscal and military crises, if not the wholesale collapse of the caliphate. The caliphs in Baghdad and Samarra were thus faced with their own version of the eternal dilemma of empire: How was one to manage the affairs of a province without providing a potential rival with his own source of money, manpower, and legitimacy?

The 'Abbāsid caliphs had no simple solution to the problem, but instead experimented with a range of options. In the early period of 'Abbāsid rule, the caliphs drew their governors of Syria from a discrete but diverse pool of candidates. Indeed, the backgrounds of 'Abbāsid governors changed significantly only well after the Fourth Civil War. Yet however trusted Syria's governors may have been, they were a constant, if implicit, source of anxiety. For the history of provincial government and provincial rebellion in Syria reminded the caliphs again and again of the limits of central control.

The Limits of Central Control, I: Early 'Abbāsid Strategies

Before the Fourth Civil War between al-Amīn and al-Ma'mūn (193-218/809-833), 'Abbāsid central government bent its efforts toward finding a way to prevent rival sources of power from gaining a foothold in the provinces. In the wake of the 'Abbāsid revolution, and given the patrimonial nature of early Islamic politics, appointing 'Abbāsid nobles to provincial posts seemed to be a logical solution. However, the 'Abbāsid caliphs soon learned that placing equally legitimate 'Abbāsid claimants to the throne in positions endowed with discrete sources of manpower and revenue could seriously exacerbate the problem of provincial government.

Al-Manṣūr and his descendants found an alternate solution in appointing the younger generation of kinsmen and the families of old revolutionaries and clients, all of whom lacked the pedigrees necessary to challenge 'Abbāsid legitimacy. Yet, although few actually rebelled against the central government, none of them were immune to the temptations offered by the dynamic of provincial power or to the caliphal anxieties that surrounded their position.

'Abbāsid Kinsmen

In the earliest months of the caliphate, when the stability of the new regime had yet to be proved, the early 'Abbāsid caliphs employed a commonsense strategy that farmed out many provincial positions to members of the 'Abbāsid ruling family (*ahl al-bayt*): usually the uncles, cousins, and sons of the caliphs themselves.[1] Of course this policy was hardly revolutionary. Such a strategy was entirely in keeping with the nature of politics in the early medieval Near East. Patronage and family ties were a prominent feature of 'Abbāsid political culture, and, more to the point, seemed at first to solve the problem of provincial rule for the newly installed government. Relatives, after all, were known quantities. They were people over whom one could expect to wield some influence. With the proper amount of circumspection, caliphs could rely upon their relatives as trusted servants who had vested interests in maintaining the regime.

Then again, some kinsmen of the caliphs also posed a unique problem for the caliphs. By their very nature, members of the ruling family shared the same genealogical legitimacy that the 'Abbāsid caliphs claimed for themselves. Given the uncertainty of provincial rule in the wake of the revolution, it may have been the only option for the caliph al-Saffāḥ and his successors, but using relatives as provincial governors could also add to the problems of the caliphate. With the right kind of support, an errant kinsman in a nearby province could threaten the center at a level of magnitude that no ordinary rebel governor could hope to muster.

The Revolt of 'Abd Allāh b. 'Alī

As it happened, it was in the province of Syria that this danger inherent in the early 'Abbāsid patrimonial arrangement first became a reality. Even before the dust of the revolution had settled, 'Abd Allāh b. 'Alī, the caliph al-Saffāḥ's uncle and the first 'Abbāsid governor of Syria, won the support of the Syrian *ashrāf* for his own bid to power. During the troubled succession struggle that followed the death of al-Saffāḥ in 136/754, 'Abd Allāh relied heavily on his Syrian supporters. He was thereby able to pose the first major internal crisis to the 'Abbāsid regime.

Yet 'Abd Allāh's revolt is a difficult subject to address. When 'Abd Allāh claimed the caliphate for himself, he automatically made himself the focus of controversy. As a result, the opposing lines of discourse within the historiographical tradition of the 'Abbāsid court preclude any historian's attempt to find a neutral record of the revolt within the Islamic historical sources. Although fragments of a pro-'Abd Allāh corpus of traditions survive, because 'Abd Allāh ultimately failed to seize power, it was his victorious rival, al-Manṣūr, and al-Manṣūr's descendants, who furnished accounts of the succession struggle.[2] What all accounts agree upon, though, is that the succession to al-Saffāḥ was not solidly secured before his death, and that 'Abd Allāh based his revolt on the claim that al-Saffāḥ had previously made him his heir as a reward for engineering the fall of Marwān II.[3]

'Abd Allāh may never actually have received al-Saffāḥ's blessing, as he and his officers claimed he did. But, to his credit, there is at least some evidence that his revolt was not a sudden decision. Rather, 'Abd Allāh had portrayed himself as an obvious successor to the leader of the new *dawla* in the few years prior to al-Saffāḥ's death. Indeed, the claims of the surviving pro-'Abd Allāh traditions can hardly have come from any other milieu, as it is unlikely that the few months of 'Abd Allāh's revolt were sufficient to generate such optimistic historicizing. They are more likely to be traces of a legitimizing strategy dating from the period in which 'Abd Allāh's succession was still a very real possibility—that is, before his confrontation with al-Manṣūr's armies in 136/754. Moreover, it seems that in the obscure period following the 'Abbāsid revolution, 'Abd Allāh claimed the charged title of "al-Saffāḥ" for himself.[4] He was, in fact, one of the most powerful men in the caliphate upon Abū al-'Abbās al-Saffāḥ's death. He had a large body of Khurāsānī and Syro-Jazīran frontier troops at his disposal. That he is treated here as the leader of a "revolt" is more a reflection of the bias in the sources than of his political legitimacy in 136/754.

Although the validity of 'Abd Allāh's and al-Manṣūr's rival claims will probably remain open to debate, it is clear that 'Abd Allāh was only able to parlay his role in the destruction of the Marwānid house and his status in Syria into a bid for the caliphate because he could manipulate the dynamic of power within the province. 'Abd Allāh's gambit for the caliphate was a revolt backed by an alliance of local interests with those of the governor. In this case, "local interests" were those of the military men of the recently toppled Umayyad government and not of the bulk of the population of the province. As a Christian chronicler put it, "He ['Abd Allāh] took command of the Arabs [i.e., Muslim troops] of the Jazīra and the Syrian districts after they had despaired and lost all hope of living."[5] Syrian elites were certainly an important part of 'Abd Allāh's support, but they did not revolt as provincials seeking to restore centrality to their province.[6] Rather, the *ashrāf* who supported 'Abd Allāh rebelled as former Umayyad elites who were unwilling to adjust to their new postrevolutionary role as mere local troops. They backed 'Abd Allāh in order to maintain themselves in the new regime in positions of power to which they were accustomed. It may have been pure happenstance that news of al-Saffāḥ's death reached 'Abd Allāh while he was preparing to lead the summer frontier raid, but it was a perfect opportunity for 'Abd Allāh to affirm the personal loyalty of the armies then under him and march toward Iraq.[7]

As the leader of a military revolt, 'Abd Allāh naturally found his main supporters among the commanders of the army that had accompanied him to the frontier. These included the leaders of the Khurāsānī army that arrived with 'Abd Allāh in 132/750. It was exclusively members of the Khurāsāniyya who testified to 'Abd Allāh's claim regarding his agreement with al-Saffāḥ.[8] Among those who gave their support were Abū Ghānim 'Abd al-Ḥamīd b. Rib'ī al-Ṭā'ī, who was a *dā'ī* or "propagandist" for the 'Abbāsid cause in Marw, who had fought alongside 'Abd Allāh at the battle of the Zāb, and who had acted as 'Abd Allāh's deputy in Damascus while he was occupied with local rebellions in 132/750.[9] Also present was Ḥumayd b. Qaḥṭaba al-Ṭā'ī, the son of the most prominent Khurāsānī general of the 'Abbāsid revolution. In 132/750, Ḥumayd had assisted 'Abd Allāh in the siege of Damascus and in subduing pockets of resistance in the countryside. 'Abd Allāh's brother, 'Abd al-Ṣamad, who had followed him to Syria and the siege of Damascus, later added his support to the revolt.[10]

'Abd Allāh's other supporters were the leaders of the Syro-Jazīran army, many of whom had previously served under the Umayyad caliph Marwān II. These supporters included men like Bakkār b. Muslim al-'Uqaylī, a Jazīran *sharīf* who had fought against the 'Abbāsids in Armenia; al-Ḥakam b. Ḍab'ān al-Judhāmī, a Filasṭīnī *sharīf* who had evidently taken control of Filasṭīn after Marwān II fled into Egypt; Zufar b. 'Āṣim al-Hilālī, a Qaysī officer whose father had been Marwān's governor of Armenia; 'Uthmān b. 'Abd al-A'lā b. Surāqa al-Azdī, a leader from Mosul who had been Marwān's governor there; and Manṣūr b. Ja'wana, a Qaysī leader from Edessa who had fought against the 'Abbāsids in 132/750.

The account of 'Abd Allāh's conversation with these Syro-Jazīran officers is improbable but still of interest because even if the account does not reflect the actual needs of 'Abd Allāh at the time of his revolt, it at least illustrates the degree to which rebellious governors were expected to rely on local support. In the account, each officer is allowed a verdict on 'Abd Allāh's claims: "I am with you (*anā sahmuka,* lit., "I am your arrow")," Bakkār exclaimed; Zufar, for his part, offered a warning against *fitna;* Ibn Ḍab'ān shrewdly equivocated; and Ibn Surāqa, an old hand at rebellion, stressed local opinion, saying "Your reputation with the Syrian army is not good, so nothing will be of use to you except someone like me who has a good reputation and supporting hands, or else a dissenting leader who hopes to attain honor in it [revolt]."[11] Once he had secured the support of most of his officers, 'Abd Allāh made his intentions public and received the oath of allegiance of his troops. He appointed his officers to various governorates, made 'Abd al-Ṣamad his heir, and wrote to the other governors of the frontier regions inviting them to join his revolt. They refused.[12]

Dissension between the Khurāsānī and Syro-Jazīran blocs of 'Abd Allāh's supporters was not long in coming and ultimately led to 'Abd Allāh's downfall. The alliance was a potentially fractious one from the beginning, not only because the Syro-Jazīran troops and the Khurāsāniyya had so recently been bitter enemies, but also because each group had a different stake in the revolt.[13] For the Khurāsāniyya, it mattered little which ʿAbbāsid they served. But for the Syro-Jazīran troops, ʿAbd Allāh b. ʿAlī offered a future, whereas al-Manṣūr offered only uncertainty. ʿAbd Allāh headed east from the frontier, making for Iraq by way of Ḥarrān, which once served as Marwān II's capital and where al-Manṣūr had left a garrison of Khurāsānī troops. It was at this point that the tide turned. For fear that they might act as a fifth column, ʿAbd Allāh moved against his own Khurāsānī supporters. The Khurāsānī leader Ḥumayd b. Qaḥṭaba renewed his allegiance to the caliph al-Manṣūr and fled ʿAbd Allāh's camp, seeking to join the approaching caliphal army.

The army was led by one of the most powerful men of the revolution, the chief propagandist Abū Muslim, who claimed that al-Manṣūr had sent him as the new governor of Syria.[14] Abū Muslim had evidently already written to ʿAbd Allāh to that effect and attempted to provide himself with a cover by claiming that he was merely headed for his new post. But the implications of the approach of Abū Muslim were not lost on many of ʿAbd Allāh's Syrian troops, who deserted ʿAbd Allāh to defend their homes and families against Abū Muslim's forces.[15] His ruse accomplished, Abū Muslim continued his march on ʿAbd Allāh. The two forces met outside Naṣībīn, where ʿAbd Allāh's doubts about the Khurāsāniyya in his ranks were realized. Abū Muslim invited ʿAbd Allāh's Khurāsanī troops to join his side, and many did. In response, according to some accounts, ʿAbd Allāh had the remnants massacred.[16]

With his forces now seriously reduced, ʿAbd Allāh faced a quick defeat. Abū Muslim's army routed ʿAbd Allāh's followers and he and his brother ʿAbd al-Ṣamad fled. The two found refuge with their brother Sulaymān at Basra and eventually won the clemency of al-Manṣūr.[17] Fortunately for the Syro-Jazīran army, Abū Muslim recognized the necessity of maintaining experienced frontier troops and secured a general amnesty for the members of the Syro-Jazīran contingents who had rebelled.[18] A delegation of leaders of the army accompanied Abū Muslim to Iraq, where they formally sought al-Manṣūr's forgiveness.[19] The delegation included the Qaysī *sharīf* ʿUthmān b. ʿUmāra b. Khuraym, whose family would go on to faithfully serve the ʿAbbāsids in the East, and al-Ḥārith b. ʿAbd al-Raḥmān al-Ḥarashī, a Damascene who had taken up the ʿAbbāsid cause while Marwān II was still in Syria.[20]

The Rise of the Banū Ṣāliḥ

The revolt of ʿAbd Allāh b. ʿAlī demonstrated in the clearest terms the danger inherent in a system of provincial government that put ʿAbbāsid kinsmen in the position of governor. As a result, al-Manṣūr was quick to assign provincial posts to clients and military men who were not kinsmen.[21] Nevertheless, ʿAbbāsid nobles remained a mainstay in the system of provincial government until the reign of al-Ma'mūn, and the specter of ʿAbd Allāh b. ʿAlī continued to haunt the central government. Indeed, after the revolt of 136/754, a brother of ʿAbd Allāh b. ʿAlī took control of Syria in the name of al-Manṣūr and began consolidating power in his own family, which rapidly assumed prominence in Syria as well as in Baghdad. This brother was Ṣāliḥ b. ʿAlī.

During the revolution, Ṣāliḥ b. ʿAlī had accompanied his brother in pursuit of Marwān II and had continued into Egypt where his forces caught up with the caliph and finally killed him in 132/750. At the time of ʿAbd Allāh's revolt in 136/754, Ṣāliḥ was governor of Egypt and Filasṭīn. When news of the revolt reached him, he marched into Syria with a contingent of Khurāsānī troops to reassert al-Manṣūr's authority there and probably to attack ʿAbd Allāh from the rear while he was preoccupied with the threat of Abū Muslim's approach from Iraq. Ṣāliḥ was delayed in Filasṭīn by the last remnants of ʿAbd Allāh's Syrian supporters, who were led by ʿAbd Allāh's governor of Filasṭīn, al-Ḥakam b. Ḍabʿān. The two forces met at Lajjūn in al-Urdunn, where Ṣāliḥ's Khurāsānī troops defeated al-Ḥakam and his Syrian army. Al-Ḥakam fled the scene and went into hiding in the region of Baalbek, where he was able to continue resisting al-Manṣūr's authority until 138/755, when Yazīd b. Rawḥ al-Lakhmī, Ṣāliḥ's agent over Baalbek, captured him and sent him to Damascus. There, the governor had him executed.[22]

Even more than his ruthless brother ʿAbd Allāh, Ṣāliḥ proved to be the one figure responsible for establishing ʿAbbāsid central authority in Damascus and Syria generally.[23] Given the lesson of ʿAbd Allāh b. ʿAlī's revolt, al-Manṣūr had every reason to be suspicious of Ṣāliḥ's growing power and wealth, as some sources allege that he was.[24] A number of Ṣāliḥ's descendants became governors of Dimashq, Qinnasrīn, and other subdistricts of Syria, and the Banū Ṣāliḥ tended to hold powerful or at least prestigious positions throughout the caliphate as a whole. Al-Faḍl b. Ṣāliḥ, for example, was one such son, second in power only to his father. In 138/755, al-Faḍl led the *ḥajj* and, in the following year, led the summer campaign on the Byzantine frontier with his father.[25] In 149/766, after Ṣāliḥ retired to Aleppo, al-Faḍl is said to have served him as governor of Dimashq. When his father died in 152/769, al-Faḍl added the *jund* of Qinnasrīn to his own domains.[26] Although he left Syria in 159/775 to become governor of al-Jazīra, he later returned to the province in 163/779 when he accompanied the caliph al-Mahdī in his visit to Jerusalem.[27]

Other members of the Banū Ṣāliḥ shared in the family's increased presence in Syria. Al-Faḍl's brother, Ibrāhīm, was governor of Egypt like his father before him, and was *amīr* of Dimashq, al-Urdunn, Filasṭīn, and Cyprus under the caliph al-Mahdī. When al-Mahdī died, the new caliph al-Hādī retained Ibrāhīm in his post and even added the governorate of al-Jazīra to his domains. Sometime shortly after 170/786, the caliph al-Rashīd removed him from this post, but he later reinstated him to Dimashq in 172/788. In 175/791, in his capacity as governor of Dimashq, Ibrāhīm negotiated a truce between warring Qaysī and Yamanī tribal factions and led a delegation of Syrian *ashrāf* to meet with al-Rashīd at al-Kūfa.[28] While in Iraq, Ibrāhīm left his son Isḥāq in charge of affairs in Syria, at which time the bloody series of factional wars led by Abū al-Haydhām erupted.[29]

In the middle of this unrest, the Banū Ṣāliḥ were faced with their own family crisis. After meeting with al-Rashīd in 176/792 in Iraq, Ibrāhīm b. Ṣāliḥ died. But unlike Ibrāhīm's provincial post, family leadership did not pass to Ibrāhīm's son, but went instead to the next eligible son of Ṣāliḥ, 'Abd al-Malik. 'Abd al-Malik b. Ṣāliḥ had served the caliph al-Rashīd as governor of Medina and had led summer campaigns against the Byzantines. By 173/789, he was serving as governor of Qinnasrīn and the newly formed region of al-'Awāṣim, though he was replaced around 177/793. It was probably at this time that al-Rashīd had 'Abd al-Malik move Ibrāhīm's family from Filasṭīn to Aleppo, a move that marked the beginning of a general ingathering of the Banū Ṣāliḥ to the *jund* of Qinnasrīn.[30]

In 178/794, al-Rashīd appointed 'Abd al-Malik governor of Dimashq in place of Ibrāhīm's son Isḥāq, with the aim of establishing equilibrium in the wake of Abū al-Haydhām's revolt. 'Abd al-Malik's brother, 'Abd Allāh b. Ṣāliḥ, assisted him by taking over his responsibilities in Qinnasrīn and the frontier and, it seems, by controlling the subdistricts (*kuwar*) of Dimashq for him. However, by 184/800 at the latest, 'Abd al-Malik had returned to his original position in Qinnasrīn and al-'Awāṣim, and after this date the Banū Ṣāliḥ no longer held positions outside of these northern districts.[31]

'Abd al-Malik's duties in Qinnasrīn did not keep him aloof from the politics of Baghdad. For reasons which remain obscure, al-Rashīd had 'Abd al-Malik arrested and imprisoned in 187/803. Like 'Abd Allāh b. 'Alī, 'Abd al-Malik b. Ṣāliḥ became a particularly controversial subject for court historians. When combined with his reputation for eloquence and statesmanship and his support of al-Amīn in the Fourth Civil War, 'Abd al-Malik's notoriety makes it virtually impossible to distinguish any genuine accounts of his conflict with al-Rashīd from the tales, speeches, poems, and soliloquies that accompany most presentations of his imprisonment.[32]

According to most of the sources, 'Abd al-Malik's eldest son 'Abd al-Raḥmān and his scribe Qumāma b. Yazīd reported to al-Rashīd that 'Abd al-Malik was planning to seize the caliphate for himself. Despite a number of fine statements in his defense (many in rhymed prose), 'Abd al-Malik was imprisoned, or perhaps kept in house arrest. Six years later, in 193/808, the caliph al-Amīn released him while the caliphate was in the midst of the Fourth Civil War. After his six years' confinement, 'Abd al-Malik's influence in Syria and the Jazīra was still strong, and he was able to raise a significant body of troops from the tribes of Syria and al-Jazīra to assist al-Amīn's cause. But the new arrivals fell into conflict with al-Amīn's garrison of Khurāsānī troops stationed at al-Raqqa, and 'Abd al-Malik died before he was able to resolve their differences.[33]

As with 'Abd Allāh b. 'Alī's claim for the succession in 136/754, the accusation that 'Abd al-Malik planned to rebel against al-Rashīd cannot be verified. According to some accounts, he himself claimed that he was the victim of a plot started by his son and Qumāma.[34] It may thus be no accident that, as a result of 'Abd al-Malik's imprisonment, Qumāma went on to succeed him as the tutor of al-Rashīd's son and third heir al-Qāsim. Then again, in his version of these events, the historian al-Ya'qūbī depicts 'Abd al-Malik as being explicitly in collusion with the tribal heads (*ru'asā'*) of Syria and al-Jazīra.[35] But what is relevant to the present discussion in 'Abd al-Malik's predicament is not his real or supposed plan to rebel, but the fact that the allegations leveled against him were guaranteed to be treated seriously. Al-Rashīd knew very well that influential provincial governors like 'Abd al-Malik had the means to rebel if they wanted to. For not only was 'Abd al-Malik a member of the 'Abbāsid ruling family, and tutor to al-Qāsim, but he also had strong ties to the frontier and the frontier troops.[36] Putting 'Abd al-Malik in prison was the toughest sentence possible given the circumstances,[37] and it was a tacit recognition of the dangers inherent in the system of provincial government.

The impact that the Banū Ṣāliḥ had on Syrian politics in the early 'Abbāsid period was significant enough that some scholars have likened the family to a "local subdynasty."[38] Others have criticized this notion, especially with regard to 'Abd al-Malik b. Ṣāliḥ, whose power was rather more limited than had previously been supposed.[39] But although it is true that a "subdynasty" implies a certain level of autonomy that the Banū Ṣāliḥ may not have possessed, this family was a dominant force in politics and society in Syria for many generations.[40] The Banū Ṣālih possessed choice urban and rural properties throughout the region, including former Umayyad holdings, in the *ajnād* of Filasṭīn,[41] Dimashq,[42] Ḥimṣ,[43] Qinnasrīn, and also in the frontier. For example, 'Abd al-Malik b. Ṣāliḥ owned a palace and a garden at Manbij that was said to have won the admiration of al-Rashīd.[44] Above all, the family had its most extensive holdings in and around Aleppo.[45] Over time, the lucrative districts of Qinnasrīn and the frontier regions became the heartland of the Banū Ṣāliḥ.

After the Fourth Civil War of 193–198/809–813, descendants of Ṣāliḥ b. 'Alī continued to be influential in the 'Abbāsid court and within Syria as a whole, especially in the *jund* of Qinnasrīn and in the region of Aleppo.[46] They owned land and slaves,[47] extended their patronage to clients (*mawālī*),[48] patronized poets,[49] and intrigued among one another just like any other princely family of the day.[50] Most of the family property remained in the hands of the Banū Ṣāliḥ for generations, having at some point been rendered inalienable as *awqāf*. In Aleppo, for example, Ṣāliḥ's son 'Īsā had his properties there established as *awqāf*, and they remained in the hands of his descendants, who could still be found living in seventh/thirteenth-century Aleppo, according to Ibn al-'Adīm.[51] Ibn al-'Adīm also noted that the descendants of 'Abd al-Malik b. Ṣāliḥ at Manbij still possessed the gardens that al-Rashīd had so admired.[52]

However, the Banū Ṣāliḥ were by no means allowed to run the province of Syria, or even the *jund* of Qinnasrīn, as though it were a family appanage. In the period before the Fourth Civil War, the caliphs appointed other 'Abbāsid nobles to positions of power within the province, perhaps as an attempt to break the hold of the Banū Ṣāliḥ over the region, yet still keeping control carefully distributed within the 'Abbāsid ruling family. Al-'Abbās b. Muḥammad b. 'Alī, for example, led summer campaigns in 138/755, led the pilgrimage in 139/756, and became governor of "Dimashq and all of Syria" for his brother al-Manṣūr in 140/757. In 142/759, he was put in charge of the Jazīran frontier, and, in 149/766 and 159/775, he again led summer campaigns against the Byzantines. In the course of the reign of al-Rashīd, he was put in charge of the pilgrimage, made governor of Mecca and of Dimashq yet again, before being assigned to al-Jazīra in 185/801, the year before his death.[53]

The majority of these 'Abbāsid nobles who were chosen to govern Dimashq and other regions of Syria were, moreover, of a generation younger than the sons of Ṣāliḥ. This new generation of 'Abbāsid nobility included sons of the Imām Ibrāhīm, in whose name, according to 'Abbāsid official history, the 'Abbāsid *da'wa* in Khurāsān was secretly conducted.[54] The province plucking 'Abd al-Wahhāb b. Ibrāhīm, for example, led campaigns into Byzantine territory in 140/757, 142/759, and 152/769, and led the pilgrimage in 146/763. By 154/770, he was governor of Filasṭīn for his uncle al-Manṣūr, and at the time of his death (in 158/774 or 159/775), he is said to have been governor of Dimashq.[55] His son Ibrāhīm succeeded him until 160/776, when he was ousted by Damascene rebels.[56]

The Khurāsāniyya and 'Abbāsid Clients

Throughout the period of direct 'Abbāsid rule, especially in the first years of the new caliphate, the 'Abbāsid caliphs were inclined to appoint members of the ruling family as governors in the province of Syria. But because of the potential political threat that highly placed, powerful kinsmen like the Banū Ṣālih posed, the 'Abbāsid central government also had to work out other less potentially disastrous strategies for governing the provinces. One of their alternate strategies was to appoint to positions of power loyal servants of 'Abbāsid interests who were not kinsmen. Prominent among them were commanders of the 'Abbāsid army, in particular men who fought in the 'Abbāsid revolution itself, and who had strong ties to Khurāsān: the "Khurāsāniyya" or "Ahl al-Khurāsān." This group includes many of the commanders of the original revolutionary army, the *ahl al-dawla,* that swept west in 132/749-50, and their descendants, the *abnā' al-dawla* (lit. "sons of the revolution").[57] As clients or members of families who had led the 'Abbāsid cause in its early stages, such men would have had a stake in continued service to the 'Abbāsid government. These were men like 'Abd al-Ḥamīd b. Rib'ī al-Ṭa'ī, and Ḥumayd b. Qaḥṭaba, who supported 'Abd Allāh b. 'Alī's revolt on the frontier, or Abū 'Awn al-Azdī, who led Ṣāliḥ b. 'Alī's army in Egypt and north Africa.[58] Beginning with the reign of al-Manṣūr, however, the *ahl al-dawla* assumed a new postrevolutionary role as military men and administrators in various areas of the government, including the provinces.[59] As a result, it is not surprising to find, for example, the prominent Khurāsānī commander Abū 'Awn al-Azdī in charge of collecting taxes in Syria for al-Manṣūr.[60]

Khurāsānī commanders and their descendants could also be used to counter the potentially more ambivalent loyalties of members of the ruling family itself. Obviously, the 'Abbāsid family members in power did not always welcome the arrival of these new men. In 140/757, al-Manṣūr decided to replace Ṣāliḥ b. 'Alī, the eponymous patriarch of the Banū Ṣāliḥ, and to remove his governors from al-Urdunn, Filasṭīn, and al-Balqā'. To do so, he sent one of the leading members of the *ahl al-dawla,* Muḥammad b. al-Ash'ath al-Khuzā'ī. Ibn al-Ash'ath was a noted military figure of the revolution, with a high record of success in Iran and the eastern provinces of the caliphate. His appointment to Syria was largely a reward for his victory in 137-38/754-55 against the rebel Sunbādh at Rayy. Despite his credentials, he was only able to assume his position in Syria after some significant resistance and delaying from Ṣāliḥ.[61]

Moreover, most members of the Khurāsāniyya and their descendants (unlike most members of the 'Abbāsid family) were experienced military men who were divorced from local politics. When a strong military presence was required, the caliph could thus usually rely upon the Khurāsāniyya to crush contention. This was what al-Rashīd did in 191/806, when the activities of the Egyptian and Syrian bandits led by Abū al-Nidā' near Ayla grew to be more than the local garrisons could handle. The caliph sent Yaḥyā b. Mu'ādh al-Khuttalī, the son of a Khurāsanī commander, at the head of a large army. With the cooperation of Egyptian troops, Yaḥyā was able to subdue Abū al-Nidā', and al-Rashīd made him governor-general of Syria.[62]

The Abnā' tended to follow in their fathers' footsteps. Thus, for example, the family of Yaḥyā b. Mu'ādh went on to serve the 'Abbāsid government for generations in various capacities, including as officials in Syria. In the reign of al-Ma'mūn, Yaḥyā's son Isḥāq was subgovernor of Dimashq for the governor-general al-Mu'taṣim. He held the position again in the reign of al-Wāthiq.[63]

In the case of the descendants of Yaḥyā b. Mu'ādh, it may be that such long-term association with Syria worked against the interests of the central government. By the reign of al-Mu'taṣim, it certainly seems like the family had developed ties to local interests. When al-Mu'taṣim became caliph, he put 'Alī b. Isḥāq b. Yaḥyā in charge of the garrison (*ma'ūna*) of Dimashq. In 226/840, it seems that 'Alī killed Rajā' b. Abī al-Ḍaḥḥāk, who was the *ṣāḥib al-kharāj* and a financial administrator in caliphal service since the reign of al-Ma'mūn.[64] 'Alī later claimed that madness drove him to this act, but the sources suggest that simple personal jealousy was the cause: the two had argued over protocol and their authority relative to one another (both were in fact answerable to the caliph). 'Alī is said to have denounced Rajā' as an infidel and a crypto-Zoroastrian, and to have stressed his own precedence as a member of the Khurāsāniyya. Moreover, it is quite possible that 'Alī was planning a provincial revolt. The evidence for this is circumstantial but provocative, given the dynamic of power in Syria.

If 'Alī was planning a provincial revolt of some kind, then this would explain why he didn't merely stop at Rajā's murder, but also killed other members of Rajā's retinue, including his scribe, his nephew, and his physician. Perhaps he intended to purge the local administration of any possible opponents. For a successful revolt in Syria, 'Alī would also have had needed local support and, indeed, he may well have dabbled in Syrian factional affairs. This would explain why, in the aftermath of the investigation of the murders, the new governor had a number of local Qaysī tribesmen rounded up and crucified, the common punishment of rebels.[65] It was only when the garrison stationed with 'Alī arrested him (instead of allying with him) and reported him to the caliph that his potential as a threat was removed.

Unlike the Abnā', 'Abbāsid clients (*mawlā*/ pl. *mawālī*), did not have an association with the leaders of the revolution. Nevertheless, they served in much the same capacity as that of the Khurāsāniyya in the central government's strategy for limiting the power of kinsmen in the provinces. In Syria, for example, Sindī b. Shāhak, a *mawlā* of the caliph al-Manṣūr himself, served as governor under potentially disastrous circumstances. In 176/792, al-Rashīd sent Sindī to quell the revolt of Abū al-Haydhām in Damascus, where Sindī acted on behalf of Mūsā b. 'Īsā b. 'Alī, then governor-general of Syria.[66] Like the Abnā', 'Abbāsid clients retained their usefulness after the Fourth Civil War.

The Limits of Central Control, II: Continuities and Changes after the Fourth Civil War

With al-Ma'mūn's victory over al-Amīn in the civil war and his arrival as caliph in Baghdad in 204/819, the Manṣūrid political elite was largely displaced. Al-Ma'mūn eagerly sought to portray his victory as one that heralded a new order, and the changes in the composition of the new elite that supported him reflected both that desire and the very real political needs of al-Ma'mūn's fragile triumph. But although the players changed after the civil war, the basic structure of provincial rule remained the same; kinsmen, clients, and military men from Khurāsān still served in provincial positions. Older elite groups like the Abnā' of Baghdad and the Hāshimī nobility had been too warm in their support of al-Amīn, so al-Ma'mūn replaced them with counterparts he could trust. He particularly favored supporters from Khurāsān like the Ṭāhirids and close relatives such as his son al-'Abbās and his brother Abū Isḥāq, the future caliph al-Mu'taṣim.[67]

The impact of al-Ma'mūn's victory was slow to come to Syria. During the civil war, many Syrian tribes had flirted with al-Amīn's cause, and some local elites had emerged as the holders of real power. To them, al-Ma'mūn's changes meant an enlarged caliphal military presence, and that Syria increasingly served as one component of a multi-province administrative domain, "the West". In 198/813, al-Ma'mūn sent Ṭāhir b. al-Ḥusayn to al-Raqqa in the Jazīra. This was the first stage in a campaign to reassert Baghdad's authority there and in all the western provinces, including Syria. But although he was al-Ma'mūn's leading general and *mawlā* from Khurāsān, Ṭāhir actually accomplished very little while at al-Raqqa: dissension in the ranks of the Abnā' who were stationed there with him and rebellions in northern Syria thwarted any progress he could have hoped to make. In 204/819, al-Ma'mūn made Ṭāhir governor-general of the western provinces, but he returned to Khurāsān in 206/821, leaving his son 'Abd Allāh in his place.[68]

Al-'Abbās b. al-Ma'mūn and the Accession of al-Mu'taṣim

Direct caliphal control over Syria was not restored until 213/828, when al-Ma'mūn's brother Abū Isḥāq al-Mu'taṣim replaced 'Abd Allāh b. Ṭāhir as governor-general of the western provinces and posted the Khurāsānī Isḥāq b. Yaḥyā al-Khuttalī as governor of the *jund* of Dimashq.[69] At this time, al-Ma'mūn's son al-'Abbās was given control of Qinnasrīn, al-Jazīra, and the frontier.[70] When al-Ma'mūn died on the Byzantine frontier in 218/833, it looked as if his new political order, so recently established in the west, would stay in place. The Abnā', integrated with al-Ma'mūn's Khurāsānian troops, were now the backbone of the caliphal army, and the Ṭāhirids continued to govern Khurāsān more or less faithfully, while their influence in Baghdad itself remained unchanged.

However, just as the basic structure of provincial rule in Syria remained unchanged, so also did its potential for instability, and it was once more an 'Abbāsid kinsman on the frontier who became a source of unrest when tensions over the succession temporarily threatened the Ma'mūnid order. The tensions were between the two men most qualified to become caliph: the caliph's brother, Abū Isḥāq al-Mu'taṣim, and the caliph's son, al-'Abbās b. al-Ma'mūn. Al-Mu'taṣim was the elder candidate and although he had originally opposed al-Ma'mūn's actions during the civil war, he had served both his brothers well. In 213/828, al-Ma'mūn named al-Mu'taṣim as governor over the western provinces of Egypt and Syria.[71] But al-Ma'mūn's son al-'Abbās could make a solid claim for the caliphate as well.

Indeed, there is every indication that al-Ma'mūn was grooming him for a future position of leadership. In 213/828, when he named al-Mu'taṣim over Syria and Egypt, al-Ma'mūn also appointed al-'Abbās as governor of Qinnasrīn and al-Jazīra. In 214/829, al-'Abbās was involved in fighting Khārijite rebels outside Mosul, and in 218/833 he was sent to oversee the rebuilding and garrisoning of Ṭuwāna on the frontier with troops from Baghdad and the other western provinces, including Syria.[72] When his father died later that year, al-'Abbās was as eligible a candidate for the throne as was his uncle, al-Mu'taṣim.

Thus, in many ways, the situation in 218/833 appears to be a mere replay of the events of 136/754 and the struggle between 'Abd Allāh b. 'Alī and his nephew al-Manṣūr. But at al-Ma'mūn's death, there were some important differences. First, there were fewer ambiguities in the succession in 218/833, as al-Ma'mūn appears to have arranged properly for al-Mu'taṣim to succeed him.[73] Moreover, at al-Ma'mūn's death, both candidates were leading armies on the frontier. Although al-'Abbās's army is said to have rioted in support of al-'Abbās when they received news of al-Mu'taṣim's succession, it is not clear which contingents were involved.[74] They may have been the troops under al-'Abbās' command for the garrisoning of Ṭuwāna (some of whom were Syrian), or they may have been from the Iranian troops who were later to instigate the revolt in his name in 223/838. In any case, al-'Abbās quickly gave allegiance to his uncle, and the army acquiesced to al-Mu'taṣim's succession.

But al-'Abbās's obedience did not settle the issue, for in 223/838 a group of commanders plotted to overthrow al-Mu'taṣim on the frontier and replace him with al-'Abbās.[75] The most noticeable difference between this struggle and earlier incidents of military unrest on the frontier was the total absence of provincial interests on the side of al-'Abbās. The plot to assassinate al-Mu'taṣim in 223/838 was instigated by established contingents of the new caliphal army—that is, Iranian troops recruited by al-Ma'mūn—who saw the rise of al-Mu'taṣim and his military reforms as a threat to their position.[76] In 223/838, the Syrian frontier was not a launching-point from which Syrian interests could enter into caliphal politics, as it partially had been in 136/754 under 'Abd Allāh b. 'Alī, and as it might have been in 187/803 under 'Abd al-Malik b. Ṣāliḥ. Rather, it was an arena to which the political struggles of the capital could be exported for final arbitration.

Syria and Samarra

As is well known, it was al-Mu'taṣim who won out. As caliph, al-Mu'taṣim made his own changes to the 'Abbāsid political order. The most prominent feature of al-Mu'taṣim's changes was the growth of a new military caste that al-Mu'taṣim had personally cultivated even before he became caliph. The new 'Abbāsid military was composed of different marginal groups, including Arabs, Iranians, and, of course, Turks.[77] Of the latter, many were manumitted slaves. To house these new units, al-Mu'taṣim built a new city, Samarra, which would serve as the caliphate's capital until 279/892, when the court returned to Baghdad. At first, the Turkish regiments were limited to the role of caliphal guard within Samarra. Only later did they attain political significance within the caliphate as a whole.[78]

The evidence for this is clear enough from Syria, and indicates that here at least al-Mu'taṣim's strategy for controlling provincial positions differed little from that of his predecessors, and that he tended to rely on men associated with the incumbent political order. These were kinsmen like 'Ubayd Allāh b. 'Abd al-'Azīz, the great-grandson of Ṣāliḥ b. 'Alī who governed Qinnasrīn for al-'Abbās b. al-Ma'mūn,[79] and familiar clients and military men like Dīnār b. 'Abd Allāh,[80] or Abū Dulaf al-'Ijlī, the Arab commander from Iraq who had risen to prominence under al-Rashīd and who had fought in al-Amīn's army during the civil war. Abū Dulaf owed his post in Damascus, and probably his life, to the patronage of 'Abd Allāh b. Ṭāhir, who interceded on Abū Dulaf's behalf when al-Mu'taṣim arranged to seize the commander's property.[81] Al-Mu'taṣim's other governors in Syria are not easily identifiable, but all appear to be what by then was the accepted norm for provincial governors: 'Abbāsid kinsmen or experienced military men of Arab or client background.[82]

Turkish officers do not begin to appear on the scene in Syria until late in al-Mu'taṣim's reign, and even then they were limited to high-level positions, whose actual impact on local politics may have been marginal. In 225/839, for example, Ashnās al-Turkī was named governor of Syria, al-Jazīra, and Egypt, but he was not directly involved in the affairs of his vast governorate. Indeed, Ashnās left the former Iranian nobleman Ṣūl Artikīn as governor of Syria. He, in his turn, placed the Khurāsānī 'Alī b. Isḥāq b. Yaḥyā in command of the garrison of Dimashq.[83] When Ashnās died in 230/844-45, it seems that the up-and-coming commander and chamberlain Abū Manṣūr Ītākh inherited his responsibilities, including that of Syria, if we are to believe an oblique reference by al-Ya'qūbī.[84]

Samarra's "new men" did not truly begin to dominate government either in Syria or elsewhere in the caliphate until late in the reign of al-Mutawakkil (d. 247/861). Prior to that time, it was men chosen from outside the ranks of the Samarran Turkish community who represented the authority of the central government in Syria, usually with mixed results. In particular, Arab commanders, with their large, armed tribal retinues, could drastically alter the balance of local tribal loyalties. Early in his reign, al-Mutawakkil appointed one of his companions, Sālim b. Ḥāmid, as governor of Syria. Sālim left for Syria with a following (*qawm*) of four thousand cavalry and infantry. The result of this new influx of evidently Qaysī tribesmen into Damascus was an unintended though bloody factional revolt that ended only after Afrīdūn al-Turkī arrived with an army from Samarra. Afrīdūn immediately quashed the revolt and replaced Sālim as governor.[85]

The Strange Success of 'Īsā b. al-Shaykh

In the period following the caliph al-Mutawakkil's assassination, central control over the provinces was weakened. The swift pace of factional politics and caliphal successions in the capital disrupted the continuity of patronage and political loyalties that ensured steady government in the provinces. The circumstances were ideal for provincial rebellions. In Syria, where a governor like Sālim b. Ḥāmid could inadvertantly disrupt the factional equilibrium, another Arab governor could set out to secure himself locally by actively manipulating these loyalties.

'Īsā b. al-Shaykh al-Shaybānī took advantage of the fact that central authority had weakened in Syria and, in a time when his own position in the capital was uncertain, he cultivated alliances among the local populace. He then used his standing in Syria as a bargaining chip to obtain a more secure future for himself in the Samarran government. 'Īsā had a history of such politicking. He first rose to prominence under al-Mutawakkil, when he served in the army of his patron, the Turkish commander Bughā al-Ṣaghīr. Bughā had been sent to subdue the rebel Ibn al-Ba'īth in Azerbaijan, and 'Īsā was able to negotiate the surrender of many of Ibn al-Ba'īth's supporters because, like 'Īsā, they belonged to the tribal confederation of Rabī'a.[86]

The Syrian phase of 'Īsā's career began in 251/865, when he is reported to have been fighting a rebellion led by one al-Muwaffaq, whom he captured. 'Īsā's exact post at this period is not known.[87] By the end of 251/865, he was definitely serving as governor of Filasṭīn. He was in that post when he delayed his oath of allegiance to al-Mu'tazz, who was proclaimed caliph at the beginning of 252/866.[88] 'Īsā's reaction to al-Mu'tazz's accession was probably motivated by the fact that his patron Bughā still supported the claims of the incumbent caliph, al-Musta'īn.[89] Al-Nawsharī (or al-Nūsharī), the governor of Dimashq, was sent out to subdue 'Īsā, and the two forces met at the river Jordan. Al-Nawsharī's son was killed in the battle and 'Īsā's troops abandoned him. 'Īsā himself fled into Egypt, although not without first stopping in Filasṭīn to collect what he could of his personal wealth. Once in Egypt, he sought the protection of a governor there who had also refused his allegiance to al-Mu'tazz. Meanwhile, al-Nawsharī occupied al-Ramla. When an army was sent into Egypt to confirm the province's allegiance to al-Mu'tazz, both the governor and 'Īsā finally complied. Al-Nawsharī was then replaced (or ousted) at al-Ramla by the Turkish general Muḥammad (or Aḥmad) b. al-Muwallad, at which point 'Īsā decided to take advantage of the situation and return to his former post, evidently fully prepared with money, supplies, and, perhaps, troops, from Egypt. Upon reaching al-Ramla, 'Īsā settled in al-Ḥusāmī, a fortress that he had had built between al-Ramla and Ludd. Ibn al-Muwallad tried repeatedly but was unable to dislodge him. The two very probably negotiated terms, for they finally left together for Samarra.[90]

While in the capital in 252/866, ʿĪsā was confirmed as governor of Filasṭīn and al-Urdunn, an appointment that some sources allege was given to him after he bribed Bughā.[91] Other sources suggest that he was rewarded because he brought with him from Egypt a large sum of money and a group of ʿAlids who had fled disturbances in the Ḥijāz.[92] While he prepared himself for his return to Syria, ʿĪsā sent a follower of his to act as his deputy in al-Ramla.[93] At some point thereafter, Bughā sent ʿĪsā to campaign in Filasṭīn. When ʿĪsā arrived in his stronghold, he began setting himself up as an independent ruler. He intercepted the tax revenues that had been brought from Egypt and distributed them to the local Arab tribes. He formed alliances with the Yamanī Banū Kalb tribe and attracted a following of his own fellow tribesmen from Rabīʿa. Eventually, ʿĪsā seized control of Damascus itself.[94]

In 255/868, when al-Muhtadī was named caliph in Samarra, he offered amnesty to all rebels who had seized power in the provinces, including ʿĪsā b. al-Shaykh. In return for amnesty, ʿĪsā was ordered to hand over the Egyptian revenues and other money that he had seized. He refused. The new governor of Egypt, Aḥmad b. Ṭūlūn, was sent against him, but he received orders to return to Egypt before reaching al-Ramla and this attempt to oust ʿĪsā came to nothing. In Ibn Ṭūlūn's place, the new caliph al-Muʿtamid sent Amājūr al-Turkī, who met ʿĪsā's son in battle outside Damascus, killed him, and routed his army. In response, ʿĪsā gathered his family and withdrew to al-Ramla where he dug in in anticipation of a siege. But it never came. Instead, in 257/870-71, a delegation arrived from Samarra, offering ʿĪsā amnesty and the governorship of Armenia provided that he leave Syria forever. Later that year, he did.[95]

The revolt of ʿĪsā b. al-Shaykh is noteworthy on two counts. First, it was a revolt that succeeded. He began his dispute with the central government more or less on his own, but he only became an intractable problem when he intercepted the tax revenues of Egypt and openly defied the caliph. For this, he needed the support of local elites, which he found among the tribesmen of Kalb and Rabīʿa—old tribes, but new arrivals to the political scene in ʿAbbāsid Syria. It was these men who most likely seized the tax caravan, and it was these men who fought off the caliph's armies. For these men in the chaotic last days of Samarra, 'Īsā seemed more of a going concern than did the caliph.

But 'Īsā's success was also due in large part to the fact that the stakes were frankly limited. 'Īsā was not an 'Abbāsid kinsman attempting to seize the caliphate for himself. Rather, he was an Arab commander trying to hold on to what security he had gained under al-Musta'īn in the face of the disadvantageous political realignment in the capital under al-Mu'tazz. For this reason, when the caliphal army could not subdue 'Īsā, they could at least negotiate with him without fear of any fundamental political threat. Because 'Īsā b. al-Shaykh and his descendants went on to play a long-lived if tumultuous role in the politics of Armenia, Azerbaijan, and al-Jazīra, 'Īsā's revolt is one of those rare instances where a rebel scored a more than temporary success against the central government.

Second, 'Īsā's revolt also illustrates the prominence of the new Turkish military elite of Samarra after the death of al-Mutawakkil and how the political maneuverings of the leaders of this new elite had repercussions beyond the palaces and garrisons of Samarra. On the one hand, 'Īsā's revolt itself was an outgrowth of changes within the Turkish community of Samarra, because his actions were so closely linked to both the fortunes of his patron, the Turkish commander Bughā al-Ṣaghīr, and the latter's relationship with the various caliphal candidates. On the other hand, it is commanders of Turkish origin like al-Nawsharī, Ibn al-Muwallad, and Amājūr that the caliphs sent to subdue 'Īsā. As in the outbreak of factional unrest in Damascus that Afrīdūn subdued, the caliphs gave Turkish commanders authority not only because they had military training, but also because they were neutral parties vis-à-vis the Arab tribal factions. Their impact on local currents of *'aṣabiyya* would be minimal, and vice versa.

Moreover, the fact that men like Afrīdūn and Amājūr were sent to Syria to crush a local revolt is the main reason we know anything about them. It is much the same with other Samarran Turks who served in Syria. It is a frustrating result of Syria's sketchy relationship with 'Abbāsid court historiography that, although we are better informed about high-ranking Turkish commanders like Ashnās or Ītākh, their experience in Syria tended to be limited to the position of governor-general or governor of the western provinces. Of the lower-ranking governors from Samarra, who would have had a more direct involvement in local affairs, we know little other than their names.[96]

The Last Governors of Early 'Abbāsid Syria

What we can say is that by the end of the period of direct 'Abbāsid rule, Turkish commanders had been governing Syria and its subdistricts for forty years. This practice was the last in a series of attempts that the 'Abbāsid central government made to appoint in provincial positions devoted servants who could remain above both 'Abbāsid family loyalties *and* local political loyalties. After the reign of the caliph al-Mutawakkil, virtually every governor of Syria and its component *ajnād* were military men of Turkish origin—clear examples of the new, highly-skilled, and increasingly active elite that emanated from the Samarran Turkish community.[97] In 256/869-70, when Amājūr al-Turkī took over as *amīr* of Dimashq for al-Mu'tamid in the wake of 'Īsā b. al-Shaykh's revolt, the expectations placed on the governor had not changed, no matter what his background happened to be. Syrian sources praised Amājūr for being a skilled administrator, a builder of public works, and a man who had established security and justice among the people. He remained in his position for eight years.[98]

One might expect that when Amājūr died a new governor would be sent from the capital to replace him, or, failing that, a local leader would step in and take his place. What actually happened demonstrated the level of power that members of the Samarran elite had come to hold. Amājūr's successor as governor was his son 'Alī, who was still a child. The Turkish commander Aḥmad b. Yidaghbāsh acted as his deputy, a sort of protoatabeg. By allowing a dynastic succession of this sort, the Turkish military elite could ensure the survival of their interests in Syria. Where they once served in short-term positions as functionaries in a larger military and bureaucratic apparatus, in the chaotic mid-third century, Turkish commanders governed like 'Abbāsid nobles did in the days of the Banū Ṣāliḥ. It is no surprise, then, to find the commander Aḥmad b. Yidaghbāsh later serving as governor of Dimashq for a second time; this time he governed for Aḥmad b. Ṭūlūn, the Turkish governor of Egypt who had taken control of Syria from an 'Abbāsid central government that was increasingly unable to govern its own provinces.[99]

Conclusion

Statistically speaking, from the 'Abbāsid revolution to the Ṭūlūnid conquest, the 'Abbāsid governors of Syria did not, on the whole, rebel frequently. Yet, it was an inevitable fact of political life in Syria that if governors could upset the local political equilibrium to their own advantage, they generally did. They did this by taking advantage of their unique position in the dynamic of provincial power, manipulating local sources of power, such as the army or local tribal groupings. Through the suasion of kinship, coercion, or bribery, they combined these resources with whatever support of their own it was that they possessed.

In this regard, Syria was in complete conformity with the other provinces of the caliphate. Except for the presence of frontier troops willing to support rebellious governors, there was nothing uniquely "Syrian" in the urge that Syria's governors had to occasionally rebel. Rather, this aspect of political unrest in Syria was only a small part of a larger phenomenon generated by the structure of provincial government throughout the caliphate. For its governors of Syria, the central government tapped many different sources of manpower. Kinsmen, Khurāsānīs, clients, and Turks: all were options taken by the central government in its attempt to ensure the loyalty of its provinces.

By the end of 'Abbāsid rule in Syria, the example of 'Abd Allāh b. 'Alī was never really repeated, not even in the success of 'Īsā b. al-Shaykh, and so the central government can be said to have succeeded in its goals. But the constant, low-lying anxiety that surrounded the position of provincial governor, the suspicions that hovered around men like Ṣāliḥ b. 'Alī and his son 'Abd al-Malik betrayed the fact that the 'Abbāsid caliphs were quite aware of the delicate nature of their success. As long as they could find the supporting hands of local elites, provincial governors were always potential provincial rebels. The infrequent but occasionally spectacular revolts of Syria's governors thus exposed the limits of the central government for all to see, and provided a lesson that many contentious Syrians would actively exploit.

CHAPTER FOUR

The Swords of Our Forefathers: Umayyads and the Alternatives to 'Abbāsid Rule

After the 'Abbāsid armies under 'Abd Allāh b. 'Alī captured Damascus and put its last Umayyad governor to death, it is said that they proceeded to the tombs of the Umayyad caliphs. Once there, they pried them open and scattered the remains of Hishām, 'Abd al-Malik, and Mu'āwiya as if to efface their presence from the Islamic historical landscape. In the same year, many members of the Umayyad aristocracy were rounded up in various locales and executed. For later generations, events like these provided a potent source for moralizing tales of the "how the mighty have fallen" genre. They served to illustrate the vengeance and brutal finality with which the 'Abbāsids overthrew the Umayyad house.[1]

But despite the best efforts of the 'Abbāsid authorities, plenty of Umayyad kinsmen survived the revolution who could legitimately offer themselves as the next Umayyad caliph. Even outside the obvious survivals in Umayyad Spain, members of the Umayyad family appear in our sources with an almost embarrassing frequency in the 'Abbāsid period. [2] Their status since the revolution had, of course, fallen, but descendants of the Umayyad caliphs could always find a foundation of support in Syria. Indeed, over the course of the 'Abbāsid period, a few of Syria's Umayyad nobles were willing and able to present potent challenges to the 'Abbāsid central government as a whole.

Sympathy for the Umayyad family after their political eclipse is one of the best known characteristics of the local culture of 'Abbāsid Syria, but the reasons for the longevity of Umayyad legitimacy are much less clear. How were such sentiments able to remain current in Syria, and how were Umayyad rebels able to make use of them? The question of Umayyad legitimacy was thrown open with the Third Civil War and the murder of the Umayyad caliph al-Walīd II in 126/744. It remained a source of contention well after the 'Abbāsid "victory" of 132/749 into the reign of al-Manṣūr, when the remnants of the Umayyad ruling elite were integrated into the 'Abbāsid military and courtly realms. Yet even after this integration, pro-Umayyad sentiment flourished in Syria in the form of a potent discourse of regional pride and apocalyptic expectation that, along with loyalties formed from kinship and patronage, could be readily manipulated to political ends at times when the survival of the 'Abbāsid central government itself was in question.

'Abbāsid "Revolution" and Umayyad "Rebellion"

When the dust settled after the violence of 132/750, the kinsmen of the Umayyad caliphs found themselves in a drastically changed environment. In their new setting, some Umayyads served as curiosities, like Marwān II's son and heir 'Ubayd Allāh, who is alleged to have escaped from his father's Egyptian debacle into Nubia, where he endured many trials and tribulations, only to be captured by 'Abbāsid authorities. After his capture, he was taken to the 'Abbāsid court to narrate his adventures and, naturally, to offer his personal wisdom on the fall of the Umayyads.[3] Other Umayyads lived on as members of the 'Abbāsid court, serving as companions and advisers to the caliphs.[4] Yet still other Umayyads avoided death, capture, or cooption, and appear in the medieval sources as random, though privileged, members of the general populace. No longer members of the ruling house, Umayyads in 'Abbāsid Syria were reduced to local notables, whose social standing was based not on their connection with the caliphal court but on their lineage and wealth.[5]

An illustrative if slightly fanciful example of such Umayyad notables appears in one account set in the reign of the caliph al-Rashīd. Here, rumors of a threateningly rich and powerful Umayyad in Damascus led the caliph to send an agent to investigate and to bring the Umayyad to Iraq in chains. The Umayyad ultimately made an eloquent defense of his loyalty to the caliph: what good fortune he possessed was due solely to the good governance of the 'Abbāsids. But what good fortune it was. The caliph's agent arrived at the Umayyad's home and met with great hospitality and honor, though not without first noting the Umayyad's large extended family, his retinue, numerous companions, clients, and slaves. During the trip to Iraq, the Umayyad significantly but casually pointed out the villages and gardens that belonged to him. No doubt the genuine Umayyad notables that inspired this account operated on a more humble scale, but the elements were the same: a status derived from noble lineage, extended kin, patronage networks, and urban and rural wealth.[6]

Despite the relatively fallen status of the Umayyad nobility under 'Abbāsid rule, there was (in theory) no shortage of people who might support whatever aspirations they had toward reclaiming the caliphate. In the first years of the 'Abbāsid caliphate, the Syro-Jazīran army was an obvious source of Umayyad loyalty. Even if the army had no strong political sentiments for a given Umayyad pretender, members of the army could be convinced to revolt if such action assured their continued access to privilege. Still another possible source of support would have been those members of the general populace who were clients of, or otherwise loyal to, the Umayyad family. Like their patrons, Umayyad *mawālī,* especially Syrians, appear regularly in the sources.[7]

As long as the 'Abbāsid authorities remained unable to control at least one of three potential sources of pro-Umayyad contention—the Umayyad notables, the Syro-Jazīran army, and loyal members of the populace—an Umayyad legitimist countercoup remained a real threat. As we have seen, after the revolt of 'Abd Allāh b. 'Alī in 136/754, the caliph al-Manṣūr integrated the Syro-Jazīran army into the 'Abbāsid ruling apparatus, thereby disarming any serious pro-Umayyad threat.

In so doing, al-Manṣūr appears to have followed the advice that the ill-fated bureaucrat Ibn al-Muqaffa' tendered to him in his "Epistle on Royal Companions." Composed in about 137/755, the "Epistle" enjoined the caliph to select certain suitable members of the *ahl al-shām* for special treatment, so as to ensure the loyalty of the larger group, which was already known for its potential for contention.[8] Whatever al-Manṣūr's impetus was to integrate the Syro-Jazīran troops in 137/755, prior to that time, an Umayyad threat still remained, and it is no accident that Umayyad legitimist revolts that combined the backing of Syro-Jazīran troops and the leadership of Umayyad nobles were the dominant form of unrest during the reign of al-Saffāḥ.

Stemming the Tide: Abū al-Ward and Abū Muḥammad al-Sufyānī

Of course, such revolts were not completely new to Syria. Revolts led by tribal-military factions backing rival Umayyad caliphal candidates were characteristic of the unrest in Umayyad Syria during the conflict that brought down the Marwānid house, the Third Civil War. Indeed, there is good reason for viewing the Umayyad legitimist revolts that took place in the reign of al-Saffāḥ (132-136/749-754) as 'Abbāsid-era continuations of the Marwānid-era conflicts that began under Yazīd III. The clearest example of the continuity of these conflicts is the joint revolt in 132/750 of the Qaysī general Abū al-Ward and the Umayyad noble Abū Muḥammad al-Sufyānī. Although this revolt was contemporary with the revolts of other former Marwānid military men, Abū al-Ward did not take up arms as his colleagues did to make a place for himself in the new 'Abbāsid army. Instead, Abū al-Ward joined forces with an Umayyad pretender in a last-ditch attempt to maintain the Umayyad caliphate and to put an end to 'Abbāsid authority altogether.[9]

At first, Abū al-Ward took a prudent attitude to the new regime. As Marwān II's last governor of Qinnasrīn, he surrendered to 'Abd Allāh b. 'Alī early in 132/750. He thereby secured a role for himself and his Qaysī troops in the 'Abbāsid military. However, it seems that Abū al-Ward's old loyalties were hard to shake off. Oaths of allegiance to the 'Abbāsids notwithstanding, in the end ties of loyalty and kinship to the Marwānid house in general and Maslama b. 'Abd al-Malik in particular moved Abū al-Ward to revolt. According to all accounts of the rebellion, a contingent of 'Abd Allāh b. 'Alī's Khurāsānī troops stationed themselves at the Euphrates city of Bālis and also at nearby Nā'ūra, where Maslama's family had estates, not far from Abū al-Ward's own holdings at his family estate at Za'ārat Banī Zufar. In fact, the proximity of the two estates was no mere coincidence, for Abū al-Ward's family had long and intimate connections with that of Maslama.[10]

Abū al-Ward's revolt is said to have started when the Khurāsānī commander at Bālis allegedly insulted the descendants of Maslama and their women in some way, at which point the women sought out Abū al-Ward for his assistance. Unfortunately, the liberties that Khurāsānī commanders took upon the women and households of 'Abbāsid subjects is a common theme of rebellion narratives in our sources. It is difficult to determine whether this particular example is a *topos* of our sources or simply a *topos* of reality, a report of a commonplace facet of life in a newly conquered province.[11] Whatever the cause, the Khurāsāniyya at Bālis were attacked, Abū al-Ward assembled a following of kinsmen and Qaysī soldiers,[12] raised the white banners of opposition to the 'Abbāsids, and revoked his allegiance to the governor of Syria, 'Abd Allāh b. 'Alī.[13] Other troops from Qinnasrīn and the Yamanī centers of Homs and Palmyra came to his aid. The Yamaniyya were led by the Umayyad noble Abū Muḥammad al-Sufyānī, a veteran of the Third Civil War who had spent the latter part of Marwān II's reign imprisoned in Ḥarrān.[14]

The arrival of Abū Muḥammad quite literally gave the revolt its specific political coloring, as he now offered himself as the next Umayyad caliph. He and his following are said to have donned red garments as a sign of their allegiance to the Umayyad house.[15] While Abū Muḥammad took on political leadership of the revolt, assembling a following and writing to other Umayyad notables, Abū al-Ward assumed control of military matters.[16] What had started as a general anti-'Abbāsid revolt against the predations of the Khurāsāniyya had become a pro-Umayyad rebellion for control of the caliphate involving the combined efforts of Qaysī and Yamanī troops. Abū Muḥammad bolstered his claims for the caliphate by presenting himself not only as a mundane Sufyānī—a descendant of Mu'āwiya b. Abī Sufyān—but also as *the* Sufyānī, a vaguely conceived figure of early Islamic apocalyptic. By the time of Abū Muḥammad's revolt, many Syrians (and particularly Ḥimṣīs), believed the Sufyānī to be a messianic figure who would wipe out 'Abbāsid rule and usher in the new age of the Mahdī and the Day of Judgment.[17] Abū Muḥammad was certainly able to manipulate such ideas to his advantage. As leader of the revolt, Abū Muḥammad was to his following both a caliphal candidate and "the Sufyānī mentioned [in Prophetic tradition]" or "the Sufyānī of whom it is related that he will reestablish the rule of the Banū Umayya."[18]

At first, the unification of Qaysī and Yamanī troops under the command of Abū al-Ward and the messianic image cultivated by Abū Muḥammad seemed to be a potent mix, but the revolt quickly crumbled. Having hastily sued for peace while combating the rebellion of Ḥabīb b. Murra in the south, 'Abd Allāh b. 'Alī sent his brother 'Abd al-Ṣamad to Qinnasrīn with a large advance force. The rebels, however, routed the 'Abbāsid troops, who fled the scene and rejoined 'Abd Allāh as he approached from Damascus. But when 'Abbāsid troops confronted Abū Muḥammad's forces a second time, they were victorious.

The 'Abbāsid troops intercepted the rebel armies farther south near Homs. During the fighting, many of the rebels were killed, particularly members of the Qaysiyya, including Abū al-Ward and his *qawm*. Abū Muḥammad, for his part, fled into the desert with a number of Yamanī troops and made for Palmyra. Disheartened, the Ḥimṣīs remained behind while 'Abd Allāh b. 'Alī secured the allegiance of the Qinnasrīnīs. He then departed south to Damascus to confront the joint rebellion of Ibn Surāqa and Ḥabīb b. Murra. To mop up the revolt in northern Syria in his absence, 'Abd Allāh sent his commander Bassām b. Ibrāhīm on to Palmyra, where Abū Muḥammad had taken refuge. Bassām was unable to take Palmyra, however, and Abū Muḥammad escaped and eventually found his way to Arabia and a hiding place in the vicinity of Uḥud. He remained in hiding there for some time, before he and his family were finally located and killed early in the reign of al-Manṣūr.[19]

In the immediate postrevolutionary period, the revolt of Abū al-Ward and Abū Muḥammad al-Sufyānī was the greatest threat that the 'Abbāsid central government faced. That this was true was in large part due to the fact that 'Abbāsid authority was still something of a novelty, and that most of the Umayyad ruling apparatus was still extant in one form or another. By manipulating loyalties toward the Umayyad house in the critical military districts of Qinnasrīn, Ḥimṣ and (indirectly at least) the Jazīra,[20] and by taking advantage of other contemporary unrest in the south of Syria and Damascus itself, Abū al-Ward and Abū Muḥammad were able to present a viable alternative to 'Abbāsid rule. Although the revolt was dispersed after a short but concerted struggle, it succeeded nevertheless as a wake up call, the message of which did not go unheard. As many of the sources indicate, it was the revolt of Abū Muḥammad al-Sufyānī more than anything else that impelled the 'Abbāsids to step up their search for other Umayyad nobles.[21]

Other Umayyad Counterrevolts

'Abbāsid efforts notwithstanding, the remainder of the reign of al-Saffāḥ saw its share of rebellious Umayyad nobles cast in the same mold as Abū Muḥammad and Abū al-Ward. In fact, a nephew of Abū Muḥammad carried on his uncle's attempt to return the caliphate to the Sufyānid house. Not long after Abū Muḥammad fled Palmyra in 133/750, al-'Abbās b. Muḥammad al-Sufyānī, like his uncle before him, donned the red colors and rose up in revolt at Aleppo. 'Abd Allāh b. 'Alī, having settled affairs in Damascus, headed north to subdue al-'Abbās. However, 'Abd Allāh's nephew, the acting governor of al-Jazīra (and the future caliph al-Manṣūr), had sent Khurāsānī troops to subdue al-'Abbās as well. Before 'Abd Allāh ever arrived, these troops had taken Aleppo by force, defeated al-'Abbās, and returned to the Jazīra with the booty. 'Abd Allāh, who may well have been put out by this meddling on the part of his nephew, continued north, and besieged the frontier town of Sumaysāṭ, where the remnants of pro-Umayyad rebels from the Jazīra had fled under the new command of Isḥāq b. Muslim al-'Uqaylī.[22]

Although the Jazīran revolt under Isḥāq b. Muslim at Sumaysāṭ was, like its Syrian wing, eventually extinguished, an Umayyad contender and survivor of the siege of Sumaysāṭ emerged on the heels of Isḥāq's surrender. Joined by other veterans of the revolt, Abān b. Mu'āwiya, a grandson of the caliph Hishām, marched against 'Abd Allāh b. 'Alī. 'Abd Allāh was leading a campaign on the frontier at this time (the summer of 133/751), and he must have received word of Abān's approach, for he sent a contingent of troops to intercept him. The 'Abbāsid troops dispersed Abān's forces, but Abān managed to escape and fortify himself in the citadel of Kaysūm, west of Sumaysāṭ. 'Abd Allāh himself was obliged to quit the frontier and march on Abān, whom he finally captured. It is said that, in accordance with one interpretation of Qur'ānic sanctions against rebels, Abān's hands and feet were amputated. He was then paraded through the cities of Syria as "Abān b. Mu'āwiya, paladin of the Umayyads (*hādhā abān ibn mū'āwiya fāris banī umayya*)," until he died.[23]

And still the fighting continued. Shortly after Abān's defeat, a grandson of the infamous Umayyad statesman al-Ḥajjāj b. Yūsuf fortified himself near the frontier and fended off a contingent of 'Abd Allāh b. 'Alī's troops by virtue of the fact (or so the sources relate) that he wielded the very sword of his grandfather. The disorder created by 'Abd Allāh's own revolt in 136-37/754-55 may have given the rebel a respite, but like his other Umayyad loyalist predecessors, he too had to succumb to 'Abbāsid troops, this time under the command of Ṣāliḥ b. 'Alī, who took over affairs in Syria after 'Abd Allāh's own bid for power was crushed in 137/755.[24]

Other Umayyad loyalists also took advantage of the distractions caused by 'Abd Allāh's revolt. 'Abd Allāh had left the now reconciled Yamanī commander Ibn Surāqa in charge in Damascus while he marched into Iraq to confront al-Manṣūr. With ʻAbd Allāh thus preoccupied and his chances of victory in doubt, Ibn Surāqa characteristically turned coat and began disparaging the Banū al-ʻAbbās from the pulpit of the Umayyad mosque. The *ahl dimashq* raised another Sufyānid notable, Hāshim (or, probably, Hishām) b. Yazīd, as their caliphal candidate, with Ibn Surāqa acting as his right-hand man. But when the new governor Ṣāliḥ b. ʻAlī arrived at the walls of Damascus, the two rebel leaders fled.[25]

Although never the subject of detailed accounts, the frequency of actively pro-Umayyad revolts in Syria in the reign of al-Saffāḥ deserves some comment, for they indicate some political realities in postrevolutionary Syria that the medieval narrative sources (and the modern scholarship that follows them) tend to obscure. The fact that revolts like that of Hāshim b. Yazīd are entirely absent from some of the more important medieval sources reminds us that here, as almost everywhere else in early Islamic historiography, we are once more confronted with the self-interested "lens" of later ʻAbbāsid imperial historiography.[26] This narrative lens not only selected some accounts for special attention and ignored others, but also framed the categories applied to the actions described in them. From the vantage point of ʻAbbāsid court historiography, these accounts privilege Abū al-ʻAbbās al-Saffāḥ as the recognized legitimate caliph starting in 132/749. They describe the ʻAbbāsid forces methodically stomping out the last hangers-on of the Umayyad ancien régime. In fact, if one factors out the distorting effect of ʻAbbāsid historiography, these Umayyad "revolts" appear as something else altogether.

For the very existence of such rebellious activity betrays the cracks in the otherwise seamless imperial mask with which later ʻAbbāsid chroniclers tried to cover the uncertain process of ʻAbbāsid state-building. These so-called Umayyad revolts against ʻAbbāsid authority suggest that ʻAbbāsid authority was still an open question, and that a stable ʻAbbāsid sovereignty only slowly emerged from a prolonged period of chaos. In such a milieu, the Umayyad claimants and their supporters were not acting as rebels against ʻAbbāsid authority but as defenders of the Umayyad regime against what to them were rebels.

In this reading of the political situation after 132/750, these pro-Umayyad revolts of the early ʻAbbāsid era should be seen as organic products (indeed, components) of the Third Civil War. As such, the claims of someone like Abū Muḥammad al-Sufyānī or

Abān b. Mu'āwiya were still on par with those of other caliphal candidates, only one of whom was the 'Abbāsid nobleman who was eventually named al-Saffāḥ by later chroniclers. In other words, the conflict over the caliphate that began with the murder of the Umayyad caliph al-Walīd II in 126/744 did not end with a revolutionary 'Abbāsid triumph in 132/750. Instead, the conflict ended in 137/755, when al-Manṣūr managed to successfully silence the claims of his rivals by integrating both Umayyad nobles and the Syro-Jazīran troops into his own governing apparatus.[27]

Umayyad Legitimacy in the 'Abbāsid Age

Once the Syro-Jazīran army and most of the Umayyad nobility had been co-opted, the 'Abbāsid caliphs after al-Manṣūr were able to put the threat of an Umayyad restoration more or less completely behind them. However, this is not to say that feelings of loyalty toward the Umayyads died with the revolt of Hāshim b. Yazīd. On the contrary, Syrian sympathy with the Umayyad house was remarkably tenacious in the 'Abbāsid period. Long after al-Manṣūr consolidated 'Abbāsid rule in Syria, descendants of the Umayyad caliphs could still find men and women who attached strong loyaties to the Banū Umayya and their legacy.

Unfortunately, the sources that point to the existence of these loyalties are difficult to handle, and it is impossible to examine how these sentiments developed over time in any detail. Still, a few points about Syrian loyalties to the Umayyads are certain. On the one hand, if regional stereotypes of the period can tell us anything, it is that extreme devotion to the Banū Umayya was held to be a quintessentially Syrian trait. Generations of scholars passed on to one another traditions of the allegedly scandalous Syrian reverence for the Banū Umayya. In one such tradition, for example, a Christian Arab of Syria educates a traveler contemplating the tomb of the caliph 'Abd al-Malik:

> [The Christian] said: "Let me tell you his story, so that you may be on your way." "And what is his story?" I asked. He said: "This is the King of the Earth (*malik al-arḍ*),whom the King of Heaven and Earth called upon and then took his spirit. Then his people came and put him here until God arrives on the Day of Reckoning with the poor and wretched of Damascus."[28]

The literati of Baghdad and Samarra portrayed this Syrian attitude toward the Umayyad caliphs as a peculiar custom of provincial bumpkins and a good basis for jokes, as in this third/ninth-century tale:

> Having found myself in Syria [the narrator said], I noticed that nobody was named ʿAlī, Ḥasan, or Ḥusayn [the names of ʿAlids] and I heard nothing except Muʿāwiya, Yazīd, and al-Walīd [the names of Umayyads]. [One day,] I passed by a man sitting on his doorstep, and, having taken a thirst, I asked him for a drink. "Ḥasan!" he called [into the house], "give him something to drink!" "Did you just say Ḥasan!" I cried. "Why yes, I have sons named Ḥasan, Ḥusayn, and Jaʿfar. Syrians [customarily] give their children the names of the caliphs of God, but since we all are always hurling curses and swearing at our children, I gave mine the names of the enemies of God; when I curse one, I am only cursing the enemies of God!"[29]

By mocking Syrian attitudes toward the memory of the Umayyads, accounts like these implicitly show that there existed pro-Umayyad sentiment in Syria that contemporaries thought was worth ridiculing or marginalizing.

On the other hand, there is also a significant amount of positive evidence to show that for many Syrians the Umayyad legacy was no laughing matter, and that the Umayyad past was, to many, a golden age. Although examples of this Syrian discourse can be found scattered throughout various *adab* (belletristic) works and the canonical collections of religio-legal traditions,[30] it is best sampled in the collections of religio-legal traditions and narratives known as *faḍāʾil* ("virtues" or "excellences"). The *faḍāʾil* works, and the traditions in them, have long been the focus of study, especially those *faḍāʾil* works concerned with Jerusalem and Filasṭīn.[31] While most of these works are later compilations from the era of the Crusades and after, these collections preserve accounts which were circulated throughout the entire period prior to their collection, with many originating from a very early period indeed.[32] As such, these later collections are virtual archives of Syrian *faḍāʾil* traditions of diverse date and origin. Moreover, given the preeminence of Jerusalem in the *faḍāʾil* genre, most scholarship has focused on traditions dealing with that city and have ignored the fact that such traditions were part of, or were at least conversant with, a wider body of discourse extolling the virtues of Syria in general.

"The Virtues of Syria and Damascus," compiled by the fifth/eleventh-century scholar al-Rabaʿī (d. 444/1052), provides ample evidence of the discourse circulating in ʿAbbāsid Syria about the Umayyad legacy.[33] Unfortunately, this material is notoriously difficult to evaluate because the precise histories of these scattered traditions are unknown. Virtually all of these traditions do bear chains of transmission that include the names of Syrian traditionists of the ʿAbbāsid period, or else reveal their age through historical references. But until a relative chronology for these traditions can be established, any attempt to identify trends in this discourse is likely to be futile. Moreover, these traditions do not indicate how widely the beliefs espoused in them were held, if at all, and what cultural meanings contemporaries assigned to them. Do these traditions reflect beliefs passionately held by the bulk of the population? Or are they only evidence of rarified, even fossilized, scholastic debates?

It goes without saying that a comprehensive analysis of the *faḍā'il al-shām* traditions is beyond the scope of this study. For the moment, all one can really attempt to provide is a "discursive snapshot" of the kinds of statements that some Syrians—predominantly *ʿulamā'*—made over the course of the ʿAbbāsid period. The most obvious theme of these statements is the special sacred status of Syria. It was a region that was blessed by God, over which His angels spread their wings, and in which His prophets lived and died.[34] Consequently, the armies of Syria (*ahl al-shām*) were styled as divine weapons: the swords or arrows of God.[35] Perhaps inevitably, the virtues of Syria came to imply the vices of other places, notably Iraq, which had been a rival of Syria since the battle of Ṣiffīn.[36] Syrian-Iraqi antipathy was particularly noticeable in Umayyad conflicts and in the ʿAbbāsid revolution, and the *faḍā'il* accounts, whatever their original discursive function, indicate that such sentiment was still current after 132/750.[37]

That "Syria" had come to imply the Banū Umayya, and "Iraq," the Banū Hāshim (or at least the Banū al-ʿAbbās) is likewise clear from an early period.[38] These associations certainly informed later sentiments like that attributed to the eminent Syrian *faqīh* Abū Mushir al-Ghassānī (d. 218/833), whose grandfather was killed by ʿAbd Allāh b. ʿAlī during the revolution and who himself was a supporter of the rebel Abū al-ʿUmayṭir al-Sufyānī (see below) and a victim of al-Ma'mūn's *miḥna:*

> I heard 'Alī b. 'Uthmān al-Nufaylī al-Ḥarrānī say: "A group of us *ḥadīth*-scholars were in Damascus at the door of Abū Mushir . . . to hear *ḥadīth* from him. It happened that Abū Mushir took ill for a few days, so we went in to visit him, and we said to him: "What's the matter with you, Abū Mushir (*aysh khabaruka*)? How are you?" He said, "I am now—God be praised—in good health, pleased with God, yet displeased with Alexander the Great (*dhū al-qarnayn*), for not building the barrier between us and *ahl al-'irāq* as he did between *ahl khurāsān* and Gog and Magog!"[39]

Yet the most striking thing about this Syrian discourse is its apolitical nature. However much the Umayyads may have styled themselves God's representatives on earth,[40] traditions *explicitly* legitimating the Banū Umayya as viable political leaders do not appear in the sources. Obviously, if such discourse did exist in the Umayyad period, it was most likely sifted out of the historical and religio-legal tradition as this corpus crystalized under the 'Abbāsids. In fact the current interpretation of the nature of Umayyad authority rests primarily on the analysis of documentary sources and poetry that was not subject to later reshaping.[41] What survives in collections like those of al-Raba'ī is a "cleaned up" discourse, that could only afford to be *implicitly* pro-Umayyad.

And yet, pro-Umayyad sentiment was not completely homogenized out of existence. When al-Manṣūr considered a plan to have the virtues of the Banū Hāshim and the vices of the Banū Umayya preached from all the pulpits of Syria, he met with violent defiance in Aleppo. In Damascus one family preserved the blood stains from the fighting of the revolution on the walls of their house. For generations afterward they pointed them out to visitors.[42] Sometimes the implicit pro-Umayyad sentiment that did survive could be downright cheeky, as when writers passed praise of the Umayyads by placing it in the mouth of 'Abbāsid caliphs:

> When al-Mahdī came to Syria on his way to Jerusalem, he entered the mosque of Damascus with Abū 'Ubayd Allāh al-'Asharī, his scribe. He said: "O Abū 'Ubayd Allāh! The Banū Umayya have outstripped us in three ways." He said: "And what are they, O Commander of the Faithful?" He said: "[First,] by this house," by which he meant the mosque of Damascus, "for which I know no other like it on the face of the earth. [Second,] by the noble quality of their clients (*bi-*

> *nubli al-mawālī*) for truly they had clients the likes of which we do not have. And [third,] by 'Umar b. 'Abd al-'Azīz, for by God there will never be anyone among us like him." Then he arrived at Jerusalem and entered the Dome of the Rock and said: "O Abū 'Ubayd Allāh! This is the fourth!"[43]

By far the most powerful pro-Umayyad discourse in circulation in 'Abbāsid Syria was apocalyptic in nature. Apocalyptic expectations, literature devoted to it, and rebels motivated by it were hardly new to an area that was, after all, the birthplace of the genre—what one historian of the phenomenon has called "the Syro-Palestinian crucible."[44] Indeed, apocalyptic expectations were an important force behind the rise of Islam itself.[45] Syria in particular was held to be a center for the study of traditions about the End, perhaps because it (Damascus in particular) was expected to play so prominent a role in the events preceding the Day of Judgment.[46]

Certainly, apocalyptic expectations were a powerful motivating force during the various political movements during the Third Civil War, of which the 'Abbāsid revolution is merely the clearest example.[47] Before the revolution, even the Yamanī *sharīf* Thābit b. Nu'aym al-Judhāmī could lead his revolt against Marwān II in 127/744 claiming that he was the Qaḥṭānī, the messianic deliverer in South Arabian versions of the *eschaton*.[48] And Abū Muḥammad al-Sufyānī (or, at least, his followers) tapped into a reservoir of relatively untrammeled apocalyptic traditions to help legitimize his own claims for worldly authority. Although they did not always follow recorded tradition to the letter, expectations of a Sufyānī or a Mahdī in Syria provided the most popular vocabulary in which to express anti-'Abbāsid and pro-Umayyad sentiments. Syrians who sought to come to terms with the changes and conflicts of their times could find solace—and inspiration—in apocalyptic discourse.[49]

Apocalyptic in Action: The Revolt of Abū al-'Umayṭir

Dissatisfied Syrians thus had before them a pool of diffuse sentiments from which they might draw to express their hopes for an end to 'Abbāsid rule. These sentiments were variously anti-Iraq, anti-'Abbāsid, pro-Umayyad, or pro-Syria, but most especially apocalyptic. However, from the period of al-Manṣūr onward, such sentiments do not seem to have amounted to much in the way of actual contention in Syria. Rather, the catalyst for converting this discursive muttering into political action came later, with the Fourth Civil War, the autonomy of the Syrian *ashrāf,* and the revolt of the self-styled Umayyad messiah ʿAlī b. ʿAbd Allāh b. Khālid, popularly known as Abū al-ʿUmayṭir al-Sufyānī.

Abū al-ʿUmayṭir's rebellion has gone largely unnoticed by the traditional narrative sources and, needless to say, by most secondary scholarship.[50] A full account of Abū al-ʿUmayṭir and his claim for the caliphate in 195/811 can only be obtained from the many accounts scattered throughout Ibn ʿAsākir's *Ta'rīkh madīnat dimashq*. Although some well-known later sources have made use of this material, much of the information in Ibn ʿAsākir's work has not been examined until now.[51]

Context and Outbreak

Like Abū Muḥammad al-Sufyānī before him, Abū al-ʿUmayṭir was a genuine Sufyānī, being a direct descendant of Muʿāwiya. At the time of his revolt, he was a typical example of an Umayyad notable. A well-off landowner, with an estate at al-Mizza in the Ghūṭa and property in the city, he does not appear to have had a politically active life. He was considered to be a man of great learning and good character (he had transmitted *aḥādīth* to students in the Umayyad mosque), a reputation doubtless based in part on his lineage and age (it is said that he was around ninety years of age when he began his revolt). Unlike Abū Muḥammad, Abū al-ʿUmayṭir was of ʿAlid descent on his mother's side and styled himself "the son of the two leaders of Ṣiffīn (*ibn shaykhay ṣiffīn*)—that is ʿAlī and Muʿāwiya. Thus—the rules of eschatology be damned—he was both Sufyānī and Mahdī in one. It is not clear whether Abū al-ʿUmayṭir was entirely persuaded of his messianic role, as some accounts suggest that others convinced him of his status. Whatever the case, Abū al-ʿUmayṭir adeptly used popular expectations of the messianic Sufyānī to great advantage.[52] Some traditions were no doubt circulated to legitimate his claims, like this one, with its obvious allusions to the campaigns and death of al-Rashīd:

> A man of the descendants of al-ʿAbbās will reside in al-Raqqa and stay there for two years. Then he will raid the Byzantines, but the affliction of the Muslims will be greater

> than the affliction of the Byzantines. Then he will return from his campaign to al-Raqqa. Then [news] that he will hate will reach him from the East. He will return to the East and will not come back from there. Then his son will rule. Under him the Sufyānī will come forth and their reign will end.[53]

Salvific themes of loyalty toward the Umayyads as well as resentment against Iraq and the ʻAbbāsids clearly had their role when Abū al-ʻUmayṭir decided to revolt in Dhū al-Ḥijja of 195/August-September 811. However, the immediate context of the revolt was the vacuum of central authority in the western provinces that had formed during the Fourth Civil War. When al-Amīn and al-Ma'mūn publicly opened hostilities against one another, Syria's *ashrāf* suddenly found that their allegiance to the central government became a simple matter of individual choice. In cities throughout the province, *ashrāf* ousted the representatives of the central government and took direct control of the affairs of their region, and occasionally conflicted with one another, while bandits and predatory tribal groups like that known as the Zawāqīl harrassed the countryside.[54]

Damascus, the provincial capital, was no exception to this trend, and, indeed, the prevailing provincial unrest probably aided Abū al-ʻUmayṭir's revolt by further weakening the forces of the central government in Damascus, which, as the provincial capital, would otherwise have been well garrisoned. It is said, for example, that the person who first put Abū al-ʻUmayṭir up to revolt was an Ibn Wajh al-Fals, a *mawlā* of the Umayyads who had come to power in Sidon on the coast. Ibn Wajh al-Fals repudiated his allegiance to the caliph al-Amīn and the governor-general, Sulaymān b. al-Manṣūr, and instead gave his allegiance to Abū al-ʻUmayṭir. Moreover, the Zawāqīl, who effectively controlled the countryside, assisted Abū al-ʻUmayṭir in expelling the governor from Damascus and preventing a replacement from reaching the city.[55]

Predictably, tribal factionalism defined many of the goals of Abū al-ʻUmayṭir's revolt. According to the Qaysī Banū Bayhas family's account, the governor Sulaymān b. al-Manṣūr had originally been sent as governor of Dimashq on the heels of an outbreak of tribal factionalism. The Banū Umayya who lived in the city exacerbated the tensions by spreading rumors about the coming of the Sufyānī, whom they took to be Abū al-ʻUmayṭir. They further claimed that as restorer of the Sufyānid house, he could only rely upon Kalb/Yaman, the Sufyānid clan's historical allies, and that he could only succeed by shedding the blood of Qays. The Banū Umayya then confronted the governor and claimed that he was corrupting his government by relying too heavily on Qays, whose leaders haughtily shunned even them, the sons of caliphs. In this way, the Banū Umayya convinced the governor to arrest the local Qaysī leader Muḥammad b. Ṣāliḥ b. Bayhas.

Once that was accomplished, the Banū Umayya took power. They then proclaimed their allegiance to Abū al-'Umayṭir, called for their followers from the Zawāqīl, and besieged the governor (and Ibn Bayhas) at his palace outside the city. In the midst of the siege, Ibn Bayhas helped Sulaymān to escape to the Qaysī badlands in the Ḥawrān, from where the two proceeded toward Iraq. But the rebels caught up with them and attacked them from behind. Ibn Bayhas retreated to the Ḥawran, while Sulaymān fled in humiliation to Iraq.[56] In the absence of any other 'Abbāsid authority, Abū al-'Umayṭir's first step after expelling the governor from Damascus was to secure the city for himself and his following.

Abū al-'Umayṭir's main supporters in Damascus appear to have been kinsmen or Umayyad *mawālī,* along with local Yamanī notables. Abū al-'Umayṭir soon expanded the area under his control, however, and it is said that he was eventually recognized as caliph in Damascus, the coastal districts, Ḥimṣ, and Qinnasrīn.[57] In these new areas, too, Yamanī notables were attracted to his cause. Despite some attempts to win over the Qaysiyya as well, their intransigence ultimately led Abū al-'Umayṭir to suppress them. In the end, his inability to supersede the faction proved to be his undoing.[58]

Some of Abū al-'Umayṭir's Yamanī followers at least were motivated by familiar Syrian sentiments. A certain Kuthayyir b. Abī Ṣābir al-Qinnasrīnī for example, reported the following tale about the Yamanī notable Isḥāq b. Quḍā'a al-Tanūkhī:

> One day I was with Isḥāq b. Quḍā'a al-Tanūkhī, when he called for his swords and began pondering them, and then said to me: "O Kuthayyir, these are the swords of our forefathers, with which they fought at Ṣiffīn. They are an object of humiliation for us until the *Qā'im* of the Sufyānid clan rises and we fight at his side with them."[59]

As much as he drew on such messianic expectations, Abū al-'Umayṭir's main concerns at this stage were quite worldly. Abū al-

'Umayṭir had a large repertoire of other historical rebellions to look to for inspiration, and he seems to have exploited the cultural lexicon of revolt with energy: he not only styled himself the Sufyānī and the Mahdī but also claimed the caliphate for himself, taking the title of "Commander of the Faithful." He even called himself "The Chosen One of the Family of Muḥammad" (*al-riḍā min āl muḥammad*), the old 'Alid title that had been exploited so well by the 'Abbāsid *da'wa*. He assembled a guard (*ḥaras*), which he posted at his door and on the walls of the city. Night and day, they were to cry out, "O 'Alī! O Select One (*Yā 'alī! Yā mukhtār*)! O He whom the Mighty has selected over the wicked Banū Hāshim!" The Banū Hāshim and their *mawālī* took the hint and fled the city. Abū al-'Umayṭir confiscated their land and dwellings, which he redistributed to local Umayyad kinsmen and their *mawālī*.[60]

Yet, judging from the mixed reactions of different members of the population, much of Damascus needed to be convinced that Abū al-'Umayṭir's intentions were pure. As the revolt broke out, some Damascenes fled the city to property in the Ghūṭa or elsewhere; others even tried to dissuade Abū al-'Umayṭir from revolting at all. Consequently, popular support for his claims had to be obtained piecemeal. His followers went door to door through the city, demanding that residents give oaths of allegiance to their new caliph; those who refused to do so had their doors nailed shut. Elsewhere in the city, groups of his supporters patrolled the streets, calling on the population to give their allegiance.

Abū al-'Umayṭir also seems to have tried to play on the financial concerns of the populace, concerns which could always find a ready audience in a city where many of the families were so dependent on military stipends. A supporter introduced Abū al-'Umayṭir to the assembled Friday congregation with these words: "O people of Damascus! Let your sons be registered for pay and let your women be given ten [dirhams of their own]! This is the Commander of the Faithful 'Alī b. 'Abd Allāh! He is more entitled to [your allegiance] than the tyrannical deceivers and the people of guile!"[61]

Abū al-'Umayṭir also attempted to foster an image of caliphal legitimacy by appropriating its symbols. In addition to his titles and his leadership of Friday prayer, Abū al-'Umayṭir occupied the Khaḍrā', the former palace of Mu'āwiya and sometime residence of 'Abbāsid governors. When he went out mounted on horseback, he was surrounded by bodyguards who cleared the way, each one of them wearing Syrian pointed caps instead of the tall black pointed caps of the 'Abbāsids, and wielding clubs that evoked the notorious *kafirkūbāt* of the Khurāsānī rank-and-file. He even publicly likened some of his followers to the great Khurāsānī commanders like Harthama b. A'yan and Sindī b. Shāhak, who had risen in rank despite their humble beginnings. Abū al-'Umayṭir also appears to have employed a number of scribes, a *wazīr,* and the *qāḍī* Abū Mushir al-Ghassānī. At the same time that he cultivated these trappings of a larger administration, Abū al-'Umayṭir may also have personally adjudicated disputes in Solomonic fashion, although accounts reflecting this practice appear to be subtle character attacks.[62]

The Qaysiyya Respond

However much he styled himself an Umayyad counterpart to the caliphs in Baghdad, Abū al-'Umayṭir still could not hide the fact that his was largely a following of Yamanī tribesmen. Despite all the caliphal rhetoric, to the Qaysiyya of the region, Abū al-'Umayṭir's revolt looked like just another case of Yamanī factionalism. And when the rebels began attacking Qaysī villages and persecuting Qaysī residents in the city, the Qaysiyya responded much as they had done in similar circumstances: they sought help from the local notable most likely to provide suitable military assistance. In this case, the notable was the fugitive Ibn Bayhas al-Kilābī, now in the Ḥawrān after having retreated from Sulaymān b. al-Manṣūr's debacle. Although Abū al-'Umayṭir had invited Ibn Bayhas to join his rebellion, Ibn Bayhas had refused. He now came to the aid of the Qaysiyya in Damascus with a force consisting of tribesmen from the Banū Numayr, the Banū al-Ḍibāb (also of Kilāb), and his own *mawālī.*

When Abū al-'Umayṭir learned of Ibn Bayhas' approach, he sent a large force led by a kinsman of his named Yazīd b. Hishām to the Ḥawrān. At first, Yazīd's force badly routed the Qaysiyya, and some Qaysī leaders fled to other regions in Syria. A certain 'Umāra fortified himself at Adhri'āt, for example, while Ṣadaqa b. 'Uthmān al-Murrī, a relative of the rebel Abū al-Haydhām, fled to Tiberias. Ibn Bayhas himself laid low in his own village. However, Yazīd's force was attacked by "the people of the valley (*ahl al-wādī*)," who were either local villagers or nomads from the desert. With this attack, the tide turned in favor of the Qaysiyya, who were able to advance as far as the walls of Damascus.[63] Henceforth, Ibn Bayhas remained camped in the Ghūṭa and simply attacked anyone who entered or exited the city, until Abu al-'Umayṭir barracaded the city gates.

After consulting with his advisers, it became clear to Abu al-'Umayṭir that the city could not withstand a protracted siege, so he called for assistance from his followers in the coastal districts, the Biqā', Baalbek, and Homs, and an enormous host came to his aid. From these troops, he sent out a large force led by his son al-Qāsim, his henchman Ibn Wajh al-Fals, and other Umayyad kinsmen to fight Ibn Bayhas. Both sides were decimated after the long battle that ensued, and Ibn Bayhas fell back and headed toward the Ḥawrān to regroup. It is said that Abū al-'Umayṭir's son al-Qāsim was among the slain, and that his son's death pushed him to send his *mawlā* al-Mu'tamir b. Mūsā with another body of troops to ambush Ibn Bayhas. The plot almost succeeded, but the last-minute arrival of extra troops gave Ibn Bayhas the advantage, and al-Mu'tamir himself was killed. It was at this point, the narrative tells us, that Abū al-'Umayṭir's standing in Damascus weakened.[64]

Ibn Bayhas, meanwhile, had become very ill and so retired to the Ḥawrān. Before leaving the vicinity of Damascus, however, he set into action a plan that would assure the downfall of Abū al-'Umayṭir in one stroke while simultaneously giving the Qaysiyya control of the city. As he left for the Ḥawrān, Ibn Bayhas assembled his followers from the Banū Numayr and told them that, because of his own illness, they should have a new leader. He selected for them another Umayyad prince named Maslama b. Ya'qūb, a descendant of the caliph 'Abd al-Malik. As such, Maslama was a descendant not of the Sufyānids, but of the Marwānids, the Umayyad ruling clan that had become so closely identified with the fortunes of the Qaysiyya in the Third Civil War. Along with Maslama's kinsmen and *mawālī,* the Banū Numayr gave him their oath of allegiance and marched straight into the Khaḍrā' palace in Damascus and put Abū al-'Umayṭir in chains.

Maslama then called for the Banū Umayya who had supported Abū al-'Umayṭir and forced them as they entered to turn their allegiance to him. With a Marwānid caliph now installed, the factional politics of Damascus were simply up-ended. Where once the Yamaniyya had had the run of Abū al-'Umayṭir's domains, now the Qaysiyya made it their own. Bearing the crimson colors of the Umayyads, the Banū Numayr took possession of the plots of land they had been assigned in the pasturelands of al-Marj outside the city. Meanwhile, every Qaysī notable in the city was allotted a dwelling.[65]

It turned out, however, that for Ibn Bayhas a Qaysī anticaliph was as bad as a Yamanī anticaliph. When Maslama learned that Ibn Bayhas was returning from his period of convalescence, he began to reconsider his own precarious position in Damascus. With Ibn Bayhas approaching Damascus with a group of his followers, Maslama feared the worst and assembled the group of tribesmen from the Banū Hawāzin who formed his inner circle. Maslama's followers assured him that they no longer followed Ibn Bayhas, and that they and their swords served Maslama alone. When Ibn Bayhas arrived at the walls of the city, Maslama and the Qaysiyya marched out against him. After a short melee, the two sides both fell back. Evidently, the sight of Qaysīs fighting Qaysīs was a sobering one for some of Maslama's following, who now reconsidered their position and abandoned the city to join Ibn Bayhas. With his forces thereby supplemented, Ibn Bayhas stormed the city.

It is said that as Ibn Bayhas' men were scaling the city walls, Maslama called for Abū al-'Umayṭir and set him free. The two escaped disguised as women to al-Mizza, where they remained hidden. Ibn Bayhas recaptured Damascus on 10 Muḥarram 198/10 September 813, but the predominantly Yamanī villages of al-Mizza, Dārayyā, and Bayt Lihyā continued to hold out against him. In the meantime, Maslama died at al-Mizza, and, shortly after him, so did Abū al-'Umayṭir. The body of Abū al-'Umayṭir, who had reigned as Umayyad caliph in Damascus for more than two years, was buried secretly for fear that his tomb would meet the same fate that the tombs of his ancestors met in 132/750.[66]

The Aftermath of the Revolt

With Damascus and the Ghūṭa now subdued, it appears that the newly victorious caliph al-Ma'mūn formally recognized Ibn Bayhas as governor of Damascus. Yet if one followed the narrative account of Ibn Bayhas' activities literally, it would appear that he was acting in al-Ma'mūn's name from the moment the revolt began. It is said, for example, that Ibn Bayhas sent the head of al-Qāsim b. Abī al-'Umayṭir to al-Ma'mūn with a note in verse announcing his victory, and that, while Abū al-'Umayṭir's war cry proclaimed Abū al-'Umayṭir as "the Select One (*al-mukhtār*)," Ibn Bayhas invoked the name of al-Ma'mūn, the "Victorious (*al-manṣūr*)." But these details appear to have been supplied to the narrative retroactively by its authors, who were, most likely, Qaysī.

In fact, when the narrative sources tell us that al-Ma'mūn appointed Ibn Bayhas "over the governorate of Damascus and he remained in that positon until 'Abd Allāh b. Ṭāhir arrived as governor-general of Syria and Egypt [in 208/823]," they are most likely referring to the period after Ibn Bayhas' final victory over Maslama and Abū al-'Umayṭir in Muḥarram of 198/September 813. For silver *dirhams* minted in Damascus in Ibn Bayhas' name have survived; the earliest of these dates from 199/814 and the latest from 206/821. Until that time, it seems that Ibn Bayhas was acting purely on his own, and as such sought only to advance the cause of the Qaysiyya in the face of what he probably saw as a Yamanī junta.[67]

The beginning of Ibn Bayhas' governorate was not the end of popular visions of an Umayyad caliphate, however. Not long after Damascus was restored to order, another Umayyad notable claimed the caliphate for himself in al-Faddayn, a village in the Ḥawrān. Sa'īd b. Khālid al-Faddaynī claimed descent from the caliph 'Uthmān b. 'Affān, and thus represented an Umayyad noble line that was entirely separate from either the Sufyānid or Marwānid houses. The precise timing of his revolt is unknown, save that it took place after that of Abū al-'Umayṭir, most likely directly after, in the year 198/813. He first attacked the nearby estates of the Banū Shuhayb of the Banū Sa'd tribe, searching out and killing all the Qaysīs he could find while aligning himself with Yaman. Ibn Bayhas sent his brother Yaḥyā b. Ṣāliḥ to deal with the rebel at al-Faddayn, where Yaḥyā besieged him and forced him to flee. Yaḥyā and his troops destroyed the fortress there and, evidently, another one at Zīzā near 'Ammān.

In the meantime, al-Faddaynī found another stronghold at Masūḥ, a village not far from 'Ammān, while a compatriot of his, Yaḥyā b. al-Ḥakam, fortified himself in 'Ammān proper. Yamanī tribesmen from the vicinity also joined al-Faddaynī's revolt, along with a group of Umayyads and other refugees from the rebellion in Damascus. Yaḥyā b. Ṣāliḥ attacked both strongholds and dispersed al-Faddaynī's forces. Al-Faddaynī himself escaped to the nearby fortress of Ḥisbān, but his ultimate fate remains unknown.[68]

Back in Damascus, Ibn Bayhas began the process of restoring the city to its condition prior to Abū al-'Umayṭir's rebellion. He returned the land that had been expropriated from the fleeing Banū Hāshim and their clients to its rightful owners. If there was any further unrest in the city prior to the arrival of al-Ma'mūn's commander 'Abd Allāh b. Ṭāhir in 208/823, it has not left any record in the sources. When 'Abd Allāh b. Ṭāhir did arrive, he inspected

Damascus and its hinterland himself. With Ibn Bayhas in his company, 'Abd Allāh visited Abū al-'Umayṭir's home town of al-Mizza and accused the populace of having harbored Abū al-'Umayṭir and Maslama in opposition to al-Ma'mūn, but the people replied that they only gave them assistance after the two rebel-leaders had abandoned their plans. In normal circumstances, 'Abd Allāh would have simply relieved Ibn Bayhas of his position, which by now he had held for ten years. However, the rest of Syria and Egypt was still in disarray, so 'Abd Allāh named another Qaysī notable, Ṣadaqa b. 'Uthmān, to act as governor until he returned from Egypt in 210/825.

It is said that Ṣadaqa warned 'Abd Allāh that of those whom he now saw wearing 'Abbāsid black in Damascus, those wearing threadbare garments were to be trusted over those whose robes were new: an indication both of Ṣadaqa's political savvy as well as of the divided and shifting political allegiances in the Umayyad capital during the 'Abbāsid age.[69]

Conclusion

Al-Faddaynī's revolt was almost the last time an Umayyad notable would attempt to replace the 'Abbāsid caliph in Iraq with an Umayyad caliph in Syria.[70] But even prior to that time, pro-Umayyad revolts were exceptions that proved the rule of Syrian acquiescence to the 'Abbāsid enterprise. All pro-Umayyad revolts came at a time when the legitimacy of the 'Abbāsid central government was already in question: either when it was just forming after the revolution, or when it was rapidly dissolving in the Fourth Civil War. At all other times, most Umayyads appear to have settled peacefully into their new roles as Syrian notables. And as with other forms of contention in Syria, a pro-Umayyad revolt relied ultimately on the cooperation and military expertise of the other, non-Umayyad elites and their factional followings. Despite their obvious caliphal credentials, Umayyads alone could hardly provide the requisite manpower.[71]

As can be imagined, obtaining the cooperation of the Qaysī or Yamanī *ashrāf* would have been a difficult task. On the one hand, the majority of Syria's factional elite were functioning—if contentious—members of the 'Abbāsid military, and they would have been reluctant to jeopardize what little security they had obtained. On the other hand, the vagaries of tribal factionalism militated against members of more than one faction backing a given Umayyad (the revolt of Abū Muḥammad appears to be an exception). Thus, the comparative rarity of pro-Umayyad revolts within the larger range of Syrian contention testifies both to the divisions within Syrian society as well as to the integration of Syrian *ashrāf* into the broader 'Abbāsid socio-political order.

In addition to the cooperation of the *ashrāf,* Umayyad rebels after the 'Abbāsid revolution made use of a legitimating discourse that had its origins in partisan, regional, and apocalyptic sentiments. The revolt of Abū al-'Umayṭir shows how these sentiments could be combined with the politics of tribal factionalism to provide the power and legitimacy needed to back a viable Umayyad alternative to 'Abbāsid rule. Nor did these sentiments die out with Abū al-'Umayṭir. That we have access to traditions supporting these sentiments at all is because they continued to be transmitted (and elaborated) throughout the third/ninth and fourth/tenth centuries.

However, the fact that these sentiments never again provided a rallying cry for an Umayyad pretender should not lead us to underestimate the power of pro-Umayyad sentiments in Syria. It is said, for example, that when the rebel governor Aḥmad b. Ṭūlūn added the province of Syria to his domains, he visited the tomb of Mu'āwiya, and ordered a peristyle to be added and Qur'ān reciters to be posted to it. In this simple but meaningful act, Ibn Ṭūlūn tacitly acknowledged the importance of pro-Umayyad sentiment in Syria by publicly renovating the edifice that earlier 'Abbāsid generals had destroyed.[72]

CHAPTER FIVE

As One Face, Your Faces Are Marred: *'Aṣabiyya* and the *Ashrāf* of Syria

Members of the Umayyad family were not the only Syrians displaced by the 'Abbāsid revolution. The revolution also had its impact on the Syrian *ashrāf,* the elites who formed the leadership of Syria's Qaysī and Yamanī tribal factions. Prior to 132/750, Syria had been the heartland of the Umayyad caliphate, and the *ashrāf* were an imperial elite, drawing their power directly from their ties to the far-flung Umayyad army or to the caliph's court. After the revolution, however, Syrian *ashrāf* were denied such sources of privilege from the new 'Abbāsid government. Detached from the centers of power and prestige, Syria's *ashrāf* found themselves in reduced circumstances as purely local military leaders. The *ashrāf* were left to make do with what local influence they could muster themselves.

Gradually, over the course of the 'Abbāsid period, they came to occupy a specific, though rather more limited, role in provincial politics. They became local notables: interlocutors with the provincial governor, the caliph's local representative. The nexus of notable and governor was the focal point for the mediation of provincial and caliphal interests, and the means by which these interests were met with the least cost to local stability. As such, it was the key to smooth government.

But provincial government was not always smooth. Like the remnants of the Umayyad family that survived the revolution and like the provincial governors themselves, the *ashrāf*-cum-notables of Syria led many destabilizing revolts throughout the period of 'Abbāsid rule. Since most of the *ashrāf* of 'Abbāsid Syria were descendants of the tribal leaders of Syria's heyday under the Umayyads, it would be easy to write off elite contention under the 'Abbāsids as irrational "tribal feuding" or as anti-'Abbāsid counterrevolts. But we should resist that temptation. Upon detailed scrutiny, the majority of Syria's *ashrāf* emerge less as counterrevolutionaries than as pragmatists who fought hard to retain the modicum of local power left to them after the revolution. Often this struggle resulted in conflict with the provincial governor and his agents; just as often, it resulted in conflict with other *ashrāf*.

The factionalism (*'aṣabiyya*) of the *ashrāf* and their followers should therefore not be viewed as movements of opposition to the 'Abbāsid state. Rather, the conflict between local elites, their tribal factions, and the caliph's representatives expressed the continuous competition between *ashrāf* for access to privilege within the 'Abbāsid political order.

A Short History of Factionalism in Syria

The tribal factionalism of 'Abbāsid Syria is a direct descendant of the factionalism of the late Umayyad period. While historians of early Islam have almost always acknowledged tribal politics as a significant element in Umayyad politics, the mechanisms and goals of tribal conflict under the Umayyads are poorly understood. Historians have viewed Umayyad tribal conflicts in a variety of ways, ranging from "natural" tribal wars that followed their own cycle of violence and retribution[1] to conflict between full-fledged political parties, complete with ideological programs.[2] It is only recently that a convincing interpretation of the development of the rivalry between tribal groupings in the Umayyad period has been made. Although the sources superficially seem to describe conflicts between different descent-groups sharing primordial rivalries, a closer look has shown that the concerns of the parties involved in a given conflict were quite topical and had less to do with blood-ties than with patronage networks. In short, the tribal strife of the late Umayyad period represents conflicts not simply between tribes, but between factions.[3]

Of course, it is easy to see why late Umayyad factionalism has been so readily misinterpreted. The agents of factional conflict in our sources tended to express themselves in tribal terms that harked back to the idealized tribal wars of the early Umayyad period and earlier. In fact, late Umayyad (and therefore 'Abbāsid) factionalism in Syria organically developed out of early Umayyad tribal politics. Therefore, later factionalism cannot be understood without some grasp of the politicking and alliances of this earlier milieu.

The Umayyad Background

Syria became the central province of the Umayyad caliphate with the accession of Mu'āwiya b. Abī Sufyān in 41/661. He drew his support from his own kinsmen, especially his own Sufyānid clan, and from alliances with the tribes of Syria, who had proved their worth at the battle of Ṣiffīn (37/657) against the Iraqi forces of Mu'āwiya's rival, the caliph 'Alī b. Abī Ṭālib. Of these Syrian tribal armies (the *ahl al-shām* of the sources), the southern Syrian tribe of Kalb and its allied tribes (known collectively as Quḍā'a) predominated. Other Syrian tribes thus competed with Quḍā'a for access to the caliph and to the patronage network that originated with him. Quḍā'a's main competitors were tribes of South Arabian origin such as Ḥimyar and Hamdān (known collectively as Yaman or Qaḥṭān) who had settled in Ḥimṣ, and the tribes of North Arabian origin known collectively as Qays, recent arrivals to northern Syria and the Jazīra.

When the Sufyānid order was challenged in the Second Civil War of 64/684, the non-Quḍā'ī tribes rallied to support the rival claimant Ibn al-Zubayr. The Quḍā'a, for obvious reasons, supported an Umayyad candidate. At the battle of Marj Rāhiṭ in 65/684, the combined forces of Qays and Qaḥṭān experienced a humiliating defeat at the hands of the numerically inferior Quḍā'a (backed by recent allies from the tribe of Kinda). The new caliph Marwān I b. al-Ḥakam brought with him to power a new branch of the Umayyad family—the Banū Marwān—but he also assured the Quḍā'a of their continued favor in the new arrangement.

But although it also focused on patronage and tribal allegiances, the politics of the Sufyānid and early Marwānid period was nonetheless quite different from the factional politics of the later Marwānid period on the eve of the 'Abbāsid revolution. Even after the Second Civil War, Umayyad politics mostly meant old style tribal politics. In Syria Umayyad kinsmen and Syrian tribal leaders still held the coveted positions as governors of the *ajnād*.[4] The first sign of the transition from tribal politics to factional politics was a shift in tribal alliances: for reasons which remain obscure, in the years after Marj Rāhiṭ, the Quḍā'a of southern Syria joined with Qaḥṭān of Ḥimṣ, forming a tribal confederacy known as Yaman. The new Quḍā'a-Qaḥṭān alliance implied a military development of some importance, for the tribal groupings had fairly coherent regional ties to individual *ajnād*: the now predominantly Yamanī *ajnād* of Filasṭīn, al-Urdunn, Dimashq, and Ḥimṣ stood face-to-face against the predominantly Qaysī districts of Qinnasrīn and al-Jazīra.

The second sign was a further change in the nature of the Umayyad military: the growing professionalization of the army. Whereas kinsmen of the caliphs had once dominated gubernatorial positions, over the course of the Marwānid period, provincial governorships (i.e., those outside Syria) tended to be granted to capable military men, regardless of their tribal background. In the course of governing a province, these governors were naturally inclined to rely on members of their own *qawm* (tribal following) and its allies for their subgovernors and other positions down to the rank and file of active troops. From the higher positions, power and wealth "trickled down" to kinsmen and other members of the same faction.

Although the overall tendency of late Umayyad factionalism is for South Arabian tribes to align with the Yaman faction and North Arabian tribes to align with the Qays faction (or "Muḍar" as its equivalent was known in the East, in contradistinction to the tribal faction of Rabī'a), in many instances this was not the case. It is quite common at the factional level to find genealogically "southern" tribesmen supporting Qays/Muḍar and "northerners" supporting Yaman.[5] It was this support network of military and tax-gathering positions within the same (roughly) tribally conceived confederation that produced the late Umayyad faction. It was this reliance on fellow tribesmen, and the genealogical shuffling and antagonism that it generated, that late Umayyad and 'Abbāsid contemporaries condemned as *'aṣabiyya,* that is, factional partisanship.

During the last years of the Umayyad caliphate, factional antagonism in the provinces quickly became polarized, thanks to the tendency of late Marwānid caliphs to rely on Qays/Muḍar for provincial appointments. Yaman, an out-group for the first time in the late Umayyad period, eagerly sought to have their men back in provincial positions. For the moment, the exception to this polarizing trend was Syria. Predicated on the competition for lucrative gubernatorial posts, factional politics were the sine qua non of provincial life, especially in the East. However, as we have seen, in Syria it was Umayyad kinsmen or members of the leading sharifian families who held the governorships of the *ajnād* and this remained true in the Marwānid period. Throughout the Umayyad period, whatever their tribal background might be, Syrian *ashrāf* were known as local tribal leaders, not as factional leaders.[6]

The Third Civil War

The Third Civil War of 126/744 changed all this.[7] For civil war in this case meant simply that the factional politics of the provinces had become a "metropolitan phenomenon" and had infected Syria.[8] It also meant a change in the basis of the power of Syria's *ashrāf*. With the arrival of provincial factionalism to the *ajnād* of Syria, authority came to be based not so much on the *sharaf* of the old Syrian families, as on reputation and factional prominence in the military. Henceforth, the old *ashrāf* either accepted these new rules—as many did—or they kept out of politics. In Syria, as in the provinces, political leadership became equivalent to factional leadership.[9] Thus, at the outbreak of the civil war, when the dissident Umayyad prince Yazīd III claimed the caliphate for himself in opposition to the incumbent caliph al-Walīd II, he did so through the support of the Yamaniyya, a factional following composed primarily of disenfranchised Syrian Yamanī tribesmen.[10]

With the murder of al-Walīd II at the hands of the Yamaniyya, the social, regional, and factional tensions in Syria came to a head. Throughout Syria, local *ashrāf* led contingents of Syrian troops against Yazīd III and chose alternative Umayyad princes as their caliphal candidates. Despite their primarily "southern" origins, many members of the *ajnād* of Syria had as much reason as did the incumbent *ashrāf* to fear for their future under the Yamaniyya. Led by local *ashrāf*, the regional army of Ḥimṣ wrote to the other *ajnād* to invite them to join with them in avenging the death of their caliph al-Walīd II. The Ḥimṣīs and their supporters swore to remain loyal to the sons and heirs of al-Walīd II as long as the boys lived, and, barring that, to support the best candidate for caliph, provided he continued to give them regular stipends and to pass the stipends along to their sons after them.

The Ḥimṣīs eventually chose as their leader a direct descendant of the first Umayyad caliphs, the ambitious Abū Muḥammad al-Sufyānī. Although Yazīd III imprisoned Abū Muḥammad and crushed the rebellion before it reached Damascus, he nevertheless gave the Ḥimṣī troops their stipends, mollified their leaders, and named a Ḥimṣī leader as governor.[11] In the *ajnād* of Filasṭīn and al-Urdunn, the troops and the *ashrāf* revolted in a similar fashion.[12]

Opposition to Yazīd III and the Yamaniyya also came from outside Syria. In 126/744, when he first learned of the death of al-Walīd II, the Umayyad nobleman and general Marwān b. Muḥammad (the future caliph Marwān II) prepared to march into Syria from the Armenian frontier, ostensibly to avenge al-Walīd II's murder and to support the latter's sons as rightful heirs to the caliphate. But, characteristically, factional unrest in his own ranks prevented Marwān from entering Syria. On the eve of Marwān's departure for Syria, Thābit b. Nu'aym al-Judhāmī, a Filasṭīnī *sharīf* and commander, conspired with those Yamanī troops who were with Marwān to desert.[13] The conspiracy was soon discovered and Thābit and his sons were apprehended. As a result, Marwān was obliged to dismiss all of the Yamanī troops and their commanders, all of whom returned to their districts in Syria.[14]

The Reign of Marwān II

When Yazīd III died in 126/744 and his brother Ibrāhīm succeeded him, Marwān renewed his plans to back the claims of the sons of al-Walīd II. As a direct result of Thābit b. Nu'aym's mutiny, Marwān now drew his military support almost exclusively from the Qays of the Jazīra and northern Syria. His commanders included Qaysī *ashrāf* such as al-Wathīq b. al-Hudhayl b. Zufar and Abū al-Ward b. al-Kawthar.[15] As Marwān and the Qaysiyya approached Damascus, they met up with a Yamanī force led by the Umayyad nobleman and commander Sulaymān b. Hishām near 'Ayn al-Jarr in the Biqā'. In the battle that followed, the Yamaniyya were routed. Sulaymān and those of his troops who were not captured or killed fled to Damascus, where, it is said, a cabal of Yamanī leaders arranged for the sons of al-Walīd II to be killed in prison. Shortly thereafter, Marwān entered Damascus and accepted the oath of allegiance to himself as caliph from the assembled troops and *ashrāf*. The first to do so was the former leader of the Ḥimṣī rebellion against Yazīd III, Abū Muḥammad al-Sufyānī, now released from prison (and, it is said, still in his fetters), followed by the Syrian army, the *ashrāf* of Dimashq and Ḥimṣ, and, ultimately, by the caliph-of-the-moment Ibrāhīm himself. Bereft of sufficient factional support, Ibrāhīm completely renounced his claim to the caliphate.[16]

Like Yazīd III, whose original coup brought the Yamaniyya to positions of authority, Marwān II was supported in his bid for the caliphate almost exclusively by the Qaysiyya. It is thus not surprising to find soon after Marwān's accession Qaysī tribesmen placed in positions of authority in Syria.[17] But we should be wary of following a "one caliph, one faction" model of Umayyad politics, even in the polarized atmosphere of civil war.[18] To understand why, one need only examine Marwān's strategy for governing in Syria. After his accession in 127/744, Marwān allowed each *jund* to select its own governor.[19] The results are vivid evidence of the variety of factional and tribal loyalties existing throughout the province shortly before the 'Abbāsid revolution. The Ḥimṣīs elected 'Abd Allāh b. Shajara al-Kindī, who is otherwise unknown, but, given his tribal affiliation, may be classified as a Yamanī. The Damascenes elected Zāmil b. 'Amr al-Ḥubrānī, whose precise affiliation is vague, but may tentatively be classified as a Qaysī.[20] The *jund* of al-Urdunn elected a Marwānid, al-Walīd b. Mu'āwiya b. Marwān, and the *jund* of Filasṭīn elected their own local hero, Thābit b. Nu'aym al-Judhāmī, a Yamanī.

Thus, of Marwān II's four subgovernors of Syria south of Qinnasrīn, only one was Qaysī after local opinion was voiced, and not even his allegiance has been solidly proved. Nor, in any case, did he remain for very long. Marwān II's victory in the Third Civil War over Yazīd III and the Yamaniyya might have been a Qaysī triumph elsewhere in the caliphate. But in Syria, the most important immediate change was that neither the Umayyad ruling family nor the local *ashrāf* retained exclusive control over the region. Despite some slight Qaysī headway into the governing positions in Syria, it would take a revolution to oust the Yamaniyya from powerful positions in Syria, one that would take the Qaysiyya—and the Umayyad dynasty—with them.

The election of the governors of the *ajnād* may have temporarily calmed the fears that the Syrian military and the *ashrāf* had about the disruption of their privileges. But later in 127/744-45, the transfer of the central treasury and the residence of the caliph to the city of Ḥarrān in the Qaysī heartland of the Jazīra quickly reawakened those fears.[21] The *ajnād* were quick to react, much as they had under Yazīd III. True to form, the first to act was the governor of Filasṭīn, Thābit b. Nu'aym, who wrote to the individual *ajnād* and urged them to move against Marwān. In turn, Marwān was forced to subdue revolts both at Homs and the Kalbī/Yamanī enclave of Palmyra, which capitulated through the intercession of Kalbī and Umayyad notables under Marwān's command. Other commanders—in particular Abū al-Ward al-Kilābī—were sent to subdue Damascus, where the Yamanī populace of the villages of the Ghūṭa had ousted their Qaysī governor Zāmil b. 'Amr and named the Yamanī *sharīf* Yazīd b. Khālid al-Qasrī in his place.

From Damascus, Abū al-Ward proceeded to Tiberias, the capital of the *jund* of al-Urdunn, which Thābit b. Nu'aym and the rebellious army of Filasṭīn had under siege. Abū al-Ward pursued Thābit to Filasṭīn, where the latter assembled his *qawm* and the local troops, only to be captured, ironically himself the victim of deserting troops.[22]

Like Marwān's first march through Syria to claim the caliphate, the pacification of Syria in 127/745 was followed by some conciliatory gestures toward the disgruntled Yamanī factional leaders, as when Marwān granted amnesty to Kalbī/Yamanī leaders from Palmyra and to Umayyad nobility like Sulaymān b. Hishām. But elsewhere, the Qaysiyya were getting hold of positions. In Yamanī-dominated Filasṭīn, for example, Marwān replaced Thābit b. Nu'aym as governor with a Qaysī member of his own guard (*shurṭa*).[23]

But the Yamaniyya had little use for Marwān and the Qaysiyya, and when the caliph directed his attentions toward rebellions in Iraq, the Syrian troops in his army gave their allegiance to Sulaymān b. Hishām at Ruṣāfa instead. Under Sulaymān's leadership, they deserted and returned to Qinnasrīn, where other Yamanī troops also arrived in his support. In the meantime, Kalbī troops arrived at the walls of Damascus with Sulaymān's brother, Yazīd b. Hishām, at their head, while the sons of Thābit b. Nu'aym overran Filasṭīn, and the garrison at Homs revolted, killing their governor and replacing him with another brother of Sulaymān. Marwān was ultimately able to crush these sons of Hishām, but Sulaymān himself managed to escape to Iraq, where he and other Umayyad elites joined forces with a Khārijite rebel.[24]

For the Yamanī *ashrāf* and their followings in Syria, hope for a return to privilege would have left with Sulaymān b. Hishām. With Qaysī followers of Marwān now dominating positions in Syria and the rest of the caliphate, the Yamanīs' access to privilege by the "usual" means of factional politics was blocked. With their numbers thinned after a year of failed rebellion, and many of their leaders and potential caliphal candidates dead, exiled, imprisoned, or in flight, any serious attempts at replacing Marwān's regime were unlikely to succeed. As is well known, the sources suggest that in Khurāsān, propagandists for the 'Abbāsid cause played on the despair of the Yamaniyya in the reign of Marwān. In Syria, Yamanī-Qaysī antagonism in the ranks of Umayyad supporters also appears to have assisted the 'Abbāsid conquest. As Marwān fled into Egypt after his defeat at the battle of the Zāb in 132/750, the cities and armies of Syria offered him only resistance. It is said that in Damascus, the former capital of Mu'āwiya b. Abī Sufyān, Yamanī tribesmen opened the gates of the city to the 'Abbāsid armies of 'Abd Allāh b. 'Alī.[25]

Initial Reactions to the 'Abbāsid Revolution in Syria

When seen in its proper context, the 'Abbāsid revolution was, of course, merely the last phase of the events that came to be known as the Third Civil War. Yet, for Syria especially, the entrance of a new 'Abbāsid ruling elite brought with it truly important changes in the dynamic of power. The responses to these changes after the 'Abbāsid movement gained control of Syria in 132/750 were varied but immediate. The Qaysī military elite in particular was reeling from a radical reversal of fortune. Once the backbone of the caliphal army under Marwān II, the ranks of the Qaysiyya were now deprived of their caliphal patron and were themselves decimated after the battle of the Zāb. Moreover, the Qaysiyya now faced a new regime that not only cultivated ties with the Yamaniyya, but also possessed a marked anti-Muḍar/Qays streak.[26] Many of Marwān II's former military men must have followed the example of Abū al-Ward, Marwān's commander who had almost single-handedly suppressed the Yamanī revolts in Syria in 127/745. He surrendered to 'Abd Allāh b. 'Alī's army in 132/750 in order to ensure for himself a continued role in the new regime.[27]

Although most of the Marwānid military men sought continued power within the military apparatus of the new regime, there were some former Umayyad elites who did not. After all, even in the aftermath of the revolution, an 'Abbāsid victory was by no means assured. As we have seen, many members of the Marwānid army fought on behalf of Umayyad pretenders against the recently arrived 'Abbāsid forces as eleventh-hour attempts to nip the 'Abbāsid *dawla* in the bud.[28] Others, however, were less eager to throw in their lot with the Umayyads in the face of the new political tide from Khurāsān, and yet they were not willing to fully surrender to 'Abbāsid terms either, as so many others did.

The Joint Revolt of Ḥabīb b. Murra and Ibn Surāqa

At a time when the future of the *ashrāf* was far from secure, the convergent fates of two Marwānid military men—Ḥabīb b. Murra of Qays and Ibn Surāqa of Yaman— demonstrate how the two rival factions could unite, if only briefly. Although the revolt was contemporary with the pro-Umayyad revolt of Abū al-Ward and Abū Muḥammad al-Sufyāni, there is no direct evidence linking them. The motives of the two revolts differ so much that the two should be seen as events born of entirely separate responses to the revolution. Whereas Abū al-Ward fought alongside an Umayyad claimant to the caliphate, Ḥabīb and Ibn Surāqa fought for the more practical goal of the Syro-Jazīran army's continued employment under the 'Abbāsids.

In 132/750, 'Abd Allāh b. 'Alī, the first 'Abbāsid governor of Syria, was encamped at Nahr Abī Fuṭrus in Filasṭīn. It was from there that he sent an army of Khurāsānī troops to pursue Marwān II into Egypt and it was also there that 'Abd Allāh allegedly massacred members of the Umayyad family.[29] Not far away, Ḥabīb b. Murra al-Murrī, a Qaysī commander from Marwān's army, revolted in the Ḥawrān.[30] He was supported by Qaysī troops from Bathaniyya and the Ḥawrān, and, it is said, was inspired by fear for his and his followers' future in the new regime.[31] 'Abd Allāh b. 'Alī marched against Ḥabīb in the Ḥawrān but granted him and his followers amnesty instead when he was forced to disengage and move against the more threatening revolt of Abū Muḥammad al-Sufyānī near Qinnasrīn.[32]

'Abd Allāh's assurances to Ḥabīb may have been welcome to the latter's Qaysī following, but they were a bald expedient for 'Abd Allāh, who, en route to Qinnasrīn, simply ordered his deputy in Damascus, 'Abd al-Ḥamīd b. Rib'ī, to take a large force of Khurāsānī and Yamanī troops and attack Ḥabīb again. The Yamanī troops were commanded by Ibn Surāqa, who would later provide valuable support in 'Abd Allāh b. 'Alī's own bid for the caliphate in 136/754. A Yamanī commander from the early stages of the Third Civil War, Ibn Surāqa had been governor of Dimashq for Walīd II, of Filasṭīn for Yazīd III, and of Mosul for Marwān II.[33]

As he was serving alongside Khurāsānī troops, Ibn Surāqa had obviously remodeled himself as a commander at the service of the ʿAbbāsids. However, in the revolutionary times following the death of Marwān II, Ibn Surāqa and his men may nevertheless have been concerned about their fate. When the ʿAbbāsid forces met up with Ḥabīb at Zurrā in the Ḥawrān, the Yamanī troops serving the ʿAbbāsids deserted, and the remaining ʿAbbāsid army was forced to retreat to Damascus.[34] Back in Damascus, Ibn Surāqa turned coat and led the Syrian troops there in revolt against the governor and the garrison of Khurāsāniyya while Ḥabīb and the Qaysī troops arrived to besiege the city.[35] With the Khurāsāniyya now attacked from within and without the city, the governor took ʿAbd Allāh's treasure and hastily retreated to Beirut.

It was at this point that Ibn Surāqa and his Yamanī and Rabīʿī troops were able to successfully negotiate their continued utility to the ʿAbbāsid government, although at the expense of their recent ally, Ḥabīb, and his Qaysī troops. Once informed of the situation in Damascus, ʿAbd Allāh b. ʿAlī wrote in conciliatory terms to the *ashrāf* of Rabīʿa and Yaman and implored them to return to the ʿAbbāsid fold: "You . . . were our partisans and our helpers in Khurāsān, you delivered the city of Damascus to us and you killed [the governor] al-Walīd b. Muʿāwiya. You are one of us, and our rise to power is due to you."[36]

Sensing danger, the Qaysī troops decamped from Damascus and rejoined Ḥabīb. By the beginning of 133/mid-750, ʿAbd Allāh had arrived at Damascus and granted amnesty to the predominantly Yamanī troops who had remained there. ʿAbd Allāh now marched again on Ḥabīb, with an obedient force of Yamanīs once more led by the mercurial Ibn Surāqa. With Ibn Surāqa's newly won support, ʿAbd Allāh finally brought the Ḥawrān under ʿAbbāsid control. During the final battle, Ḥabīb b. Murra is said to have escaped into the desert.[37]

The joint revolt of Ḥabīb b. Murra and Ibn Surāqa is a particularly striking example of the ways in which factional rivalries were manipulated in the chaotic months following the ʿAbbāsid revolution. But more striking than ʿAbd Allāh's "divide and conquer" strategy (or Ibn Surāqa's last-minute treachery) is the fact that Ḥabīb, Ibn Surāqa, and their men were able to unite, if only briefly, as fellow former servicemen in the Marwānid army. Factional rivalries are an undeniable commonplace in the history of ʿAbbāsid Syria, yet such rivalries could also be temporarily set aside when needed. In this case, Qays and Yaman found common cause in an attempt to win assurances of continued survival for both groups under the ʿAbbāsids. Such common concern would resurface later, as when the Syro-Jazīran armies united again in 'Abd Allāh b. 'Alī's bid for the caliphate during the succession struggle of 136/754.[38] Even after al-Manṣūr emerged as the victor from that struggle, the Syro-Jazīran armies were pardoned for backing 'Abd Allāh and were accorded a continued role in the 'Abbāsid government.

The Crisis of the *Ashrāf*

Al-Manṣūr's decision to incorporate the former Umayyad armies of Syria and the Jazīra into the 'Abbāsid ruling apparatus was probably motivated as much by the 'Abbāsid government's military needs of the moment as by the willingness of the Syro-Jazīran troops to fight for their continued utility. Yet whatever lay behind it, the decision worked: after al-Manṣūr accorded amnesty to the Syrian army in 136/754, we hear little of unrest or rebellion in Syria.[39] By all accounts almost no one in Syria rose up against the 'Abbāsid government until the reign of al-Rashīd.[40] If there had been unrest, it is not surprising that it was not reported by the sources of the time, given their historiographical preoccupations, and their tendency to ignore events in Syria. Yet, one cannot get around the fact that in the forty years after 'Abd Allāh b. 'Alī's defeat, whenever ones does encounter Syrians in the sources, they are obedient 'Abbāsid subjects. Perhaps, as one source suggests, the main source of dissent, the army, was simply too exhausted to bother with rebellion.[41] Then again, this period of stability coincides exactly with the rise of the Banū Ṣāliḥ in Syria, and it may be that this powerful governing family could somehow maintain the proper factional equilibrium more effectively than the military men of later, more turbulent periods.[42]

The only exception to this period of calm seems to have been a minor incident in 160/776, when a change of governors provided the opportunity for Damascene troops to burn the government pay rolls, oust the new governor, and appoint the Yamanī *sharīf* Ma'yūf b. Yaḥyā al-Ḥajūrī in his place. Ma'yūf b. Yaḥyā al-Ḥajūrī (the Elder) supported the Yamaniyya in the Third Civil War, and went on to become a prominent commander of the Syrian army for the 'Abbāsids, leading many raids on the frontier. From the one brief notice of this revolt, it is not clear what exactly was at issue. However, the troops' focus on the pay rolls, and their support of a prominent Yamanī *sharīf*, suggest that factional interests were the main concern. It may have been dissatisfaction with the existing allocation of stipends and a desire to have a local Yamanī in charge that motivated these rebels. The ultimate fate of Ma'yūf is not known, though his family continued to be prominent in factional politics in Syria for generations thereafter. By combining factional grievances with the ambitions of the *ashrāf,* his revolt set an important precedent for future *'aṣabiyya* in Syria.[43]

The events of 160/776 aside, the prevailing silence of our sources with regard to Syria also obscures a momentous change in the status of the Syrian *ashrāf*: their transformation from members of an imperial ruling stratum into precariously poised provincial elites. Given the polarized politics of the Third Civil War, it might have been expected that the supporters of at least one faction would emerge unscathed from the 'Abbāsid revolution. Indeed, Marwān II's Qaysiyya obviously stood to lose the most from 'Abbāsid success. The Yamaniyya who aided the cause of the 'Abbāsids may have had good reason to hope that they would again rise to prominence on the coat-tails of the revolution.[44]

But, if factionalism has any rules, it is that there can be only one faction in favor at a time.[45] In the context of the aftermath of the revolution, the fears of factional leaders like Ḥabīb b. Murra and Ibn Surāqa were understandable. To Qaysī and Yamanī *ashrāf* alike, the 'Abbāsid *da'wa* must have seemed like a variation on a threatening theme: an opposition movement led by Qurashī noblemen who were backed by a Khurāsānī superfaction that threatened to displace the Syro-Jazīran army altogether. Although the revolution of 132/749-50 may have started as a Yamanī countercoup,[46] this does not account for the subsequent anxiety of Syrian leaders of both tribal factions—Qays and Yaman—over their relationship with the new regime. One can better appreciate the anxiety of Syria's *ashrāf* with a look at their career options after 132/750, and a reminder that this was, after all, an 'Abbāsid revolution.[47]

The impression one gets from the medieval sources is that, if Syrians held important offices under the 'Abbāsids as they did under the Umayyads, then one has to look hard to find them. After 132/750, there were very few Syrians who held governorships outside of Syria, and who could thus be called caliphal elites in any meaningful way. An important exception seems to be the family of the Banū Khuraym, who were staunch Murrī/Qaysī supporters of Marwān II and who thrived under the early 'Abbāsids as governors of Armenia, Azerbaijan, and Sīstān. Indeed, the devastating revolt of Abū al-Haydhām al-Murrī in Damascus was touched off by the family's sudden fall from grace under al-Rashīd. Other Syrians in service outside Syria are few and far between.[48]

Moreover, if posts outside Syria were not being filled by individual Syrians, the Syrian troops as a whole did only slightly better. With a Khurāsānī caliphal army housed in Baghdad, the Syro-Jazīran troops were little used outside Syria. One startling exception is the use of Syrian contigents in north Africa. In 154/771, al-Manṣūr appointed Yazīd b. Ḥātim governor of north Africa. Before departing, he accompanied the caliph to Syria and Jerusalem, where he mustered the Syrian and Jazīran troops who were to accompany him. Yazīd is said to have disbanded the left-over Umayyad Syrian troops who were in north Africa when he arrived and to have replaced them with Khurāsānīs, but, strangely, the fate of Yazīd's own Syrian contingents is unclear. In any case, there were still Syrian troops being used in north Africa in 183/799 when the governor Tammām b. Murra faced a revolt by the Syrian and Khurāsānī troops posted with him.[49] Apart from these troops in north Africa, the Syrian troops were almost entirely confined to Syria.[50]

Yet, even in their home province, the horizons were limited for the Syrian *ashrāf* of the 'Abbāsid age. When Syrians appear as officeholders in the individual *ajnād* of the province, it is usually in exceptional circumstances. While data are lacking from the three *ajnād* of Filasṭīn, al-Urdunn, and Ḥimṣ, the record is fairly complete—and very telling—from Dimashq and Qinnasrīn (see Appendixes A and B). In Dimashq, Syrians generally appear as governors only at two points in time: in the early years immediately after the revolution, and in the chaotic years of the Fourth Civil War, when local elites were recognized as officeholders *faute de mieux*. The exception appears to be the two Syrians who were proclaimed governors of Dimashq in 160/776 after a revolt of the troops. In Qinnasrīn, the pattern is the same: Syrians appear in office in the wake of 'Abd Allāh b. 'Alī's revolt and during the Fourth Civil War, but 'Abbāsids, Khurāsānīs, Turks, and Transoxanians predominate throughout.[51]

The sole official capacity in which Syrians appear consistently throughout the 'Abbāsid period is during the annual campaigns against the Byzantines on the Syro-Jazīran frontier. In almost every other year from 132/750 to 218/833, Syrians are mentioned fighting on the Syrian frontier. The sources describe contingents of Syrian troops, such as those that accompanied 'Abd Allāh b. 'Alī in 136/753 or those that accompanied al-Rashīd himself in 190/806, usually alongside other Jazīran or Khurāsānī troops.[52] Occasionally, the sources mention specific Syrian commanders, who were presumably in charge of a larger Syrian following, such as the Damascene al-Ḥārith b. ʿAbd al-Raḥman al-Jurashī, who led the summer campaign in 135/752, or the Qinnasrīnī Yazīd b. al-Mukhallad b. Hubayra, who campaigned with al-Rashīd in 190/806 and 191/807.[53] But Syrians do not appear consistently in any other ʿAbbāsid province.

It appears, then, that prospects were certainly bleak for the Syrian *ashrāf* of the ʿAbbāsid period. It is true that in the early years after the revolution, various Syrian *ashrāf* negotiated a continued position for themselves in the military, not to mention other realms of the ʿAbbāsid political order.[54] But the position that they negotiated for themselves was a limited one. Even with their place in the ʿAbbāsid military assured, Syrian *ashrāf* were, by and large, conspicuously absent from the ranks of the ʿAbbāsid caliphal elite. Syrians fought Baghdad's battles without the benefit or the likelihood of obtaining governorships and privileged positions as they used to under the Umayyads. Moreover, whatever benefits or profits that they obtained as Syrian frontier troops were seasonal, temporary, and, in most cases, shared with Jazīran, Khurāsānī, and, later, Turkish troops.

It should come as no surprise, then, that what little influence Syrian *ashrāf* and factional leaders could hope for they obtained not as ʿAbbāsid officials but as "protonotables," local elites who acted as intermediaries with local governors, and yet, at the same time, technically served the state as soldiers and commanders in the Syro-Jazīran army. When the Syro-Jazīran troops were disbanded under the caliph al-Muʿtaṣim, the transformation of Syria's long-lineaged *ashrāf* into archetypal local notables was complete. By then, they also faced other rivals in the struggle for notability.[55]

When they were not acting as commanders and soldiers on the Syrian frontier, then, the *ashrāf* of ʿAbbāsid Syria tried to bolster their power as local notables and factional leaders. In these roles, they were mired in a highly unstable relationship with local governors, who, when they did not avoid factional politics altogether, might or might not favor the desired faction. As a result, the *ashrāf* often had to contend with one another. For unlike the factionalism of the Marwānid period, Syrian *ʿaṣabiyya* under the ʿAbbāsids could no longer be about winning control of lucrative positions in the provinces. Rather, it focused on currying partisanship with the local governor—or at least on ensuring his balanced impartiality—

and, as a result, gaining an edge on the competition for whatever scarce local military positions or privileges were to be had.

It would be reductive, however, to see 'Abbāsid-era factionalism as merely the business of soldiers, however central the military might have been to the fortunes of the *ashrāf*. Not all Syrians were soldiers, of course, but—economic diversity being the key to success—any family that wanted to get anywhere tried to place at least some of its sons in the military.[56] As a result, the civilian kinsmen of solidiers also indirectly benefited from the patronage of factions, and it is thus not always clear whether the agents of *'aṣabiyya* are soldiers or not.

Given the history of early Umayyad conflicts, the tendency of families to include members from various social ranks, and the tendency for tribes to embrace a spectrum of lifeways, tensions between civilian tribesmen always had the potential to escalate into conflicts that could only be resolved at the level of the faction. Likewise, factionalism of the 'Abbāsid period always had the potential to "spill over" into nonmilitary realms. Eventually, the inherent opportunity for conflict between Syria's protonotables and local governors, when combined with existing tribal-factional tensions, produced in Damascus an explosive sequence of events that vividly illustrates the response of the *ashrāf* to their new relationship with the central government and with one another.

The Revolt of Abū al-Haydhām al-Murrī

The revolt of the Qaysī protonotable Abū al-Haydhām al-Murrī in 177/793[57] extended over eight months and ravaged most of the fertile lands of the Ghūṭa, divided the populace of Damascus, ruined the career of at least one governor, and cost numerous lives from both of the tribal factions of Syria and from the Khurāsānī troops sent from Baghdad.[58] As is so often the case with their coverage of events in Syria, most of the medieval sources provide only a few scant lines about Abū al-Haydhām's revolt. However, Ibn 'Asākir preserves a number of longer accounts of the revolt, including a minutely detailed narrative by al-Madā'inī (d. ca. 225/840), excerpted by Abū al-Ḥusayn al-Rāzī (d. 347/958).[59] Yet the accounts compiled by Ibn 'Asākir differ slightly over the precise origins of the revolt.

Al-Madā'inī alludes to factional brawls already in progress when Abū al-Haydhām finally rose up in revolt. Ultimately, this original conflict was resolved by a visit of a delegation of the *ashrāf* of Syria (one of them being Abū al-Haydhām) and the local governor, Ibrāhīm b. Ṣāliḥ, to the court of al-Rashīd.[60] After Ibrāhīm's death, his son and deputy, Isḥāq b. Ibrāhīm, was appointed governor of Dimashq, but in that capacity, Isḥāq disrupted the balance that made government in Syria work. According to al-Madā'inī, the governor's favoritism toward Yamanī tribesmen and the liberties that Yamanī officeholders took provided the political context for Abū al-Haydhām's revolt.[61]

The other accounts preserved by Ibn 'Asākir make no mention of such a context in preexisting factional fighting, but they do agree with al-Madā'inī that personal vengeance of some kind was the trigger that brought Abū al-Haydhām into open revolt. According to the account of al-Marzubānī (d. 370/980), Abū al-Haydhām and his Qaysī following were seeking vengeance for his brother 'Uthmān, who had been sacked as governor of Sīstān and killed by his Yamanī replacement.[62] But according to al-Madā'inī, he was seeking revenge for a more distant relative of his who had been killed by Yamanīs in the *'aṣabiyya* in Damascus that preceded his revolt.[63] It is said that the mother of the slain man came to Abū al-Haydhām in the Ḥawrān with the bloodstained shirt of her son in her hands, begging him to obtain retribution.

The Revolt Erupts

Whatever the case, Abū al-Haydhām resisted getting involved at first, saying that he would bring the matter up with the governor (Isḥāq) first, and if the governor would not listen, then he would bring it before the caliph himself. Isḥāq learned of Abū al-Haydhām's involvement and, to bring him to Damascus, Isḥāq sent Ibrāhīm b. Ḥumayd al-Marwarrūdhī, who was his tax agent over the Ḥawrān and a Khurāsānī commander of some repute. Eventually, Abū al-Haydhām obeyed the summons and was taken to the city with a group of other Murrī *ashrāf*, including his son Khuraym. The governor, however, never admitted him to his presence. Their attempt at negotiation thwarted, Abū al-Haydhām and his companions simply left, and the factional violence proceeded apace.[64]

Abū al-Haydhām first took up arms when, in the middle of Muḥarram of 177/early May 793, Qaysī villagers pleaded for his assistance after Yamanī tribesmen razed their homes. With a few companions, he marched straight to the door of the governor's residence and demanded the removal of Ibn Ghawth, the Yamanī official who was behind much of the governor's decision to favor the local Yamaniyya. The governor sent out a local Qaysī leader to meet with him. After Abū al-Haydhām insisted that he had not thrown off his allegiance to the caliph, the governor conceded reluctantly to his demands and replaced the Yamanī Ibn Ghawth with a Qaysī official.

The local Yamanī troops resented this change in the factional makeup of the local governing corps, probably because they most likely owed their positions in the *jund* to the patronage of Ibn Ghawth. Encouraged by the resentful governor, they pursued Abū al-Haydhām and his companions to the Jābiya (western) Gate of the city. Abū al-Haydhām was able to force his attackers back, and, before returning to the Ḥawrān, he set free the occupants of the prison, Qaysī and Yamanī alike. In al-Madā'inī's account, Abū al-Haydhām is made to exclaim, "I have set free the people as a whole, without preferring anyone over another. This is an affair that I have ventured upon [solely] because of what is between me and the Commader of the Faithful. If he pardons me, then it will be due to his grace; if he punishes me, then let it be so." The Yamaniyya, for their part, swore to expel Muḍar/Qays from Syria once and for all.[65]

Although the origins of Abū al-Haydhām's revolt were limited geographically to Damascus and its hinterland, the conflict brought in support for both contending factions from more distant regions. On one side, the governor, Isḥāq b. Ibrāhīm, tacitly supported the Yamaniyya, who were themselves led by wellknown *ashrāf* from Damascus hailing from both old *sharīfal* families and families of the newer factional elite of Marwānid times. Familiar names include a descendant of Baḥdal b. 'Unayf al-Kalbī, the family of Ma'yūf b. Yaḥyā, a granddaughter of Ziml al-Saksakī[66] and the family of al-Ḥārith b. 'Abd al-Raḥmān al-Jurashī.[67] In addition to this core of local notability and tribesmen, the Yamaniyya of Damascus were assisted by Yamanī tribesmen from al-Urdunn, the Jawlān, and the Biqā', including a number of Kalbī subtribes.[68]

On the other side, the Qaysiyya were led by Abū al-Haydhām and his *qawm* of Murrī tribesmen from the Ḥawrān, among whom his sons, Haydhām and Khuraym, figure prominently. Abū al-Haydhām was assisted by three groups: a contingent of Numayrī tribesmen from Iraq; the enigmatic Zawāqīl from the Syrian countryside; and a number of otherwise unknown Qaysī tribesmen from the vicinity of Damascus, including a *mawlā* of that other earlier Murrī rebel, Ḥabīb b. Murra.[69]

In light of the revolt's complexity, the following discussion divides the events of 177/793 into three phases. The first phase, lasting from mid-Muḥarram to mid Ṣafar 177/early May to early June 793, centered almost entirely on the city of Damascus and the villages of the Ghūṭa. In the course of this first phase, the Qaysiyya occupied the city and shut out both the governor, who was at that time in his residence outside the Jābiya Gate, and the Yamaniyya, who were encamped not far away at Dayr Murrān on the slopes of Jabal Qāsiyūn. After weeks of destructive attacks and reprisals, the Yamanī leaders of the villages of the Ghūṭa sued for amnesty.[70]

The second phase of the revolt began after a few weeks of peace and lasted until early Rabīʿ II 177/mid-July 793. It was a period of raised stakes for both sides, and one in which the ʿAbbāsid central government decisively entered the fray. With his *qawm* and supporters dispersed after the brief peace, Abū al-Haydhām remained in Damascus with a small group of companions. But before Abū al-Haydhām could return to the Ḥawrān, ʿAbbāsid troops from al-Urdunn and Filasṭīn arrived with orders from the caliph al-Rashīd for Isḥāq. At this, the local *jund* of Yamanī soldiers reminded the governor that Abū al-Haydhām was now virtually alone. Because the arrival of the caliph's orders and troops signaled that the central government now officially considered Abū al-Haydhām a rebel who had to be subdued, Isḥāq could march openly against him, which he did in mid-Ṣafar 177/early June 793, with a combined force of Yamanī and Khurāsānī troops.

Then, in the middle of the fighting, an Umayyad notable and a small group of Qurashī companions arrived at Damascus en route to the frontier. After arranging a reluctant truce between the two sides, the Umayyad stayed to put a peace agreement in writing. But before it could be carried out, Yamanī tribesmen under Ibn Baḥdal arrived from Ḥimṣ and, presumably unaware of the truce, attacked a Qaysī village in the Ghūṭa. Outraged at this breach of the truce, Abū al-Haydhām immediately sent a group of Qaysī tribesmen to exact retribution from a village near Homs, while the remainder of the Qaysiyya burned and plundered the Yamanī villages of the Ghūṭa.[71]

In the wake of this destruction, the city returned to a relative calm for a few months, until the beginning of Rabīʿ II 177/mid-July 793, when Khurāsānī troops arrived from Baghdad under the commander Sindī b. Shāhak. A group of Yamanī tribesmen intercepted Sindī and warned him that Abū al-Haydhām had thrown off his allegiance to the caliph. At the same time, Abū al-Haydhām sent a group of Qaysī leaders to assure Sindī that, Yamanī claims to the contrary, he was still loyal. With fresh troops now on the scene, Isḥāq hoped to force the issue. As he received Sindī and his troops, he sent a group of Yamanī soldiers to foment conflict between Sindī and Abū al-Haydhām. However, Abū al-Haydhām sensed Isḥāq's hand in the matter, and, despite a few casualties, full-scale conflict was averted.

As a new presence in Damascus, Sindī's first order of business was to write in conciliatory terms to Abū al-Haydhām, granting him whatever it was he wanted. In turn, Abū al-Haydhām sought the verdict of the populace of the city, offering to march out and rout Sindī or die in the process, if they so wished. However, the Damascenes were by now eager to put an end to the conflict and replied to that effect to Abū al-Haydhām, saying that they were obedient to the caliph, that they had only risen up to combat the Yamaniyya and their oppressive acts, and that now all they wanted was a pardon. Sindī and Abū al-Haydhām then worked out a formal agreement for the return of direct 'Abbāsid control to the city, and a week later Abū al-Haydhām and his large following of Qaysī horsemen left the city and returned to the Ḥawrān.[72]

Dénouement

Abū al-Haydhām's exit from Damascus should have marked the end of his revolt, but the Yamaniyya, who had lost a great deal in the conflict, were still clamoring for retribution, and so the conflict continued even after the 'Abbāsids retook Damascus. The third and final phase of the revolt began in mid-Rabī' II 177/early August 793, when the Hāshimī nobleman Mūsā b. 'Īsā b. 'Alī arrived to replace Isḥāq as governor of Dimashq. Mūsā's appointment brought about some minor reshuffling of posts at the local level in Damascus. He brought with him another contingent of Khurāsānī troops under Harthama b. A'yan, which now supplemented the troops under Sindī. Ibrāhīm b. Ḥumayd, once Isḥāq's agent in the Ḥawrān, was now made the head of Mūsā's guard. With this force behind him, and, encouraged by the Yamaniyya, Mūsā entertained hopes of finally capturing Abū al-Haydhām. Not long after he arrived in Damascus, Mūsā gathered together a group of Khurāsānī troops and the *ashrāf* of the Yamaniyya and set out for the Ḥawrān. But despite Mūsā's best efforts, Abū al-Haydhām remained hidden in the rough country of the Ḥawrān and the Lajā. After more than a month of pursuit, Mūsā returned empty-handed to Damascus.[73]

The search for Abū al-Haydhām continued. Not long after Mūsā abandoned his attempt to capture Abū al-Haydhām, one Ibn Riyāḥ al-Murrī offered Mūsā a deal. Ibn Riyāḥ was, like Abū al-Haydhām, from the tribe of Murra/Qays, and came from a family that was particularly well connected with the 'Abbāsid ruling house. Ibn Riyāḥ and Mūsā agreed that, if Ibn Riyāḥ captured Abū al-Haydhām for Mūsā, then Mūsā would make Ibn Riyāḥ his agent in the Ḥawrān. By this time, Abū al-Haydhām had returned to some property of his at Bostra, and a group there had informed Ibn Riyāḥ of his presence. Ibn Riyāḥ marched on Bostra with almost the entire garrison of the Ḥawrān behind him, but Abū al-Haydhām was able to round up support from tribesmen of the region, and they forced Ibn Riyāh back to the Ḥawrān. In the meantime, deceived by Ibn Riyāḥ's self-confidence, Mūsā b. 'Īsā had written to al-Rashīd prematurely informing him that he had killed Abū al-Haydhām, and that he would soon be sending his head to the caliph. Ten days later, al-Madā'inī says, the caliph withdrew Mūsā as governor of Dimashq.[74]

Mūsā left as his replacement the Khūrasānī commander 'Abd al-Salām b. Ḥumayd, who was the brother of the head of Mūsā's guardsmen. Upon hearing that Abū al-Haydhām was approaching the Ḥawrān, Ibn Riyāḥ assembled his kinsmen and the leaders of his supporters and sent them out to meet with him. As a Murrī who had conspired with the government against a fellow Murrī and failed, Ibn Riyāḥ was in an awkward position. Ibn Riyāḥ begged a full pardon from Abū al-Haydhām, and the two sides agreed that the two of them would meet in Bostra to arrange the details. Ibn Riyāḥ arrived with a small contingent of Khurāsānī troops, and Abū al-Haydhām approached with a small number of companions and kinsmen. During the meeting, Abū al-Haydhām reprimanded Ibn Riyāḥ for his behavior, and reminded him of the acts of treachery against fellow Qaysīs that Ibn Riyāḥ's father had performed. Cowardice, it was implied, was a family trait. Tempers flared, and Abū al-Haydhām killed Ibn Riyāḥ and one of his companions.

Abū al-Haydhām then proceeded to Damascus, where he informed the new governor 'Abd al-Salām that he should have nothing to fear from him and that he was merely making sure that the Yamaniyya had not again managed to assert themselves over the populace of the city. But, he assured the governor, he saw that the Khurāsāniyya were strong and the Yamaniyya weak, so he was returning peacefully to the Ḥawrān. Despite these assurances, the governor sent a small force to pursue Abū al-Haydhām to the

Ḥawrān, where, on 10 Ramaḍān 177/19 December 793, they intercepted him. Abū al-Haydhām held the 'Abbāsid force at bay and was able to escape, though a son of his was killed in the conflict.

On the next day, according to al-Madā'inī's account, a group of horsemen with veiled faces arrived in the Ḥawrān and spoke with Abū al-Haydhām. Al-Madā'inī's account explains that these horsemen bore a message from a brother of his, asking him to stop the killing. Whatever the reason, it is said that Abū al-Haydhām next called for the leaders of his supporters and sent them on their way. He then put his affairs in order and was never heard from again. According to Ibn 'Asākir, Abū al-Haydhām died in 182/798 in unknown circumstances.[75]

Ibn 'Asākir's coverage of Abū al-Haydhām's revolt does have its problems. The precise sequence of events and identification of the persons involved in the revolt is difficult and, at times, impossible to fully fathom. Even the crucial point of what caused the revolt is disputed in the sources adduced by Ibn 'Asākir: al-Madā'inī suggests it was both oppositon to Yamanī partisanship and revenge for the death of a distant relative in Syria, while al-Marzubānī suggests it was revenge for the death of a brother in Sīstān. Can they both be right? At first glance, al-Marzubānī's version would seem to be the weaker of the two, as it ultimately rests on the evidence of some poetry attributed to Abū al-Haydhām. In these verses, Abū al-Haydhām expresses grief for his slain brother. By way of explanation, al-Marzubānī states that Abū al-Haydhām rebelled in Syria after al-Rashīd's governor in Sīstān killed his brother. The account goes on to say that al-Rashīd eventually had another of Abū al-Haydhām's brothers intercede and bring Abū al-Haydhām to al-Raqqa. Impressed by his ability to improvise verse, the caliph let him go.[76]

Now, just as poetry was often used to add poignancy to historical narratives, so also were historical explanations contrived to explain obscure fragments of verse. Whether there is any truth behind al-Marzubānī's account is open to question. While the authenticity of the verses is a question best left to others,[77] the outlines of al-Marzubānī's story about the brother in Sīstān produced to explain them does, in fact, have independent support. As it happens, Abū al-Haydhām did in fact have a brother, 'Uthmān b. 'Umāra al-Murrī, who was killed in Sīstān. 'Uthmān was one of the Syrian *ashrāf* in the delegation that sought amnesty from al-Manṣūr for their participation in the revolt of 'Abd Allāh b. 'Alī in 136/754, and he later served as governor of Armenia and Azerbaijan for al-Mahdī. In 172/788, al-Rashīd appointed him governor of Sīstān.[78] There, he amassed a considerable sum of money, and when he was replaced by the Yamanī Da'ūd b. Bishr al-Muhallabī, 'Uthmān met the fate common to wealthy governors on the "out": his wealth was confiscated, and he was imprisoned and killed.[79] The circumstances and date of 'Uthmān's removal from office, Rabī' I, 176/July 792, suggest that it is strongly connected with Abū al-Haydhām's revolt nine months later in Muḥarram 177/April 793.[80]

Yet even allowing for the possibility that Abū al-Haydhām sought blood-revenge from local Yamanī leaders, it seems unlikely that a simple personal desire for retribution provoked a reaction of such magnitude as the ensuing revolt. Abū al-Haydhām's revolt makes better sense in light of the broader crisis experienced by Syrian *ashrāf* after the 'Abbāsid revolution. In this context, Abū al-Haydhām's revolt did not only express his grief for his brother, but also his frustration at seeing his family's main source of privilege eradicated.

There is no direct evidence that Abū al-Haydhām received benefits from his brother's powerful position in the East, but, given the nature of patronage, factionalism, and provincial politics, it is reasonable to assume that he did. Abū al-Haydhām's family had a long history of provincial positions in the East,[81] and to have their unique foothold in the prestigious and profitable upper echelons of government so suddenly removed would have been a serious blow to dependents back home in Syria, especially given the new and limited role that the 'Abbāsid government allotted to Syrian *ashrāf*. If the governor of Dimashq was openly favoring Yamanī tribesmen for local positions and privileges as al-Madā'inī states that he was, then Abū al-Haydhām's need to redress wrongs would have been felt all the more urgently.

Despite the murkiness surrounding issues like this in Ibn 'Asākir's account, the general features of the revolt at least are clear. Abū al-Haydhām's revolt shows how highly localized elite conflict over patronage issues could escalate into full-fledged *'aṣabiyya:* from a small-scale outburst of dissent toward the local governor's preferential treatment of the Yamaniyya, combined with Abū al-Haydhām's own personal grievances resulting from the fall of his family's fortunes in Sīstān, the conflict became a genuine revolt in which both Qaysī and Yamanī factions drew on supporters from all over Syria and even farther abroad. On this account, the central government was obliged to send in troops on more than one occasion. With this broadened base of manpower went a correspondingly broadened scope for conflict and retribution. The impact of the violence of the revolt can still be gauged in the impressions left by later generations of Syrians, who considered it the most severe *fitna* in the city's history, more so even than the later pro-Umayyad revolt of Abū al-'Umayṭir.[82] Other writers understood the tribal factionalism of the revolt in terms of divine retribution, retrospectively providing "prophecies" that predicted a "barbaric movement (*da'wa jāhiliyya*)" in which Islam would be lost altogether.[83]

The revolt also clearly demonstrates the new set of relations between Syrian *ashrāf* and the central government. The governors who had a role in this revolt were all outsiders, backed by Khurāsānī troops and periodic reinforcements. Their ability to govern rested upon local support, in this case on the Yamaniyya at the expense of the Qaysiyya. This fact led subsequent governors to be easily led into the conflict. The revolt is overwhelmingly concerned with the partisanship of the local governor, and the competition of the local protonotables over access to the governor's favor, or over finding a suitable replacement for him. Abū al-Haydhām's first appearance was itself in the classic mode of the local notable, mediating between the governor and aggrieved Qaysī civilians, a role he maintained until the end of the revolt.

Not all Syrian *ashrāf* supported the revolt outright, of course. One Qaysī *sharīf,* for instance, was so well connected with the governor that he thought it better to negotiate with the governor privately, rather than taking part in the revolt, although he did supply a few mounts for members of his *qawm.*[84] Such examples remind us not to paint too monolithic a picture of this fluid social group. Combining the plight of Syria's *ashrāf,* the competition of factions, and the demands of provincial government, Abū al-Haydhām's revolt set the pattern observable in most subsequent *'aṣabiyya* in Syria.

As the revolt was born of the politics of protonotables, so it died. Shortly after Abū al-Haydhām rode off with his mysterious horsemen, Mūsā b. Yaḥyā al-Barmakī arrived as governor of Syria and Dimashq. Accompanied by a new body of military and administrative personnel from Baghdad, Mūsā was able to negotiate a firm peace between the two tribal factions. He assembled a delegation of the leaders involved in the revolt and returned to Baghdad, where they received an offical pardon.[85] But whether factional intriguers, docile intermediaries, or contentious rebels, the *ashrāf* of Syria could climb no higher. It was only by selling out his fellow tribesman that Ibn Riyāḥ was able to obtain briefly a place, humble as it was, among the ʿAbbāsid governing elite. In most other cases, the sons of once powerful Syrian families appear throughout the revolt as supporters or opponents of the governor, but almost never as holders of positions in Syria themselves.

When notables acted on their grievances, the ʿAbbāsid central government generally responded immediately and firmly. Although revolts had to be suppressed through brute force, it was negotiation, not extermination, that was the usual solution for the complaints of Syria's *ashrāf* and their followings. Yet, while this may have been the proper solution to the particular problems that surfaced in a particular revolt, negotiation could only be a temporary solution. *ʿAṣabiyya* was such an integral part of the dynamic of provincial power in Syria that the governors and protonotables of Syria—try as they might—could hardly avoid factional competition altogether.

Other Early Outbreaks of Factionalism

After Abū al-Haydhām's revolt, Qays-Yaman conflict necessitated caliphal intervention several times in the reign of al-Rashīd, but the details are far from clear. The first conflict occured in 180/796-797 and required a large army led by Jaʿfar b. Yaḥyā al-Barmakī, al-Rashīd's closest companion, to subdue it. Both the location and the principal actors are uncertain. Al-Yaʿqūbī gives the location as Ḥimṣ, but al-Ṭabarī says that Jaʿfar appointed Ṣāliḥ b. Sulaymān as subgovernor of the Balqāʾ after settling the dispute, suggesting that southern Syria had been involved as well. Contemporary non-Muslim sources support this supposition, for this conflict was surely related to that of 180/797 that devastated the monastery of Mar Saba and the coastal cities of southern Palestine. As regards the participants, al-Ṭabarī mentions that Jaʿfar "killed their Zawāqīl and their Ṣaʿālīk," while the non-Muslim sources imply that local tribes from Palestine and Transjordan were involved. Given its chronological proximity to Abū al-Haydhām's revolt and the presence of the Zawāqīl, who figured in the revolt in Damascus as well, it is likely that these two conflicts represent "fallout" from Abū al-Haydhām's revolt in the district of Ḥimṣ and in southern Syria.[86]

Another smaller conflict followed in 187/803, and, like the beginning of Abū al-Haydhām's revolt, it involved the tribal groups living in Damascus. Conflict between the Qaysiyya and the Yamaniyya broke out again in Damascus, and for familiar reasons: the governor, Shu'ayb b. Khāzim b. Khuzayma, favored the Yamaniyya over the Qaysiyya, and a number of Qaysīs were killed in the factional fighting that resulted. Al-Rashīd therefore sent Muḥammad b. Manṣūr b. Ziyād to quell the unrest and to look into local political affairs. Muḥammad settled the dispute by offering amnesty and by paying the blood-money for both factions out of the local treasury. The immediate crisis resolved, Muḥammad consulted with the *ashrāf* for advice and assistance in suppressing the conflict for good. He ordered Shu'ayb to be withdrawn, and allowed the two factions to choose a new governor. Muḥammad then left for Iraq with a delegation of twenty Syrian *ashrāf*. In Damascus, the factions selected the Hāshimī aristocrat Ibrāhīm b. Muḥammad b. Ibrāhīm, who arrived from Iraq with a new contingent of Khurāsānī troops in 188/803-804.[87] In 190/806, a similar incident occured in Homs. When the populace rose up against their governor, al-Rashīd himself marched at the head of an army to quash the rebellion. But when he reached Manbij, a delegation of Ḥimṣīs arrived to reaffirm their obedience to him and to ask for a formal audience. Al-Rashīd granted them their request, pardoned them for their actions, and, taking advantage of his visit to Syria, left to lead a campaign against the Byzantines.[88]

The *Ashrāf* of Syria and the Fourth Civil War

Between 132/750 and the start of the Fourth Civil War in 193/809, the *ashrāf* of Syria contended with local officials and with one another to maintain what little power they still had, given their new, humbler position within the 'Abbāsid political order. Yet while most Syrians never obtained access to positions of any great influence, as long as 'Abbāsid central government remained stable, Syrian *ashrāf* and their followings continued to be important to Baghdad on a smaller scale, at least, as members of the Syro-Jazīran army. With the outbreak of the Fourth Civil War, however, the blocking influence of the central government evaporated, and many of Syria's *ashrāf* emerged as autonomous power-holders in cities and towns throughout the province. When al-Ma'mūn's victorious but overextended troops arrived in 198/813 to reestablish central control, the Syrian *ashrāf* found themselves in a position of relative strength. As a result, Syrian *ashrāf* and the Syro-Jazīran armies were kept on in al-Ma'mūn's governing order, and they retained their local influence at least for a time after the end of the civil war.

The importance of Syrian elites is clear from the central, if ultimately fruitless, role that the Syro-Jazīran army played under al-Amīn. At the outset of the Fourth Civil War, when al-Amīn began preparing for a confrontation with al-Ma'mūn's new army from Khurāsān, he relied heavily both on the military support of the Khurāsānī Abnā' in Baghdad, and on whatever troops he could raise from Syria and the Jazīra. As we have seen, in 193/809, al-Amīn released 'Abd al-Malik b. Ṣāliḥ from prison in the hope that, given 'Abd al-Malik's strong connections with the tribes and armies of Syria and the Jazīra, he of all the members of the 'Abbāsid ruling elite would be able to raise support from them for al-Amīn's claims.[89]

From the Jazīran city of al-Raqqa, about midway between Baghdad and Damascus, 'Abd al-Malik wrote to the leaders of the Syro-Jazīran army. According to al-Ṭabarī, the response was overwhelming. Among the groups specifically named who responded to 'Abd al-Malik's invitations were the Qaysī Zawāqīl from the Jazīra and Yamanī tribesmen from the Banū Kalb of Ḥimṣ. However, for reasons which remain obscure, conflict soon broke out between the Zawāqīl and the Abnā' stationed at al-Raqqa, and the Syrian tribesmen returned to their homes.

Syria under the Ashrāf

While these tribesmen headed home to Syria, the *ashrāf* were also repositioning themselves vis-à-vis the central government. At the beginning of the civil war, Syria, Egypt, and north Africa had slipped from Baghdad's control as local elites took advantage of the chaos in Baghdad and seized power in their different areas.[90] While al-Amīn struggled to push back al-Ma'mūn's siege of Baghdad, Syrian *ashrāf* emerged as local leaders in virtually every major city of the province. Many of these "rebels" were no doubt bent on keeping 'Abbāsid authority out of their domains for good, as was the case for Abū al-'Umayṭir al-Sufyānī, who rebelled in Damascus in 195/810.[91] Others probably hoped at least to dictate their own terms when the inevitable surrender to al-Ma'mūn's troops finally came.

While the Zawāqīl defiantly held on to most of the Jazīra, the *thughūr* were under the control of al-Amīn's Khurasānī governor there, Thābit b. Naṣr al-Khuzā'ī, who seems to have taken authority in the area into his own hands.[92] Another Zawāqīl chieftain, ʿAbbās b. Zufar al-Hilālī, controlled the region around Qurūs/Cyrrhus in the ʿAwāṣim, and he joined forces with Naṣr b. Shabath on more than one occasion to attack their mutual rivals and pillage the countryside.[93] Elsewhere in northern Syria, the Qaysī *sharīf* ʿUthmān b. Thumāma had come to power, although his exact domains are contradicted in the sources. His influence evidently also extended into the Jazīra, as he is said to have granted permission to the monastery at Qēnneshrē on the Euphrates to rebuild its church, which had recently been destroyed, and he made sure that local tribal leaders did not prevent the monks from their task. Although the Zawāqīl chieftains ʿAbbās and Naṣr at first attacked ʿUthmān and his domains, he later joined them, only to surrender peacefully in 208/823 to al-Ma'mūn's general, ʿAbd Allāh b. Ṭāhir.[94]

From their extramural settlement (*ḥāḍir*) at Aleppo, the tribe of Tanūkh rebelled against the ʿAbbāsid Banū Ṣāliḥ, who were exercising their hereditary authority over the city itself. The Tanūkh were led by the *sharīf* al-Ḥawārī b. Ḥiṭṭān, who is also said to have controlled nearby Maʿarrat al-Nuʿmān and Tall Mannas. The besieged Banū Ṣāliḥ enlisted the aid of the Zawāqīl under ʿAbbās and Naṣr, who ousted the Tanūkh from Aleppo and sacked their settlement. The remnants of the population fled to Qinnasrin, which they attempted to take over for themselves. The populace of that city expelled them, and they dispersed as refugees into Iraq and Armenia. Al-Ḥawārī, however, was eventually granted amnesty by al-Ma'mūn.[95]

Early in the reign of al-Amīn, the factional disputes of the *ashrāf* erupted in Homs. Once again, the precise cause of the conflict is unknown, but local *ashrāf* loomed large in the disturbance. The governor involved was none other than Abū al-Haydhām's old nemesis Isḥāq b. Sulaymān, who had been transferred to Ḥimṣ when the revolt in Damascus became a serious threat. For reasons that are unclear, the populace of Homs attacked Isḥāq, ousted him from the city, and forced him to take refuge at his family's estate at Salamiyya. Al-Amīn sent a new governor, the Qaysī commander ʿAbd Allāh b. Saʿīd al-Ḥarashī, who killed some of the leaders of the revolt, among them the Yamanī *sharīf* ʿAbd Allāh b. al-Simṭ al-Kindī and two of his sons. Other leaders were imprisoned, and the agricultural region around the city was razed. After the central government's brutal response, the populace sought the new governor's clemency, but even though they received it, they soon rose up against him as well, and had to be violently subdued a second time.[96] Significantly, it was the sons of the *ashrāf* involved in this revolt, the Banū al-Simṭ, who emerged once more as local leaders in the city of Homs proper during the civil war.[97]

Further south, Palestine was once more overrun. According to Christian sources, in the early years of the civil war, the Zawāqīl ravaged the countryside, harrassed Jerusalem, and looted the monasteries in its vicinity. During the same period, Saʿīd b. Sarḥ came to power in the regional center of Ramla. Ibn Sarḥ was a local Qaysī leader who had been governor of Yemen for al-Amīn, but he had recently been withdrawn from that post. Unlike many other former governors in his position, Ibn Sarḥ managed to hold on to the proceeds of his tenure and used them to build up his own estates in Filasṭīn.[98]

Even after al-Amīn was killed in 198/813 and al-Ma'mūn came to power as caliph, local leaders in Syria and the western provinces retained control over autonomous areas.[99] Given the geopolitical realities of the Fourth Civil War, this state of affairs formed a serious obstacle to any plan that al-Ma'mūn may have had to reinstate central authority in the west. With military resources already stretched thin, immediate and direct central control over the provinces was simply unfeasible. With Naṣr b. Shabath and the Zawāqīl in control of the Jazīra, al-Ma'mūn's new army faced an intractable impediment to their march west. A further obstacle to restoring central power lay in the provincial capital of Damascus itself. There, as we have seen, the Umayyad rebel Abū al-ʿUmayṭir al-Sufyānī had expelled al-Amīn's governor, and had proclaimed himself caliph; and it was the *sharīf* Ibn Bayhas who restored order in Damascus in the absence of any central power.[100]

Central Authority Restored

Even when al-Ma'mūn became caliph in 198/813, he merely acknowledged Ibn Bayhas as governor and did not really address the situation in Syria until a decade later in 208/823, when ʿAbd Allāh b. Ṭāhir arrived in Damascus. Along with the five years of civil war, this ten-year period created a hiatus of central authority in Syria that left its impact: "All of Syria was without a king for fifteen years," as one Syriac chronicler put it.[101] This chronicler's notion of provincial authority is worth noting. For, while chaos reigned until a suitable "king" was sent from Baghdad to restore central authority, someone was in fact governing Syria: not the caliph's men, but the local *ashrāf*.

Although Ibn Bayhas nominally supported al-Ma'mūn, he was removed when 'Abd Allāh b. Ṭāhir arrived in 208/823. Before 'Abd Allāh continued on to Egypt, he named as his deputy another local Qaysī, Ṣadaqa b. 'Uthmān al-Murrī, the nephew, in fact, of the rebel Abū al-Haydhām. When 'Abd Allāh returned to Syria from Egypt in 210/825 with prisoners in tow, he replaced Ṣadaqa with officials from Baghdad. The Khurāsānī Naṣr b. Ḥamza b. Malik was named *amīr* and al-Ḥasan b. Wahb, *ṣāḥib al-kharāj*. 'Abd Allāh then continued on to Baghdad, accompanied by Ibn Bayhas, who died shortly thereafter.[102]

But the presence of a Khurasānī governor and financial official (if indeed they were resident in Syria) did not yet mean that Baghdad could extend direct control over Syria. Shortly after 'Abd Allāh and Ibn Bayhas left in triumph for Baghdad, an anonymous *amīr* of Damascus, probably the Khurāsānī Naṣr b. Ḥamza or a subordinate, sought out a suitable local man to govern Damascus in his place. He first approached Aḥmad b. Yazīd b. al-Ḥakam al-Ḥajūrī, an elderly *sharīf* from one of the Yamanī tribes of the Ghūṭa. He declined the *amīr*'s offer because of his age but suggested his kinsman Ma'yūf b. Yaḥyā.[103] Ma'yūf was an ideal choice: a member of the Syrian *ashrāf* whose status came from generations of service to the 'Abbāsid state, beginning with his grandfather, the elder Ma'yūf b. Yaḥyā. Once appointed, the younger Ma'yūf remained in power only briefly, but he was succeeded by his son, Ḥumayd. Ḥumayd himself was not new to 'Abbāsid service: he had previously acted as head of the Syrian fleet and governor of the Mediterranean coast under al-Rashīd.[104]

But Ḥumayd b. Ma'yūf was the last of Syria's *ashrāf* to enjoy such a position of authority, for, in 213/828, al-Ma'mūn named his brother (and successor) al-Mu'taṣim governor of Syria, and subsequent governors and subgovernors were all trusted members of the 'Abbāsid ruling elite. The autonomy that the *ashrāf* of Syria gained as a result of the Fourth Civil War was purely temporary. Once central control of the provinces was restored, the *ashrāf* returned to their previous role as local intermediaries, a role which grew even more circumscribed as time passed. This change is best illustrated by the activities of the Qaysī Banū Bayhas of Damascus in 226/840.

Once virtual governors of the city, after the Fourth Civil War they were forced back into the limited positions of local power that men such as Abū al-Haydhām once held. Like Abū al-Haydhām, the Qaysī leaders were once again obliged to use violence against the local governor to redress factional grievances.

At the time of the Qaysī revolt, Damascus was still reeling from the recent trial of the former governor, 'Alī b. Isḥāq, who had murdered Rajā' b. Abī al-Ḍaḥḥāk, one of the financial officials serving with him. 'Alī claimed that he was driven to his crimes by the whisperings of Satan. But a more likely source of inspiration lay in the murmurings of local *'aṣabiyya,* especially given the sudden independence that local *ashrāf* of both tribal factions gained in Damascus during the civil war and their subsequent disappointment.[105]

In the wake of the investigation into 'Alī's crimes, the new governor, Abū al-Mughīth al-Rāfiqī, had a number of Qaysī tribesmen executed. Shortly thereafter, a group of Qaysī tribesmen from the Banū Numayr raided the governor's stables and made off into the desert with a number of his horses. The governor sent his henchman Muḥammad b. Azhar to retrieve the horses. Strangely, the Yamaniyya offered the governor no support against the Qaysīs. In fact, it appears that Yamanī tribesmen waited for Ibn Azhar outside the city, ambushed him and his troops, and made off with their weapons and horses.

Meanwhile, in the Ḥawrān, a descendant of the Qaysī Ibn Bayhas who had come to power in Damascus during the Fourth Civil War marched on Damascus. Assisted by another Qaysī leader named Mazyad, he put the city under siege. The Qaysīs encamped at Kafr Baṭnā, where they attracted the support of residents of other villages in the Ghūṭa. At this point in 227/842, the Khurāsānī commander Rajā' al-Ḥiḍārī arrived at the head of an army. He entreated the Qaysī rebels to abandon their siege, and they agreed, provided that Abū al-Mughīth be withdrawn as governor. However, the time when the *ashrāf* could dictate their terms had passed. On 4 Jumāda I 227/19 February 842, Rajā' attacked the Qaysiyya before they were fully prepared for battle. There were many casualties on both sides, including the rebel leader Mazyad. Ibn Bayhas fled with his *qawm* to the Ḥawrān, where Rajā' caught up and captured him.[106] Although this younger Ibn Bayhas may have hoped to win at least a temporary Qaysī predominance in Damascus like his ancestor did during the civil war, the times had changed. 'Abbāsid control in Syria was, for the moment, irresistable.

The End of the Ashrāf

The last clear case of old-fashioned factional conflict in Syria took place in the reign of al-Mutawakkil (r. 232/847-247/861), when Yamanī and Qurashī notables led the factional fighting in Damascus introduced with the arrival of the governor Sālim b. Ḥāmid. Significantly, the fighting was said to be over a long-standing dispute inherited from the days of the Third Civil War.[107] Yet even factionalism of this sort was undergoing changes, as Syria's *ashrāf* had to contend with even greater threats to their sources of authority. With the military reforms of al-Muʿtaṣim and his successors, the Syro-Jazīran frontier troops appear to have been disbanded, or at least drastically cut back from even their post-revolutionary state: the last unquestionable record of Syrian troops in service is that of the contingents sent to the frontier with al-ʿAbbās b. al-Ma'mūn to garrison Ṭuwāna in 218/833.[108] For the *ashrāf* of Syria, many of whom were only the youngest members of long lines of military men, demilitarization meant the further constriction (if not the total elimination) of their favored path to privilege, and an even greater need for local political equilibrium to be maintained.

Now completely detached from the ʿAbbāsid ruling apparatus, the *ashrāf* were left only with their own local standing to support themselves. The *ashrāf* of Syria had, in short, become full-fledged local notables. With their scope for authority now reduced further than ever before, the notables of Syria began to draw support from realms outside the usual factional circles, as in 226/840, when they provided a vital military edge to what had been a disorganized peasant revolt in support of the messianic Sufyānid, al-Mubarqaʿ.[109] At the same time, the decline in the fortunes of Syria's notables made possible the rise of new local-political leaders, whose origins are obscure. It would be imprudent to make too sweeping a statement given the spotty coverage of Syria in the sources and the slippery terminology used in them. But, although it is still articulated in terms of Qays-Yaman rivalry, the political activity of notables after the Fourth Civil War appears to be more concerned with civilian interests than ever before. The predominantly Yamanī city of Homs is a case in point. After al-Ma'mūn re-imposed central authority, Homs and its vicinity became the dominant arena for unrest in Syria. The Homsī poet Dīk al-Jinn lamented in verse his city's embarrasingly provincial propensity for in-fighting even when congregated in common worship:

They heard the prayer upon the Prophet repeated
So they broke away as a group saying: No, no!
Yet their *imām* continued the prayer
So they broke up into gangs, men smiting men.
O tribe of Ḥimṣ! Having fallen from her shame,
Disgrace and evil deeds befall you.
As one face, your faces are marred, so long as
Its nose cleaves to the ground and is abased.[110]

Dīk al-Jinn's contemporary verses suggest that tribally articulated conflicts could thrive well after the demise of the military faction as a facet of Syrian politics, and the narrative sources confirm this.[111]

In 240/854, the Homsī populace rebelled against the local military and financial officials and expelled them from the city. According to al-Ṭabarī, this uprising was in response to the actions of the local military official, Abū al-Mughīth al-Rāfiqī, who, for reasons unknown, had killed one of the local notables. The caliph al-Mutawakkil sent a body of troops and offered to replace Abū al-Mughīth with a new military official, Muḥammad b. ʻAbdawayh. The caliph also threatened to send an even larger force if his offer was not accepted. The Homsīs agreed to the arrangement, and it is said that the populace favorably received Ibn ʻAbdawayh during his initial tenure. A year later, however, the populace, including a number of Christians, rose up against him. Al-Mutawakkil ordered Ibn ʻAbdawayh in no uncertain terms to put an end to the uprising, and he sent troops from Dimashq and Filasṭīn to assist him. However, Ibn ʻAbdawayh was unable to follow the caliph's commands to the letter—they were unrealistically brutal in any case—and was only able to apprehend ten of the rebel leaders, whom he sent to Samarra. Like many caliphs before him, al-Mutawakkil wished to make a public statement about the consequences of rebellion, and so he sent two of the leaders of the rebellion back to Homs, where they were publicly beaten, executed, and crucified on the city gates. Other rebels were apprehended later.[112]

Despite the suppression of this revolt, in 248/862, virtually the same sequence of events took place when the populace rebelled against al-Mustaʻīn's governor, the Sogdian commander Kaydar b. ʻUbayd Allāh al-Ushrūsanī, and expelled him from the city. While the governor sought refuge in the nearby city of Hama, the rebels in Homs killed a number of the governor's soldiers and crucified them. In response, the caliph sent the commander al-Faḍl b. Qārin.

The populace approached al-Faḍl with every indication of obedience and submission, and, by way of explanation for their uprising, they complained to him of the injustices that Kaydar had inflicted on them. Al-Faḍl settled the initial disturbances, but it soon became clear that rebellion was brewing again, and so al-Faḍl captured a group of the rebel leaders (*ʿuyūnuhum*), and dismantled the city walls.[113]

By 250/864, the populace had clearly broken with al-Faḍl's government, and they sought the assistance of the Kalbī/Yamanī tribes of the area, who were led by one ʿUṭayf b. Niʿma al-Kalbī. Under the leadership of ʿUṭayf, the populace—including Christians and Jews—rioted in the streets. Al-Faḍl took refuge in the governor's residence, but the men with him capitulated to the rebels and handed him over to the mob, who pillaged his residence, then crucified him on the north gate of the city. In anticipation of the caliph's expected response, the Homsīs marched out toward Damascus, which was then under the control of the Turkish commander al-Nawsharī. But when al-Nawsharī faced them at the head of his garrison, the Homsis dispersed and returned to their city. At that point, the caliph al-Mustaʿīn sent an army under the Turkish commander Mūsā b. Bughā to put a definitive end to the rebellion. The Homsīs and Kalbīs were routed, and Mūsā entered the city without difficulty. A number of the rebel leaders were captured, but ʿUṭayf al-Kalbī escaped into the countryside with a group of bedouin.[114]

ʿUṭayf had not disappeared for good, however. Shortly after he fled into the countryside, ʿUṭayf joined forces with the Tanūkhī/Yamanī notable Yūsuf b. Ibrāhīm al-Fūṣayṣ, perhaps the last member of the old Syrian sharifian families to dabble in the politics of notables. Al-Fuṣayṣ had rebelled at Maʿarrat al-Nuʿmān before assembling a following of his tribesmen and fortifying himself at Qinnasrīn. At this point, in 252/866, the Turkish commander Aḥmad b. al-Muwallad arrived from Samarra to secure Syria's allegiance to the new caliph al-Muʿtazz. At Homs, local leaders swore allegiance to the new caliph, but ʿUṭayf himself resisted briefly before being captured as a rebel and executed. When he received news of his partner's execution, al-Fuṣayṣ fled for the security of the Jabal Lukkām, in northwest Syria. At Homs, the remnants of ʿUṭayf's Kalbī/Yamanī following offered some resistance to Ibn al-Muwallad. Eventually, the Homsīs were able to push back Ibn al-Muwallad's forces, forcing him to continue northward while he secured the region for al-Muʿtazz and eventually arrived at Aleppo.

Meanwhile, al-Fuṣayṣ had returned to Qinnasrīn, where he

had a change of heart and launched an attack on his former allies among the Banū Kalb. By pure good fortune, Ibn al-Muwallad was at this moment replaced by the commander Abū al-Sāj al-Ushrūsanī, who thought it more expedient to placate his rivals in Syria peacefully. Abū al-Sāj granted al-Fuṣayṣ amnesty and appointed him governor of Lādhiqiyya and its vicinity.[115] As for the fate of the contentious populace of Homs and the Kalbī tribes of its countryside, the sources are unfortunately, but typically, silent.[116]

Conclusion

The ʿAbbāsid revolution of 132/750 created radical changes among the ruling elite of the Islamic world. Yet, in many ways, the emergence of local leaders like ʿUṭayf is a more meaningful articulation point in the social history of Syria. Syrian society was not cataclysmically overturned during the revolution. Most of the sharifian families of Syria after the revolution had roots among the *ashrāf* of the Sufyānid period, or else were descendants of the new class of military leaders that emerged in the course of the Marwānid period. The political changes wrought by the ʿAbbāsid revolution radically constricted the fortunes of these families, but until the middle of the third/ninth century, many of these families nonetheless remained influential in Syria. Abū al-Haydhām may thus evoke his predecessor Ḥabīb b. Murra, but if newcomers like ʿUṭayf al-Kalbī and his followers evoke anything, it is the "bedouin dynasts" and urban militias that so characterize Syria in the fourth/tenth century.

Much of the durability of the sharifian families of Syria at this time was due to the continued service of the Syro-Jazīran army. As long as it remained a part of the ʿAbbāsid governing apparatus, the military continued to be a realm where Syria's populace could find wealth, prestige, and power, however limited these may have become after 132/750. But the continued utility of the Syro-Jazīran army was not taken for granted in the heady days of the revolution, and the *ashrāf* of Syria had to fight to maintain it. Even with the place of the Syro-Jazīran army assured, Syria's *ashrāf* had to struggle to hold onto what little influence they had left and found themselves enmired in a Janus-faced role as both provincial intermediaries and frontier commanders. Because they were part of a network of factional ties, protonotables such as Abū al-Haydhām kept a close eye on the wavering equilibrium of local politics. If a negotiated solution to perceived inequities could not be obtained, *ashrāf* were willing to fight to protect their access to privilege within the 'Abbāsid governing order.

The relationship between Syria's *ashrāf* and the 'Abbāsid government could hardly be called irenic. But the *ashrāf* were not opponents of 'Abbāsid central government, as a superficial view of the revolts of Syria's noble families might suggest. The relationship between center and province in Syria was characterized by competition, but it was competition between local elites over the particular configuration of social and political alignments at a given time, not between rivals for any higher authority. The *'aṣabiyya* that so dominates the picture of Syria in our sources should be seen as a function of the 'Abbāsid dynamic of provincial power, not as a gesture of opposition to it. Although the central government and its chroniclers may have viewed any impediment to the smooth functioning of provincial administration as "rebellious," the majority of Syria's contentious *ashrāf* were not bent on destroying the 'Abbāsid caliphate. They were instead desperately clinging to their own limited place within it.

CHAPTER SIX

Worst Elements: The Impolitics of Unnotables in 'Abbāsid Syria

So far, this study has examined the contentious acts of the elite groups of Syrian society: the revolts of governors, the larger claims of Umayyad pretenders, and the factional competition of notables. Even in the traditional Arabic sources, which generally have little to say about Syria, elite contention is one of the few well documented aspects of Syrian history. Yet the bulk of Syrian society was not, of course, composed of elites, but of members of social strata far removed from the high politics of the military or the caliphal court, and whose direct access to power was virtually nonexistent: the urban masses, peasants and bandits of 'Abbāsid Syria.

If the relationship of local Syrian elites to the center made them "notables" to our literary sources, most Syrians were considered "unnotables" and are only rarely encountered. Rarely encountered, that is, but not entirely absent. Typically, when our sources do take note of ordinary Syrians it is only on the very odd occasion when they become involved in rebellious activity. Why was contention among the lower strata of Syrian society so rare? Obviously, the silence of our sources on Syrian affairs, especially rural affairs, is partly to blame here. Another obvious answer might be that members of these strata were too oppressed, or just too busy, to be anything but apolitical. In a sense, this is true; the quotidian constraints imposed upon Syria's "unnotables" could be overwhelming. In the countryside, the agricultural cycle, the fragility of the agrarian economy, and the demands of village life posed clear obstacles to peasant contention. But this picture of constraints is only partly valid. In fact, the fragmentary evidence that exists suggests that the lower strata—whether in urban or rural settings—were no more apolitical than the rest of Syrian society. In particular, the political activity of the lower strata of Syria appears most clearly in three forms of contention: urban violence, rural rebellion, and banditry.

Urban Violence and the Lower Strata

Given the overwhelmingly urban focus of the sources, one might expect that the lower strata of Syria's urban populations would figure prominently relative to the rural population. Unfortunately, this is not the case. Even though urban violence in Syria is a commonplace in most of our sources, with the exception of the *ashrāf* and their followings who were involved in incidents of factionalism, the precise composition of the groups involved is not known. There is no information on the background, occupations, or beliefs of the members of these armed urban crowds, even if they may well have formed a substantial proportion of the participants in a given incident of *fitna* or *'aṣabiyya*, and the same may be said for the rest of the 'Abbāsid caliphate as well. Only in Baghdad, the capital, have the sources given some attention to the "rabble (*'ayyārūn*)," or to the "common folk (*al-'āmma*)" especially because of their role in the defense of the city during the Fourth Civil War.[1] Given this dearth of information, any conclusions made about the lower strata of Syria's cities must necessarily be tentative, and must be informed by a certain requisite amount of speculation.

Only in two recorded instances is there any direct testimony of the political activity of Syria's urban masses. The first instance, alas, appears to be a didactic tale. It is said that during the reign of al-Amīn, prior to the revolt of Abū al-'Umayṭir al-Sufyānī, the governor of Dimashq and his *ṣāḥib al-shurṭa* conspired to steal a crystal vase that hung in the old *miḥrāb* of the Umayyad mosque, allegedly, as the account suggests, to please the caliph. Unfortunately, the account is suspect. That the account eventually ends with the caliph al-Ma'mūn returning the vase to its rightful place after al-Amīn's death would suggest that the account emanated from the polemical aftermath of the Fourth Civil War. Even so, it can at least convey some sense of 'Abbāsid-era attitudes about urban contention. When the vase was discovered missing, the crowd (*al-ghawghā'*, "riff-raff") turned violent. The group assembled and marched on the governor's residence, demanding his removal and that he be replaced by a local man. The governor acquiesced, and fled the city by night with his accomplice.[2]

The account, if it contains any truth, suggests that the motivations of the crowd could be complex. First, the crowd evidently viewed the theft symbolically. It was not the theft in and of itself that warranted action, but the violation of norms about the proper relationship between the government and the local community. "Your vase has been stolen!" was the cry that the prayer leader who discovered the theft is reported to have made to the crowds, stressing the personal nature of the affront. Along with this, the theft and/or its account could also have been taken as a comment on the Umayyad legacy, a subject of some sensitivity among the populace of Damascus. However, it is likely that the incident was only the immediate manifestation of a deeper problem, as the revolt eventually focused on the issue of local rule and the illegitimacy of the local governor, who, Ibn 'Asākir notes, faced many riots from the Damascenes before this.[3]

We are on steadier ground with the second case, which comes some fifty years later in the city of Homs, during the revolt of 248/862. In this conflict, the populace of the city ousted their governor, and successfully defeated an attempt by the local troops to crush them, steps which subtly revealed the ideals guiding their actions. The presence of members of the lower strata in the conflict is far from clear, but ideas about the proper functioning of government were certainly in play. When the crowd killed some of the soldiers in combat, they took the bodies and crucified them. At first glance, this may appear to be an example of the wanton cruelty of the mob. In fact, however, it is a gesture with a clear political meaning. As the populace of Homs knew only too well, crucifixion was one of the Qur'ānic punishments for rebels. By crucifying soldiers of the local garrison the crowd was both turning the tables and asserting that the troops (and by extension, the governor) had transgressed the bounds of political order, and were themselves the rebellious parties in the conflict.[4]

At first, the populace peacefully accepted the new governor, al-Faḍl b. Qārin. But it soon became clear that another rebellion was planned and so al-Faḍl took precautionary steps. He rounded up men alleged to be the leaders of the revolt, dismantled the city walls, and tore up the cobblestone pavements of the streets, in one stroke depriving the crowd of leadership, defensive structures, and ammunition. However, the populace was still disgruntled, and they themselves repaved the streets. Led by the Kalbī ʿUṭayf, the crowd, made of Christians and Jews as well as Muslims, marched on al-Faḍl's residence. When al-Faḍl's men finally handed him over, the crowd plundered his residence, killed him, and defiantly crucified him on the northern gates of the city adjacent to the marketplace, there to be seen by the public and by anyone (such as troops from Iraq) who might enter the city from the north.[5]

On the basis of these few examples, it would be unwise to press any conclusion too far. The precise social composition of these violent crowds is very far from clear, and the degree to which the urban poor actively took part in the revolts and adhered to the concepts that motivated them is uncertain. Nor is it easy to define the relationship between these broader concepts and shorter-term motives for a given revolt, such as factional tension or military unrest. Yet although our grasp of the situation of urban nonelites is slim, a close reading of the accounts of these incidents of urban violence suggests at least one conclusion: the crowds of Syria's cities had fairly clear ideas of what the proper political order should be, and they were capable of forcefully articulating these ideas when required.

The Constraints upon Rural Contention

While the urban populations of ʿAbbāsid Syria had few qualms about expressing their social and political grievances, the rural population of the region appears quiet, even tame. The prevailing silence of the Syrian peasantry at this period is especially striking in comparison with rural life in other regions, such as early medieval western Europe, where peasant contention was not uncommon, or even in comparison with other provinces of the ʿAbbāsid caliphate, which were wracked by rural unrest. In contrast to the contemporary Coptic uprisings of the central Delta, or the Khārijite revolts of the Jazīra, the Syrian peasantry seems positively aquiescent.[6] What accounts for this evident quietude on the part of the Syrian peasantry? In what follows, I argue that certain structural features of rural life in Syria militated against collective action on the part of the peasantry, although it did not render it an impossibility. Moreover, armed conflict was only one of a range of options that Syria's rural population might take to address perceived wrongs.

Part of the silence of Syria's rural population is, of course, an illusion produced by the historiographical constraints on the period and the region mentioned in chapter 1, constraints compounded by the particular problems that medieval rural life poses as a subject of modern historical inquiry: we simply know next to nothing about it. Our sources are, as noted, overwhelmingly urban sources, with all the disinterest or disdain that such sources have for the rural populations. At a time when the Syrian rural population was predominantly illiterate and non-Muslim, the anecdotes of literate urban Muslim elites about the peasantry must be used with caution. Rich accounts of rural life have been produced for (most obviously) medieval western Europe, where Bloch, Duby, Ladurie, and others have made the most of sparse but precious documentation and comparison with contemporary ethnographic observation. But early Islamic Syria lacks even these meager resources for reconstructing its rural history. There exist at present exactly three papyrus documents that deal with rural life in ʿAbbāsid Syria, all from the same year and the same locale.[7] While the contemporary (or, at least, recent) Syrian countryside has been the subject of a number of important studies, such as those of Weulersse and Latron, it is unlikely that one can extrapolate much information on early Islamic rural life from studies of the peasantry of the French Mandate era. After all, the peasants of that period had already been subject to varying social and economic pressures of which the Ottoman Land Reform of 1858 is only the most recent pre-Mandate example.[8] Localized studies of periods closer to the early Islamic period exist, such as the excellent case studies of the Crusader Lordship of Tyre and the Roman Ḥawrān, but the lifestyles and agricultural practices analyzed in them are hardly applicable to other regions of Syria.[9]

Archeological evidence is one possible source of valuable contemporary evidence that could remedy the gaps in our historical knowledge of the Syrian peasantry, but here too there are great gaps. For obvious reasons, most archeological work in Syria is concerned with the urban or the monumental, not with rural farmsteads. While a number of extremely important regional surveys exist, particularly from southern Syria, they can tell us only about "the big picture": settlement patterns in a large region over a long period of time.[10] Although single rural settlements have been investigated archeologically, with the excavation and ethnoarcheological study of the site of Khirbet Fâris in central Jordan being the most promising case, these projects are still in progress.[11] At this point, our knowledge of the organization of village life in early Islamic Syria is shadowy at best, and one is forced to agree with R. Stephen Humphreys, that "a pessimistic (or realistic) assessment" of the sources available suggests that a complete history of rural society in the medieval Islamic world, and especially in Syria, is currently impossible.[12]

But if it is impossible to provide a detailed picture of Syrian rural history, it is still possible to speculate on the general constraints that rural life in Syria imposed on the likelihood of peasant rebellion. The underlying assumption taken here is that, given a peasantry willing to rebel against the central government, peasant rebellion is most likely to occur where there exist elite groups with shared interests, and where opportunities for alliance and collective action with these groups are frequent.[13] Peasant unrest in medieval western Europe, for example, was facilitated by the fact that peasants were involved in long-standing patronage and land-tenure arrangements with local landowners who often shared the interests of the peasantry vis-à-vis the central government and who had a long history of social and cultural interaction with them.[14] Although historical information on Syrian rural life is admittedly slim, I suggest that the relationship between the Syrian peasantry and local elites was somewhat different than that in medieval Europe, and was not as conducive to rebellion on the part of the peasantry.

Based on what little the sources tell us of rural life in 'Abbāsid Syria, the relationship between the peasantry and local elites was not likely to have been characterized by close interaction, but rather by disjunction. At perhaps the crudest level, the Muslim Arab or Arabicized local elites would have had little in common with the predominantly non-Muslim, non-Arab peasantry. The barriers of ethnicity, language, and confessional identity could seriously hinder alliances between the two social groups.[15] On the other hand, it must be conceded that ties of kinship or patronage would have linked a certain portion of the rural population to a particular *qawm* of a given notable family. It is likely that much of the factionalism of the period in fact hides a certain amount of peasant contention, insofar as some of the factional fighters are likely to have been peasants.

For those peasants who did have some kind of tenure arrangements with local landowners, it is doubtful that they could easily unite with their landlords in an armed movement. Large portions of the agricultural lands of the province were former Umayyad lands, which were later confiscated by members of the 'Abbāsid family, few of whom ever lived on the lands that they managed (the Banū Ṣāliḥ appear to be an exception).[16] Moreover, many local landowners were participating members of the Syro-Jazīran army, and they were likely to be absent as well, either on campaign or very rarely serving in some distant military post. Thus, it seems likely that other functionaries of the local government often intervened between the peasants and local landowners at tax collection time, which would otherwise be a good time for expressing collective complaints. Indeed, some local elites may well have seen tax collection time as an opportunity for turning a profit, ideal for ploys like buying peasant grain at low prices, or extending eleventh-hour loans in exchange for labor, livestock, or even property. Far from finding common cause with local elites, the peasantry often had every reason for attacking them.[17]

When peasants and local elites were not in conflict, their relationship could be beneficial as the peasants could turn to local elites to help solve certain problems. Yet even so, peasants could also turn to other men who performed mediating functions. The *'ulamā'* provided the most readily available foci of pietistic loyalty, and a number of prominent Syrian religious scholars won considerable notoriety as champions of orthodoxy and justice among Muslims and non-Muslims, often at the expense of the caliph and the central government.[18] For example, later generations considered the jurist al-Awzā'ī (d. 157/773) as the Syrian *'ālim* par excellence, in no small part due to his immense popularity during his lifetime.[19] The few epistles attributed to him that survive show how it was expected that he could intercede directly to the caliph on behalf of the local populace, or even on behalf of the local governor.[20] Moreover, on rare occasions, the populace could make their complaints directly to the caliph himself, with positive results.[21] Thus, the ability of rural populations to redress grievances nonviolently through mediators like members of the *'ulamā'* further diminished the likelihood of peasants finding common cause with local elites in an armed rebellion.[22]

In addition to the often disjointed relationship between the peasantry and local elites to inhibit peasant rebellion, there were also the inherent constraints of rural life to contend with. That agriculture was readily susceptible to the damage of poor weather, pests, flood, and human destruction was a simple fact of life that forced peasants to prepare for the worst. Disaster could strike at any time, and it often came without respite: a drought could lead to poor harvests, resulting in a famine that could, in turn, leave the populace open to plague. In the time of al-Rashīd, pestilence, poor harvests, and tribal warfare forced many peasants from their land near Nābulus and elsewhere in Filasṭīn, forcing the government to take over the abandoned land and attract cultivators to it. The description of local conditions that the Samaritan chronicler Abū al-Fatḥ (fl. 1355) provides is in the same vein as the jeremiads of other confessional minorities, but it is worth citing at length as a record of the fragility of the rural economy and the despair that such disasters (natural and human) can bring:

> During [al-Rashīd's] reign, a great infestation of locusts came, the likes of which had never been seen. They ate up all the green plants and all the pasturage of the land . . . and covered the surface of the land from the sea to [the River] Jordan . . . so that nothing remained on the face of the earth, and the land stood empty.
>
> In the next year, conflict broke out between the Muslims and a great massacre was caused among them. They broke out into two factions, and would go out and fight one another in great enmity, killing each other without mercy. Those Samaritans and others who lived among them were in the greatest distress. [The Muslims] would enter the villages and plunder the crops, the gold, silver, brass, and clothing. . . . The people fled, their villages empty because of the trials and tribulations inflicted upon them. And if [the Muslims] came across a woman, they would practice upon her the deeds of the people of Sodom. . . . The people lived in the mountains and in caves after they were deprived of everything that they had owned; they stood stripped of everything. The great among them who had dependents gave their wealth and extended their protection to them, but those who had no patrons remained wandering about the mountains and caves and wadis. When [the Muslims] came, they would come in and take everything and set the houses and grain-stores on fire, so that nothing remained that had not been razed and the land was in ru-

> ins. It remained that way for nearly a year, until God took pity and set them apart from one another.
>
> In the next year, a great dearth came upon the people and a plague without mercy . . . the price of bread climbed, and the people were utterly starving such that they forgot what it was like to be satiated. . . . It is said that a woman ate her own child in a village called Arba' . . . How may people died in the roads without burial! The street became a cemetery, and the Gentiles used to dig pits alongside the street and allot to them a certain number of corpses for each pit, topping them off with whatever corpses could not be assigned a tomb. How many Samaritan high priests, prayer-leaders, and learned men died without any mourning or burial as is proper, other than the few who were buried in earthen pits without tomb or coffin. How many children were separated from their fathers and fathers separated from their children only to die without the one knowing anything about the fate of the other! . . . People's behavior was transformed, so that not a father remained who enquired after his son or a son who asked after his father, nor a brother who enquired after his brother. Woe to whoever saw by his own eyes this calamity! Blessings to whoever suffered this ordeal and emerged from his trial and obtained relief! . . . After that the rains came and mercy arrived. The peasants returned weeping, possessing neither livestock nor seed. Those who imported seeds from distant lands plowed the earth with their own hands, or with donkeys, mules, and all their other beasts.[23]

As Abū al-Fatḥ's account shows, rebellion might be one way out of a tight situation but, for the most practical reasons, most peasants preferred other alternatives to rebellion. When circumstances became unbearable, peasants could, and did, simply abandonn the land. In addition, the peasants who fled to the hills and caves of Filasṭīn may not have been entirely without resources. The fluidity and flexibility of rural lifeways in the mixed pastoral/agricultural economy of Syria meant that some peasants could avert disaster by complementing (or replacing) their farming with full- or part-time pastoral nomadism. Finally, in a tribal society like that of early Islamic Syria, kinship networks (and, as Abū al-Fatḥ indicates, patronage networks as well) would have provided avenues for care and assistance to let peasants scrape by without recourse to more drastic measures.[24]

However, despite all these obstacles and alternatives, peasant rebellion was not completely precluded. By no means were all landowners absent from their lands, nor were they unknown to their peasants. As Abū al-Fatḥ mentioned, desperate peasants could seek the "protection" of local elites (*al-kibār*), a phenomenon familiar to the Jazīra as well.[25] Peasants were also capable of gathering together for certain purposes, providing the potential cradle for violent collective action. For example, although our knowledge of the organization of labor in rural Syria is virtually nil, the necessities of farming would most likely have brought peasants into contact with one another on a regular basis.[26] Moreover, periodic market fairs brought together peasants of diverse origins, abilities, and social status, often in regional centers where they could interact with townsmen.[27] Thus, even if the conditions outlined above made peasant rebellion unlikely in 'Abbāsid Syria, it was not impossible. The peasantry had before them an array of strategies for averting the worst disasters. Armed rebellion against the government was only the most difficult and least popular of these strategies.

So, when did peasants in 'Abbāsid Syria choose the strategy of opposition over the other strategies of simply "making do"? The two incidents of peasant rebellion in 'Abbāsid Syria that have been recorded suggest that, assuming that the conditions of elite leadership and collective organization are met, rural rebellions fourished especially in remote areas at times when the central government appeared to be in flux. In addition, both recorded incidents were motivated by millenarian expectations, a feature common to peasant social movements.[28]

The Revolt of Bundār / Theodore

The first instance of peasant unrest in 'Abbāsid Syria took place during the reign of al-Manṣūr among the population of the Lebanon Mountains, historically a stronghold for ascetics, rebels, and heterodoxy, and an area where village life was likely to have been largely free of any significant interference from the Muslim central government or its local representatives, and where the peasants had a history of contention under the leadership of certain local elites.[29]

Little is known of the particularities of village life in the

Lebanon Mountains at this time, but the population, like that of the rest of Syria, was likely to have been predominantly Aramaic-speaking Christian free peasants (known to the Arabic sources as *Anbāṭ,* "Nabataeans"). They were therefore required in theory to pay both the poll-tax (*jizya*) and tax on their lands (*kharāj*). The exception to this rule was a community of Christians known as the Jarājima (perhaps those known to the Greek sources as Mardaites), who, in return for auxiliary service on the Taurus passes as guards and spies against the Byzantines, were formally allowed to maintain a certain level of autonomy.

However, the Jarājima had a checkered past with the Muslim authorities. Under the Umayyads, they were known to have openly colluded with the Byzantines in attacks against the Muslims, and were on occasion joined by Christian peasants and runaway slaves from the region. At other times, they attacked the baggage of Muslim troops headed for the frontier. Nevertheless, the Jarājima remained an important element in the Marwānid frontier defenses, and their position does not seem to have changed with the 'Abbāsid revolution, nor was their special status questioned until the time of al-Mutawakkil.[30] Insofar as the peasantry of the region had already joined in raids with the Jarājima in the past, it was not long before the peasantry once again provided the backing of another leader. This time, in 142/759, as the caliph al-Manṣūr was only beginning to consolidate 'Abbāsid rule in the provinces, some peasants of the Mount Lebanon region rallied behind one Bundār, or Theodore as he should properly be called, self-proclaimed "King" of the Jarājima.[31]

According to the lengthy account of Ibn 'Asākir, after Theodore "took the name of king, crowned himself, and displayed the Cross," he acquired a following among the local Christian peasantry. The peasants were in arms against an undefined inequity in taxation. It is said that they told Theodore, "We went to see Isma'īl b. al-Azraq and al-Jazarī (?), who was in charge of the *kharāj* in Baalbek, and they just grew angry with us." Their attempt at negotiation rebuffed, the peasants under Theodore decided to fight the local officials. Their numbers began to grow, and they traveled about plundering villages in the Biqā', killing Muslims, and looting their property.

Theodore next directed the movement toward the source of the peasant's complaints, Baalbek, the center of the local administration. A contingent of Muslim cavalry from Baalbek intercepted

Theodore, however, and after suffering great losses, he fled with the survivors to a nearby "citadel" in the mountains, perhaps a cave or mountaintop stronghold. At this point, the governor of Syria, Ṣāliḥ b. 'Alī, learned of the situation, and wrote to his governor of Dimashq, the Qaysī general Riyāḥ b. 'Uthmān al-Murrī, to assist the Muslim forces at Baalbek. Riyāḥ assembled a large force of soldiers and irregulars from Dimashq (including merchants and other volunteers) under the command of his brother Yazīd, as well as a second force from the troops stationed in the coastal districts under the command of another brother, al-Walīd. The Muslim forces besieged Theodore and his followers in their citadel, and eventually forced them to surrender. Theodore, along with a group of followers, fled to the safety of Byzantine territory.

The peasants who were captured during the siege escaped serious reprisals at first, and were merely sent back to their villages, where they could continue to be productive for the provincial government. However, Ṣāliḥ b. 'Alī soon reconsidered, and with an eye to securing the frontier region, he ordered that all the Christian peasants of the Lebanon Mountain region be removed and forcibly settled throughout the rest of the province. This action produced a response from the Syrian jurist al-Awzā'ī, who wrote to Ṣāliḥ b. 'Alī decrying the punishment, stating that it was contrary to Qur'ānic principles and the explicit *sunna* of the Prophet. The peasantry deserved fair treatment, he argued, "for they are not slaves to be moved about from town to town, but rather free, protected peoples, whose virtue is to be protected from abomination, and to whose women we give equal rights when we marry them as we do our own women in inheritance, divorce, and the inter-marriage waiting-period." It is not known whether al-Awzā'ī's protestations had any effect, as the final fate of the deportees is unknown.[32]

Various historians have discussed the revolt of Theodore, but few with any analytical interest, other than to note that the revolt was at base a tax revolt.[33] Only Crone has attempted to go beyond this obvious point, noting that it, along with other fiscally motivated revolts elsewhere in the caliphate, "clearly reflect the shift from a loose conquest society to an integrated state." While Crone's interpretation is no doubt true, it and the other interpretations have missed what makes this revolt socially significant for the Christian peasants themselves. For Theodore's revolt was not (just) a simple tax revolt, or merely an indicator of larger socio-political processes.

It was also a startlingly rare occurence for early Islamic Syria, a movement of perhaps the most politically impotent social group in the province against the supreme political power. What, besides taxes and the extention of central control, motivated these peasants in their rebellion?

Upon close inspection, Theodore's revolt bears all the marks of a movement influenced by traditions of popular kingship. Comparative evidence to support this hypothesis is not difficult to find. The similarities between the revolt of Theodore and the various revolts of popular messianic "Kings" in Roman Judea are particularly striking.[34] Theodore's "coronation" and defiant use of the Cross, recently prohibited by Muslim authorities, has already been mentioned.[35] Like the Judean "Kings" before him, Theodore, too, appears to be of peasant origin, from the village of al-Munayṭira, according to the account in Ibn 'Asākir. Finally, like these other revolts, Theodore's movement was nativist. That is, it encompassed a discrete, indigenous social grouping, and was directed against another group that was viewed as extraneous to the local societies of the Lebanon Mountains. As in the case of the Judean revolts, unfair taxation was an important catalyst to revolt.

In light of these and other similarities,[36] it is worth asking if Theodore's "kingship" was also messianic in nature, as in the case of the Judean revolts. Unfortunately, there is simply no direct evidence, no slogans or writings from Theodore's followers. Nonetheless, the movement could hardly be otherwise. For if Theodore was proclaimed king, what was he king of? He was surely not a pretender to the Byzantine throne, and the Anbāṭ had no traditions of independent monarchy on which to draw. Either Theodore had introduced a radical idea into the political thought of the Anbāṭ of the Lebanon Mountains (and was a Lebanese nationalist ahead of his time), or he and his peasant followers were drawing on traditions of another, messianic king, not unlike the traditions of the "son of David" that motivated the nativist movements of Roman Judea. In fact, Christian expectations of an "Emperor of the Last Days" are well documented from the Marwānid period, exemplified most prominently in the *Apocalypse* of pseudo-Methodius, although it is not clear to what degree this literary tradition impacted on the unlettered peasantry. However, the popular messiah-kings of Judea on the one hand, and the royal messiahs of medieval Europe on the other suggest that such ideas could attain wide popular acceptance, if in an altered form.[37]

Abū Ḥarb al-Mubarqaʿ

Messianic traditions of a different stripe were at work in the second reported incident of peasant unrest in ʿAbbāsid Syria. The unrest evidently began in an area of al-Urdunn not far from the region that had featured prominently in the revolt of al-Faddaynī. Like al-Faddaynī's revolt, expectations of the Sufyānī informed this incident of peasant unrest. In this case, however, the focus of these expectations was not a (genuine) descendant of the Banū Umayya, but a local outlaw named Abū Ḥarb, who, in the course of his revolt, adopted the sobriquet of al-Mubarqaʿ, "the Veiled One."[38]

As Eisenstein has noted, the various accounts of Abū Ḥarb's revolt are all more or less derivative of the account that al-Ṭabarī provides, with the exception of the brief notice of al-Yaʿqūbī and, one should add, the local perspective of Abū al-Fatḥ. Al-Ṭabarī does not name his source, merely referring to him as "one of my acquaintances, who stated that he was familiar with the story," but the account has all the features of a classic outlaw narrative. As in many other such accounts, the brazenness of the ʿAbbāsid military vis-à-vis the civilian population serves as the catalyst for contention. In this case, a soldier sought lodging in Abū Ḥarb's home while he was away. When Abū Ḥarb's sister (or wife) refused to let the soldier in, the soldier beat her. When Abū Ḥarb returned, his sister complained of the incident to him, and he sought out the soldier and killed him.

With the central government seeking his arrest, Abū Ḥarb took up the life of an outlaw, covering his face with a veil and hiding out in the hills of al-Urdunn. While in hiding, Abū Ḥarb began to attract a following from among the local peasants and he began to preach to them of the evils of the central government: "he would mention the central government and how it oppressed the people and speak scathingly of it." He exhorted his followers "to command the right and forbid the wrong [*al-amr bi-al-maʿrūf wa-al-nahy ʿan al-munkar*]," a popular Muslim moral injunction with its roots in the Qur'ān and early *aḥādīth,* and entirely consonant with the concern for social justice observed in other peasant movements.[39] Perhaps inevitably, given local traditions of resistance, Abū Ḥarb claimed Umayyad ancestry, and, probably early in 226/840, his followers proclaimed him to be no less than the Sufyānī, a millenarian harbinger of the end of time. Abū Ḥarb's reputation soon spread beyond the peasantry, and he attracted the support of local Yamanī tribal notables as well as a few members of the troops of Dimashq.[40]

Side by side with Abū Ḥarb's message, socio-economic factors would also have pushed the peasants of southern Syria to consider rebellion. According to Michael the Syrian, Abū Ḥarb's followers consisted of "3,000 starving and destitute men." Michael elsewhere describes the year in which the revolt took place (1153 of the Seleucid era) as one in which natural disasters crippled agriculture in Syria and the Jazīra. After an extremely cold and dry winter, spring brought only hail and storms that damaged crops and locusts that ravaged the harvests. If, as is likely, the southern regions of Syria are to be included among the regions affected, then Abū Ḥarb's message of the justice of the people versus the injustice of the central government (not to mention his low tax rate of less than four *zūzas* a head) would have been an appealing one to the local peasantry.[41]

Abū Ḥarb and his followers made first for Filasṭīn, probably, as al-Ṭabarī suggests, intending to attack al-Ramla, the local administrative center and the most obvious sign of the presence of the central government in the region. But the group may also have been attracted by the wealthy cities of the region, particularly the wealth so obviously on display in the hands of the various religious establishments. Although a Muslim messianic leader like Abū Ḥarb may have had his own polemical reasons for attacking non-Muslims, it is possible that his peasant followers included a certain number of Christians (the bulk of the peasantry of the region having not yet converted). We might therefore ask if the depredations of Abū Ḥarb's group on the region were motivated less by sectarian tensions than by a desire to reclaim the ill-gotten booty of the rich and powerful. Certainly, by all accounts, the looting ignored confessional boundaries. When the group approached Jerusalem, Christians, Jews, and Muslims fled, while both mosques and churches were plundered. In an attempt to save the churches of the city from destruction, the Patriarch paid off a large amount of gold as ransom. Likewise, the city of Nābulus was attacked, and the inhabitants fled, among them the Samaritan high priest, who died of wounds received during his flight to Hebron.[42]

It was most likely at this point that a small force of local troops under the commander Rajā' al-Ḥiḍārī arrived from Damascus, where al-Mu'taṣim had sent him to crush the outbreak of Qaysī factionalism there led by Ibn Bayhas al-Kilābī.[43] Abū Ḥarb's following greatly outnumbered Rajā's force, and so the commander bided his time, waiting until autumn in late 226/840 or early 227/841, when many of the rebel following returned to their fields. With the rebel numbers now decreased, Rajā' attacked them, and captured Abū Ḥarb. He returned with him to Iraq where Abū Ḥarb, along with the Qaysī Ibn Bayhas, was put in prison.[44]

Like so many peasant rebellions, the revolts of Theodore and Abū Ḥarb were largely efforts of sound and fury with little or no benefit accruing to the peasantry in the end.[45] Indeed, the peasants of the Lebanon Mountains suffered greater deprivations in retaliation for Theodore's revolt than they did before it. As we have seen, many of those punished were not even participants in the rebellion. For the peasant followers of Abū Ḥarb, the constraints of the cycle of agricultural labor proved too much, and, after some profitable looting of the towns of Filasṭīn, they chose to return to their fields rather than risk destruction at the hands of the 'Abbāsid army. Even when the peasants of 'Abbāsid Syria could find a charismatic leader like Theodore or Abū Ḥarb, and even when that leadership provided them with the necessary organization to attempt to change their position with the central government, to many peasants, the ends of rebellion simply did not justify the means.

Banditry and the Zawāqīl

With examples like the revolts of Theodore and Abū Ḥarb, there is little wonder that the peasants of 'Abbāsid Syria preferred other ways to counter adversity. As we have seen, most peasants chose one of the other routes open to them to surmount social or economic hardship, like making appeals to local elites, seeking assistance from kin, or simply fleeing the land. Peasant flight often brought cultivators and pastoralists to the cities in search of new ways to make a living, but sometimes it brought them only as far as the steppe, where they could also make a living as bandits (*luṣūṣ, quṭṭā' al-ṭuruq*). Poised between city, field, and desert, the geographical context of bandits in Syria mirrored their social and political ambiguity. Syria's bandits made a living off this ambiguity, cultivating ties to the rural population, to local elites, and even to the central government.

This ambiguous social role of bandits is nowhere more clearly demonstrated than in the activities of the group known as the Zawāqīl. Virtually every aspect of the Zawāqīl's origins, activities, and demise are obscure. Among western scholars, only Ayalon has attempted to fully understand them, showing that the term refers to a confederation of Qaysī tribesmen, whose activities (when Ayalon wrote) were known only in connection with the revolt of Naṣr b. Shabath of 196/811 during the Fourth Civil War. However, a great deal of new information on the Zawāqīl has come to light since Ayalon wrote, particularly from Ibn 'Asākir, and we are now able to provide a more refined picture of the Zawāqīl.[46]

Unknown to Ayalon and others, the Zawāqīl first appear in the revolt of Abū al-Haydhām in 176–77/792–93, when some Qaysī tribesmen approached a group of the Zawāqīl in the Ḥawrān to ask their assistance in exacting retribution for a kinsman who had been killed by a Yamanī. The Zawāqīl, among them one Di'āma b. 'Abd Allāh, proceeded to the Ghūṭa, where they took their revenge and were subsequently called in to assist Abū al-Haydhām and the Qaysiyya against the Yamaniyya and the 'Abbāsid army. From this evidence, it is clear that the Zawāqīl are indeed a Qaysī group (as Ayalon has shown), and, moreover, that they are a mercenary group of some kind, with a reputation for military, or perhaps simply criminal skill.[47]

The connection of the Zawāqīl with banditry can still be made clearer. As Ayalon has shown, the medieval lexicographers clearly connected the Zawāqīl with brigands, treating the two terms as virtually synonymous, and the Zawāqīl and their leaders were certainly no angels. 'Amr b. 'Abd al-'Azīz al-Sulamī, for example, was an escaped convict, a former soldier who had murdered his commander, when he began his predatory attacks on the villages and towns of southern Syria before joining up with Naṣr b. Shabath. Di'āma b. 'Abd Allāh, who figured prominently in the Zawāqīl contingent in Abū al-Haydhām's revolt, is surely the same Di'āma who is named as a colleague of Yaḥyā b. Irimiyā, the Jewish bandit from the Balqā' active in the 180s/ca. 800. Contemporaries were aware of the shady pasts of many members of the Zawāqīl; al-Ma'mūn's letter to Naṣr b. Shabath described his followers in these terms:

> A confused band from the near and distant corners of the lands, with their scum and worst elements, those thieves and robbers who have rallied to your side and those whom

> their land has spewed forth or whose tribe has expelled because of their bad reputation within it.[48]

Although they inhabited the steppe, Syria's bandits were no strangers to the local government or the benefits it offered. For example, in the early 180s/late 790s, there emerged a triumvirate of bandit leaders, all of whom refused to give allegiance to the new governor, Ibrāhīm b. Muḥammad al-Mahdī. One of these bandits was Di'āma b. 'Abd Allāh, the Zawāqīl leader. The others were a certain Nu'mān, who, like Di'āma, was a *mawlā* of the Umayyads, and Yaḥyā b. Irimiyā, a Jew from the Balqā' in southern Syria. Rather than marching out against these three separate bandit chiefs, Ibrāhīm wisely chose to open negotiations first.[49]

The different fates of each of the bandits is instructive of how bandits frequently played off the interests of the government. Nu'mān was the first to reply to the governor, and he agreed to obey him. However, a previous oath prevented him from actually making the symbolic gesture of obedience in person, so Nu'mān sent Di'āma to Damascus to meet with the governor. In return, Ibrāhīm made Di'āma one of his retainers (*ja'alahu min khāṣṣatihi*). For his part, Yaḥyā still refused to submit to Ibrāhīm even after some negotiation (conversion to Islam allegedly being one of the conditions), and he returned to the Balqā'. When the caravan bearing the tax revenues from Egypt headed toward al-Ramla, Yaḥyā could not resist, and prepared to ambush it. However, his colleague Nu'mān informed Ibrāhīm of the plan and intervened, killing Yaḥyā and retrieving the tax money. Clearly, both Di'āma and Nu'mān were happy to be on good terms with the central government when it suited them. In the end, they both became retainers of the local governor, and Nu'mān was even used to thwart the activity of other bandits.

Moreover, the Zawāqīl were not just limited to serving the interests of the peasantry (if they ever did) or the local government. In their role in Abū al-Haydhām's revolt, the cause that the Zawāqīl served in this revolt was, after all, that of *ashrāf* (and landowners), not that of the peasantry. The Zawāqīl were no less innocent than the rest of the followers in both factions by joining in the fighting and sacking of villages. Much the same could be said of the role of the Zawāqīl in the revolt of Abū al-'Umayṭir in 195/810, when, after pillaging the countryside of much of southern Syria, they were enlisted to help oust the governor of Dimashq. The fact that they were a predominantly Qaysī group assisting an Umayyad pretender backed by Yamanī notables did not seem to deter them.[50]

Finally, bandit groups have commonly had some kind of connection with the military: frequently, either bandits had been soldiers or vice versa. Thus, it is not surprising to see the Zawāqīl benefiting from the needs of the military, just as they had profited from that of the *ashrāf*, the local governor, and perhaps the peasantry. After all, when the Zawāqīl under Naṣr b. Shabath and others appeared at al-Raqqa in 196/811, it was in answer to a call for the tribesmen of Syria and the Jazīra to join the army of al-Amīn. They were stopped, however, when a member of al-Amīn's contingent of Abnā' stationed at al-Raqqa noticed his horse among those used by the Zawāqīl. The owner was evidently a veteran of Abū al-'Umayṭir's revolt, during which the Zawāqil had taken the horse. For the Zawāqīl, playing with both sides could have obvious drawbacks.

When the two contingents of troops gathered to confront each other, the Syrian troops persuaded themselves that, even though fighting for al-Amīn had seemed to present an opportunity to raise their station, conflict with the caliph's army would only end in their own deaths. "To Syria! To Syria!" one Syrian is said to have shouted. "To your home! To your home! A Filasṭīnī death [i.e., an honorable one] is better than a Jazīran life!" Thus incited, the Syrian troops deserted and returned to their homes.

As it turned out, the Syrian troops had chosen wisely, if not courageously. The Zawāqīl, left by themselves to fight against the Abnā', were almost immediately routed. Despite this setback, however, the leader of the Zawāqīl, Naṣr b. Shabath, was still able to round up a significant body of support to resist al-Ma'mūn's reconquest of al-Jazīra. He even negotiated a role for himself in al-Ma'mūn's military after al-Amīn's defeat. When Naṣr b. Shabath was finally defeated, the Zawāqīl were evidently absorbed as part of 'Abd Allāh b. Ṭāhir's army, as they are said to have accompanied him to Khurāsān, where they were decimated in battle in 213/828. Still others may have joined later, since al-Mutawakkil had a contingent of Zawāqīl in his new army housed at Balkuwārā.[51]

Similarly, the Egyptian army probably produced the bandit leader Abū al-Nidā', who was executed at al-Raqqa in 192/807 and who was certainly no friend of the peasants. Abū al-Nidā' was himself a *mawlā* of the tribe of Balī, but his followers were mostly tribesmen from the eastern Nile delta (*ahl al-ḥawf*), a long-lived source of manpower for the Egyptian military. In the previous year, Ḥawfī tribesmen had refused to pay the *kharāj* to the governor of Egypt. Abū al-Nidā' and his followers began attacking villages and holding up travelers near the town of Ayla and elsewhere in southern Syria. Although other tribesmen joined his ranks, a combined army of both Egyptian and Iraqi troops was able to capture him and disperse his followers.[52]

The "rebellious" activity directed against the 'Abbāsid authorities by bandit groups like the Zawāqīl, then, is only one side of the complete story of banditry in Syria. Although they did often pose a threat to the interests of the local and central governments, Syria's bandits were also happy to serve those interests as well, whether as informal "men-on-the-scene" like Di'āma and Nu'mān, or as members of the military. The bandit groups of Syria, like the peasants who knew them, were contentious only when it suited them, and never when other options were possible.

Conclusion

In the cities of 'Abbāsid Syria, the urban poor almost certainly joined the crowds who periodically took up arms against perceived injustice, while in the countryside, peasants had a number of ways to redress wrongs. Despite the unlikelihood of peasant-elite cooperation and the realities of peasant life that worked against collective action, from time to time Syria's peasants could and did take up arms against the local government. Moreover, peasants, ex-soldiers, and other marginal groups were the source of bandits like the Zawāqīl, who became adept at "working the system," playing off the social and political interests of peasants, the local elite, and even the central government in order to survive.

Yet even with all this political activity, Syria's lower strata could only achieve the shortest-term ends: a certain amount of loot, a temporary tax break, a more secure source of income. The crowds who tried to reorder Syria's cities, like the notables who led them, were fighting to *maintain* the customary political order, not to topple it. Similarly, even if the peasantry could fend off the interference of the local government, they simply could not escape the limits that rural life imposed on their activity on the one hand, and the decisive military might of the central government on the other.

Banditry provided the one means whereby common people might raise their social standing, perhaps as heroes among the local peasantry, but more likely as servants of local elites or even as soldiers in the 'Abbāsid army, rubbing elbows with the *ashrāf*. Occasionally rebels but never revolutionaries, Syria's "unnotables" were political actors whose impolitic acts most frequently served the interests of others.

CHAPTER SEVEN

Conclusion: Standards of Revolt

> Dorothy: Someplace where there isn't any trouble. . . do you suppose there is such a place, Toto?
>
> *The Wizard of Oz* (MGM, 1939)

In the aftermath of the 'Abbāsid revolution, the new caliphate absorbed Syria into its emerging constellation of territories governed directly from Iraq. Formerly the Umayyad metropolis, Syria was now a functioning province of the 'Abbāsid caliphate, in which members of the populace paid taxes, served in the army, and occasionally staffed positions in the central government. Yet Syrians also periodically gathered, brandished weapons, and, in their different ways, used violence to reinforce their various claims. Why were Syrians so keen to rebel?

This study has sought to answer that question by treating Syrian unrest not as isolated, irrational events of violent ingratitude toward the 'Abbāsid government, but rather as a single array of differing but related genres of contention united by their common interest in making claims about central authority, local power, and legitimacy. Writing the history of Syrian unrest in this way has required a local yet long-duration perspective, a perspective that has been possible to adopt only because of the wealth of new information available from local sources like Ibn 'Asākir and Ibn al-'Adīm.

So what has this perspective gained us in our attempt to understand Syrian unrest? In the first place, it is clear that a number of factors directly triggered Syrian contention in the 'Abbāsid period, but that the system of provincial government created a context in which the various personal sources of discontent could escalate into violence deemed rebellious in Iraq. At the heart of the 'Abbāsid system of government was a dynamic of provincial power, according to which smooth provincial government rested upon the cooperation of provincial governors and local elites (the *ashrāf*), who mediated parochial interests with those of the center. Just as the *ashrāf* enhanced their local status through their connections with the government, provincial governors needed the *ashrāf* to be able to govern effectively. Given the strains placed on both of these closely interdependent social groups, their relationship was highly subject to conflict, and it was this unstable dependent relationship between province and center that created a setting favorable to the kinds of contention that have been explored in this study. Although such a setting was common to other provinces, and, indeed, to other states, it was new to the former Umayyad metropolis.

What is more, this setting was a *constant* feature of Syrian history under the 'Abbāsids, as much in operation immediately after the revolution as it was over a century later. Given the unwavering context of instability in the dynamic of provincial power in the 'Abbāsid period, the high frequency of Syrian contention comes as no surprise. Syrians did not take up arms in revolt so much because they resented the fact that their province once had been the center of the caliphate and then suddenly was not. Rather, it was the fact that *Syria was a province* that provided the Syrians with both the materials and the opportunities for revolt.

In general, opportunities for unrest were smaller for those Syrians less deeply involved in the system of provincial government. The rural populations and the common people of the cities were the least inclined toward independent contention, because they were quite far removed from the loci of provincial power (insofar as much can be said about them at all). Rebellion and banditry were but two elements in a complex calculus that rural and urban populations alike might draw upon to defend their interests.

Like these "unnotables" of Syria, Umayyad kinsmen made their claims somewhat (but not entirely) independently of the system of provincial rule, and so, after the first Umayyad counterrevolts, Sufyānid claims for the caliphate were rare. By comparison, the governors of Syria were responsible for more political instability than either the common folk or any Umayyad pretenders. Provincial governors could easily use their position in the system of provincial rule to make their own claims. By importing court politics into the provinces, Syria's governors were as responsible as anyone else for the region's reputation for discord.

The provincial governors were matched in their propensity for unrest only by the *ashrāf*, who were by far the most active contributors to Syrian contention. After they had fought for their continued utility in the new 'Abbāsid ruling apparatus, Qaysī and Yamanī factions intensified their competition as the path toward privileges narrowed for factional leaders, their kinsmen, and their followers. When it became necessary, Syria's *ashrāf* could call upon their constituencies among their kinsmen and the urban populace to back their claims. However, as long as the authority of the central government remained intact, the contention of Syria's *ashrāf* was never a serious threat. Governors might be killed, taxes delayed, the countryside raided, but the general legitimacy of the 'Abbāsid government was never contested. Only in situations where 'Abbāsid authority was plainly in question—as during the Fourth Civil War—could Syria's *ashrāf* emerge as autonomous leaders. Even then, their actions toward the central government were often not defiant but instead pragmatic.

Aside from their independent forays into contention, Syria's *ashrāf* also played decisive roles in the contention of others. In the messianic revolt of Abū Ḥarb al-Mubarqa', some of the *ashrāf* threw in their lot with Abū Ḥarb's peasant following and, bringing their own military expertise and factional followings, probably contributed to its capacity for violence. For Sufyānid claimants like Abū Muḥammad and Abū al-'Umayṭir, the crucial element in their success, and, ultimately, in their failure, was the cooperation of factional leaders: in the case of Abū al-'Umayṭir, his predominantly Yamanī regime was overturned with the appearance of the Qaysī Ibn Bayḥas and his own candidate. Most importantly, because of their placement in the system of provincial government, the *ashrāf* of Syria could provide provincial governors like 'Abd Allāh b. 'Alī with the local support and military backing that they needed to make their own claims against the center. In short, contention in Syria was never solely driven by the interests of one social stratum, but by the confluence of many claims, all of them in one way or another connected with the system of provincial government.

When seen from this perspective, Syrian contention cannot be considered, as so many have maintained, to be a symptom of any general political or socio-economic decline attributable to the passage from Umayyad to ʿAbbāsid rule.[1] In fact, if we view the history of Syria over the *longue durée,* the Umayyad period was an exceptional interlude of primacy for Syria and its populace; the ʿAbbāsid revolution merely returned the region to its historically prevailing role as a province within a larger unitary state, be it Hellenistic or Roman, Mamluk or Ottoman. True, after 132/750, Syria was no longer the metropolitan province of the ruling elite. Its *ashrāf* found themselves in less amenable surroundings than that to which they had been accustomed under the Umayyads. But decline is always a matter of perspective; the crisis of the *ashrāf* did not spell crisis for Syria as a whole.[2] However unhappy some Syrians may have been, the large-scale political breakdown and socio-economic collapse of ʿAbbāsid Syria that modern scholarship has posited for so long has no historical basis. Indeed, in certain cases, contention—especially interelite competition like that of Syria's *ashrāf*—can be seen as a kind of backhanded compliment to the success of ʿAbbāsid state-building and an affirmation of its legitimacy. Political life in ʿAbbāsid Syria was certainly different from that under the Umayyads, but, all things considered, it showed little change for the worse.

The View from Syria

By recognizing that contention in Syria was not a symptom of decline but was a feature inherent in the ʿAbbāsid system of provincial government, we are now in a position to appreciate how Syrians might have understood the history of their province after the apogee of Umayyad power. Before the death of the caliph Hishām in 125/743, Syrians had been at the center of a flourishing civilization and expanding state. Syrian centrality under the Umayyads was both geographic and—more importantly—social and political. For it was Syrians who made up the Umayyad imperial elite, who oversaw the caliphate as soldiers, commanders, governors, and administrators, and this centrality continued even in the midst of crisis. When the caliphate was plunged into its third civil war with the accession of Hishām's successor, al-Walīd II, it was natural that it was the troops of Syria and the Jazīra who fought for the causes of their own caliphal candidates.

In the early days of the civil war, it might have looked like Qays or Yaman could one day lose all, but general Syrian supremacy was never in question. Even late in the reign of Marwān II, when the supporters of the Hāshimiyya movement raised their black banners in Khurāsān, Syrian troops were sent to crush them, as they had done to provincial rebellions many times before. When, in 132/749, it became clear that the 'Abbāsid family now openly led the movement and that it was not going to just dry up, the 'Abbāsids and their Khurāsānī army arrived as late comers to a Syrian conflict that was already in progress. Even when the 'Abbāsids killed Marwān II, it was a setback only for his Qaysī followers: the Syrian tribal factions had plenty more Umayyads where he came from.

But long years of in-fighting and even longer years before that on the frontiers under Hishām had weakened the army. Syrian military men found themselves outmatched by the Khurāsānī army and the growing ranks of supporters for the 'Abbāsid family's caliphal candidate, al-Saffāḥ. Even while Marwān II still lived, some Syrians threw in their lot with the 'Abbāsid forces. One by one, the factional followings that lined up behind Umayyad candidates like Abū Muḥammad al-Sufyānī faced defeat, flight, and death. And some, such as Ḥabīb b. Murra and Ibn Surāqa, were just fighting to hold on, whatever the tenor of the caliph who would rule them. But for many Syrians, an 'Abbāsid caliph supported by a Syrian army began to look better and better. With Umayyad candidates a bit thin on the ground after al-Saffāḥ's massacres, and with the death in 136/754 of al-Saffāḥ himself, 'Abd Allāh b. 'Alī was just the man for the job.

However, 'Abd Allāh's young nephew al-Manṣūr proved to be a problem. Solidly supported by the Khurāsānī army, al-Manṣūr and his general Abū Muslim easily thwarted 'Abd Allāh's supporters and put an end to their hopes to remain a caliphal elite. Consequently, under al-Manṣūr's caliphate, Syrians, elite or not, felt the first decisive shock of their new status as 'Abbāsid provincials. For the peasant followers of the Christian rebel Theodore, the changes going on around them were signs of a greater, more glorious transformation to be wrought by a hero-king of their own. But Theodore's movement was destroyed and his followers dispersed.

The *ashrāf*, meanwhile, were pardoned for their association with 'Abd Allāh and remained as frontier troops ready to assist the Khurāsānī army when necessary. What was left of the Umayyad ruling family in Syria cultivated what little wealth and local power was left to them; some even tried to make a home as caliphal companions in the court of Baghdad. From the reign of al-Manṣūr onward, Syrian contention became less a story of raising white banners than one of finding ways to live under black ones.

In this respect, the *ashrāf* found it hardest to adjust. It was a slow process. Some hung on to influential posts in distant provinces, as did the Banū Khuraym. Some made it as courtiers in Baghdad. And campaigning on the Byzantine frontier did offer some genuine benefits, particularly under a caliph like al-Rashīd, who was so personally involved in expanding the frontiers of the Islamic world. Nevertheless, most Syrians saw their only hope for influence embodied in one figure: the 'Abbāsid governor. If the *ashrāf* could court the favor of a governor for themselves and their factional followings, the pain of adjustment might be buffered, the connection to privilege prolonged. Just as importantly, the governor's patronage wonderfully aggravated one's factional foes, as the Yamanīs learned when they attempted to confront the outraged Qaysī supporters of Abū al-Haydhām.

But just when it looked like Syrians had established a relatively settled pattern of relationships with Baghdad, a momentous change occured: al-Rashīd was dead, and central government collpased. During the Fourth Civil War, the *ashrāf* dispensed with the governors, and, indeed, endeavored to usurp them. Long dormant Umayyad loyalties found an outlet even among a generation that had never known Umayyad sovreignty. To many Syrians at the time, in the absence of any viable 'Abbāsid alternative, Sufyānīs like Abū al-'Umayṭir were a logical place to seek authority. And in the troubled days of the Fourth Civil War, with Umayyads, 'Abbāsids, Qaysīs, and Yamanīs all in need of a little extra manpower, bandits and mercenaries like the Zawāqīl made a killing.

However, the political breathing space that the Fourth Civil War provided for Syrians was short-lived. For those old enough to make the comparison, al-Ma'mūn's victory against al-Amīn and the campaigns of 'Abd Allāh b. Ṭāhir in the west might have seemed like a replay of the events of 132/750. But the similarity was superficial; for Syrians, and the *ashrāf* especially, the world had changed irrevocably since 132/750. Now, Syrians who resisted the restoration of 'Abbāsid authority were killed or imprisoned. The bulk of the *ashrāf* quietly resumed their antebellum roles as frontier troops and competitive local elites for al-Ma'mūn, his successors, and their governors. Moreover, those roles themselves were changing. Al-Mu'taṣim deprived the *ashrāf* of their last connections to the military and they were left to compete with one another and with new elements from the urban and rural populace as local notables.

As the old Syrian sharifian elite dwindled under al-Mu'taṣim's successors, political action by others came to the forefront. In the countryside, for the first time, peasants formed the core following of a Sufyānī, al-Mubarqa'. It was also the last time that Umayyad legitimism, tribal factionalism and rural grievances would find common cause. In the cities and towns, power came to be exercised by non-Arab governors and tribal dynasts; urban crowds either protested on their own or they made do under local notables, like 'Uṭayf of the Banū Kalb, who were increasingly drawn from new groups, including nomads from the countryside. The Syrians who fought alongside 'Īsā b. al-Shaykh were not seeking Syrian centrality or access to the privileges of the caliphal elite; they were just tribesmen from the provinces hoping to profit from confusion in the center. Syria might have been a troublesome province, but it was also an undeniably 'Abbāsid one. Indeed, by the time Aḥmad b. Ṭūlūn gained control of Syria in 264/877, Syrian provincial life and Syrian contention looked much like that of the rest of the medieval Islamic world.

Contextualizing Syria

One deceptively obvious implication of this view of Syrian history is that Syrian contention can hardly be regarded as exceptional. Indeed, provincial contention is a consequence of early Islamic provincial government, and is to be found in comparable forms and frequency in other provinces of the 'Abbāsid caliphate. Elton Daniel, for example, has made the point that Khurāsān, despite its reputation for being the bastion of 'Abbāsid support, was in fact as prone to contention as any other province.[3] Nor did Syria have a monopoly on any forms of contention. In Khurāsān, as in Syria (and perhaps more so), local Khurāsānī elites such as Sunbādh or al-Muqanna' led rural revolts that tended to be articulated as nativist or millenarian movements. Also as in Syria, the region had its share of ambitious provincial governors and military factionalism and was soon lost to the direct control of the central government.[4] In Egypt, pro-Umayyad contention was not unknown, and the factionalism of the Arabs of the Ḥawf had their analogs in Syria, too.[5] Peasant resistance to taxation was another feature common to both Egypt and Syria.[6] Likewise, the Jazīra, of course, could offer Shaybānī and Hamdānī Khārijites in addition to the *'aṣabiyya* of factional notables and the rebellions of governors.[7]

The timing and frequency of contention in Syria was also part of a broader pattern shared by other provinces. Provincial contention peaked notably in two periods: immediately after the revolution, and during the Fourth Civil War. In Khurāsān, the Jazīra, and Egypt, as in Syria, 'Abbāsid rule was a debatable issue in its early days. In every province, the Third Civil War was still being fought well after 132/750. True, in the Jazīra, the 'Abbāsids got their message across with the Mosul massacres of 133/751.[8] But for Egyptian elites, as with the Syrians, the issue was only settled with al-Manṣūr's victory over 'Abd Allāh b. 'Alī.[9] And although resistance to al-Manṣūr still continued for a time in Khurāsān, it came from supporters of the 'Abbāsid revolution who contended with the 'Abbāsids over the direction of the revolution and the memory of Abū Muslim.[10] During the Fourth Civil War, the autonomy of Syria's *ashrāf* was mirrored in the local rebel governors of Egypt and the Jazīra, and in the bids for autonomy by Khurāsānī elites after al-Ma'mūn's return to Baghdad.[11] Contention was not a Syrian trait—it was a *provincial* one.

But if contention was a common, panprovincial phenomenon, was there *nothing* unique in the way it was expressed locally? What made Syrian contention distinctively Syrian? Obviously, local conditions significantly affected the forms and frequency of contention in Syria. For example, the proximity of the Byzantine-Islamic frontier territories and their garrisons greatly facilitated the ability of governors to mobilize and supply troops for their own ends.[12] With pay in their pockets and a charismatic commander at their head, troops that had been mobilized to fight external foes could easily be redirected against internal rivals. Also (although the sources cannot stretch this point too far), it does seem that the particular structure of peasant society in Syria militated against rural contention in ways unlike peasant society in other regions of the caliphate. Peasants rebelled in Syria, but Syria never produced rural revolts as tragic or as cataclysmic as the Coptic revolts of

Egypt. Syrians also had a unique interpretation of their place in history to enervate them, producing the distinctive apocalyptic traditions about Syria and the Umayyad past that set the stage for the occasional Sufyānid revolts of the period. When a few anonymous Mizzīs fearfully buried Abū al-'Umayṭir in secret, they were responding to the lessons of the past that only Syrians could appreciate.

What made Syrian contention especially unique were the claims of Syria's elites, elites that had felt the impact of 'Abbāsid rule like no other social group in the caliphate. Unlike Syria's *ashrāf*, Egypt's Arab military elite were easily integrated into 'Abbāsid provincial politics; after all, they had been experts at it under the Umayyads.[13] And factional competition, though common to the Jazīran *ashrāf*, was, in Syria, shaped by the particular fortunes of dominant notable families like the Banū Bayhas and the Banū Khuraym.

The revolt of Abū al-Haydhām, a watershed by any estimation, is not just the story of one man's private fury; the revolt also speaks of the concerns of a multitude of Syrian tribes. Syrian *ashrāf*, formerly the traditional imperial elite under the Umayyads, had to negotiate for survival under the 'Abbāsids in a quite different way than did the elites of Egypt, Khurāsān, or even the Jazīra. For the Syrian *ashrāf*, the transition was sharper, the competition steeper, and the sense of loss once the *ashrāf* faded away was far keener than elsewhere. Every province had local elites, but the passing of those who used to command the world produced a different void than did the passing of those who had never done so. For the *ashrāf* of 'Abbāsid Syria, it was their understanding of their collective histories that quite literally became the rallying cry for revolt.

Questions

Syrian contention in the 'Abbāsid period was thus a distinctive local expression of a broader pattern of state-society relations in the early Islamic period. For Syria cannot be said to have been an exclusively contentious province; neither was it the sole province that contended with the central government. Rather, in becoming a province, Syria was integrated into a system of power relations common to the caliphate as a whole. Yet the very banality of Syrian contention at this level raises an important question: if contention was not particularly unique to Syria—despite its peculiar local expressions—but common enough to other provinces, then why were 'Abbāsid contemporaries so ready to privilege Syria as the contentious province *par excellence*? Or, to put it another way, why is it not a petulant Egyptian soldier who buttonholes al-Ma'mūn in the anecdote that opened this study?

Clearly, there were other factors behind the development of Syria's image than an observable trend toward ceaseless discord. Certainly, the pro-Umayyad, pro-Syrian, and anti-Iraq, anti-'Abbāsid sentiments recorded in works like the *faḍā'il* collections sound defensive, and perhaps this implies that they were responding to a substantial line of argument that was anti-Umayyad and anti-Syrian. The derogatory traditions and anecdotes about the customs of Syrian rubes cited in this study may only be the tip of the iceberg. Perhaps—paralleling the physical conflicts in 'Abbāsid Syria—there existed a discursive struggle over the meaning of Syria that was just as fierce as the combat in the countryside and the melee in the city streets. But the contours of this discursive debate and its relationship with the realities of Syrian history remain to be studied.

A proper understanding of contention in 'Abbāsid Syria also provokes questions about Syrian contention beyond the period of direct 'Abbāsid rule. For as long as Syrian society remained part of the 'Abbāsid system of provincial government, the forms of Syrian contention remained more or less constant. Conversely, when the system of government in Syria began to change, so did the forms and scale of contention. To be more precise, the late third/ninth century saw the collapse of 'Abbāsid authority in Syria, the rise of various "successor dynasties" like the Ṭūlūnids, and a significant transformation in Syrian contention. Choosing the Ṭūlūnid period as this study's stopping point for examining unrest in Syria was therefore not an arbitrary decision.

It is true that, on the one hand, many aspects of provincial government under the Ṭūlūnids remained essentially the same as they had been in 'Abbāsid times. When Aḥmad b. Ṭūlūn took control of Damascus and the rest of Syria and added it to his Egyptian domains late in 264/877, he was not introducing a radically new political order. Rather, Ibn Ṭūlūn's actions were based on a pattern of provincial politics (and provincial contention) established long ago. Although power over Syria now rested in a Turkish dynasty based in Egypt, neither Turkish commanders nor Egypt were new to the Syrian political vocabulary. Since the time of al-Rashīd, Syria had frequently been grouped with Egypt and other western provinces as a western "superprovince" to be governed at the discretion of powerful military men. That these men were now predominantly of Turkish origin was almost incidental and, by 264/877, it was in any case the established procedure. From the point of view of the Syrian populace, what was new was merely the destination of their tax payments; whether they ended up in the treasury in Baghdad, Samarra, or Ṭūlūnid al-Qaṭā'i' mattered little.[14]

On the other hand, the Ṭūlūnid conquest did initiate significant change in Syria. The Ṭūlūnid period marked the first time in Islamic history that much of the province of Syria was subordinated to a central administration in Egypt, an arrangement that would remain in place until the establishment of Saljuqid authority in Syria around 480/1087.[15] It is also the beginning of a period of raised stakes in Syrian local politics, one which witnessed the rise of local dynasties like the Ḥamdānids and the Jarrāḥids, sectarian movements like the Qarāmiṭa, and the added threat of a new, muscular Byzantine presence in the north. These changes in provincial administration and in the local Syrian political scene generated subtle changes in the nature of Syrian contention.

Of course, the contentious Syrians of the second/eighth and third/ninth centuries did not disappear with the Ṭūlūnid conquest in 264/877. Even after Ibn Ṭūlūn took power, urban crowds still sometimes murdered their governors, elites displaced from their former positions still fought over dwindling privileges, and the last Sufyānī audaciously, if vainly, claimed the caliphate. But despite these surface similarities, the collapse of caliphal authority brought with it a sea change in the forms and intensity of Syrian contention. As new actors entered the scene from the governing ranks of Egypt and the nomadic populations of the desert, repertoires of contention were slowly altered. In the cities, garrisons of foreign troops and armed urban militias (*aḥdāth*) intensified urban violence, while the rural-based militant Shī'ī movement of the Qarāmiṭa made the depredations of the Zawāqīl seem generous by comparison. Although the Ṭūlūnid conquest may seem to have been a simple reshuffling of governing elites, this study suggests that changes in the nature of provincial government had a direct impact on contention in Syria.[16]

Yet (keeping in mind the frailities of the sources), the potential impact of other factors on contention in the early Islamic period remains an open question. Certainly, the many studies of European contention by Tilly and others have highlighted the interrelationship of economic change and contention during and after the rise of industry. But to what degree does this interrelationship apply to Syria in the period *before* industrialization, when agriculture was the dominant mode of production and had been for millenia? When and why did contention in Syria significantly change *after* the 'Abbāsid period? To what degree did changes in the system of land-tenure—such as the spread of prebendal holdings (the *iqṭā'āt*)—affect contention in Syria after the 'Abbāsids? In the case of the early Islamic period, the spread of the *iqṭā'* system and the changes in the nature of provincial government are obviously related, but the precise relationship between these transformations and changes in contention remains unclear. For the moment, our sources, miserly with economic information at best, can only provoke more questions.

That Syrian contention in the 'Abbāsid period was linked to the way Syria was governed may appear to be self-evident, but it has never drawn the attention of historical inquiry. This study has tried to show concretely the particular ways in which Syrians responded to the imposition of 'Abbāsid rule on their province. More than any other factor, it was the system of 'Abbāsid provincial government that tied governors, *ashrāf*, Umayyad nobles, peasants, rabble, and bandits into a network of power relations that permitted—and occasionally pushed—people to make a stand for their own interests, even when the latter did not accord with the interests of the caliphs in Iraq.

In Syria, this system of government allowed contention to be expressed in particularly Syrian terms: the antagonism of Qays and Yaman, the demise of the *ashrāf*, the advent of the Sufyānī, the raising of the white banners. But the contention itself was far from uniquely Syrian. In this respect, the experience of the Syrian populace after the fall of the Umayyads was at once intensely rooted in the local history of Syria and also indicative of broader patterns throughout the caliphate.

APPENDIX A

Governors of the *jund* of Dimashq (based on Ṣafadī, *Umarā'* esp. 202–6, with minor modifications)

al-Saffāḥ	132–136/749–54
ʻAbd Allāh b. ʻAlī	132/750
ʻUmar b. Shurayḥ al-Ḥaḍramī	
ʻAbd al-Ḥamīd b. Ribʻī	132/750
ʻUthmān b. ʻAbd al-Aʻlā b. Surāqa	
Ṣāliḥ b. ʻAlī	136/754
Riyāḥ b. ʻUthmān al-Murrī	

al-Manṣūr	136-158/754–775
Yazīd b. Rawḥ al-Lakhmī	138/755
Muḥammad b. al-Ashʻath	140/757
al-ʻAbbās b. Muḥammad b. ʻAlī	140/757
Ibrāhīm b. ʻAbd al-Wahhāb	157/773
al-Faḍl b. Ṣāliḥ b. ʻAlī	
ʻAmr b. Muḥammad b. ʻAbd al-Muṭallib	
ʻAbd al-Wahhāb b. Ibrāhīm	
Ibrāhīm b. ʻAbd al-Wahhāb	

al-Mahdī	158–169/775–785
Muḥammad b. Ibrāhīm al-Imām	159/775
Ibrāhīm b. ʻAbd al-Wahhāb	???–160/776
Maʻyūf b. Yaḥyā al-Ḥajūrī	160/776 [rebel]
al-Ḥārith b. ʻAbd al-Raḥmān al-Jurashī	160/776 [rebel]
Ibrāhīm b. Ṣāliḥ	169/785

al-Hādī	169–170/785–786
Ibrāhīm b. Ṣāliḥ	169/785

al-Rashīd	170–193/786–809
Muḥammad b. Ibrāhīm al-Imām	??? -172/???-788
['Abd al-Ṣamad b. 'Alī]	
Ibrāhīm b. Ṣāliḥ	172–175/788–791
Isḥāq b. Ibrāhīm b. Ṣāliḥ	
Mūsā b. 'Īsā	176/792
Sindī b. Shāhak	
Mūsā b. Yaḥyā b. Khālid	176/792
'Abd al-Malik b. Ṣāliḥ	177–179/793–795
Isḥāq b. 'Īsā b. 'Alī	179–???/795–???
Shu'ayb b. Khāzim b. Khuzayma	187–188/802–803
Ja'far b. Yaḥyā b. Khālid	188
'Īsā b. al- 'Akkī	
Ibrāhīm b. Muḥammad b. Ibrāhīm b. Muḥammad	188–189/803–804
Sulaymān b. 'Abd Allāh al-Manṣūr	189–190/804–805
Ṣāliḥ b. Sulaymān	
al-'Abbās b. Muḥammad b. 'Alī	
'Alī b. al-Ḥasan b. Qaḥṭaba	192–193/807–808

al-Amīn	193–198/809–813
'Alī b. al-Ḥasan b. Qaḥṭaba	193/809
Manṣūr b. Muḥammad al-Mahdī	193–194/809–810
Aḥmad b. Sa'īd al-Ḥarashī	194/810
Sulaymān b. 'Abd Allāh al-Manṣūr	194–195/810
Muḥammad b. Ṣāliḥ b. Bayhas	195–198/810–813

al-Ma'mūn	198-218/813–833
Muḥammad b. Ṣāliḥ b. Bayhas	198–205/813–820
Ma'yūf b. Yaḥyā	
Ḥumayd b. Ma'yūf	
'Abd Allāh b. Ṭāhir	205–207/820–822
Ṣadaqa b. 'Uthmān al-Murrī	
Naṣr b. Ḥamza	
al-Mu'taṣim	213/828
Isḥāq b. Yaḥyā al-Khuttalī	

al-Mu'taṣim	218–227/833–842
al-Qāsim b. 'Īsā, Abū Dulaf	
Muslim b. Muḥammad, Abū al-Ṣāliḥāt	
Dīnār b. 'Abd Allāh	225/839
Muḥammad b. al-Jahm al-Sāmī	225/839

Mūsā b. Ibrāhīm al-Rāfiqī, Abū al-Mughīth

al-Wāthiq	227–232/842–847
Mūsā b. Ibrāhīm al-Rāfiqī, Abū al-Mughīth	
Isḥāq b. Yaḥyā al-Khuttalī	
Ashnās al-Turkī	
Muslim b. Muḥammad, Abū al-Ṣāliḥāt	
'Abd al-Raḥmān b. Ḥabīb	
Mālik b. Ṭawq	232/847

al-Mutawakkil	232–247/847–861
Mālik b. Ṭawq	
Sālim b. Ḥāmid	
Afrīdūn al-Turkī	
Ṣāliḥ al-'Abbāsī al-Turkī	
al-Fatḥ b. Khāqān	244/858
Kiliyātikīn al-Turkī	
Aḥmad b. al-Mudabbir	
Yūnus b. Ṭārja	247/861

al-Muntaṣir	247–248/861–862
'Īsā b. Muḥammad al-Nawsharī	

al-Musta'īn	248–252/862–866
'Īsā b. Muḥammad al-Nawsharī	
Ṣāliḥ al-'Abbāsī al-Turkī	

al-Mu'tazz	252–255/866–869
Aḥmad b. Khālid al-Shaybānī	
Yamakjūr al-Turkī	

al-Muhtadī	255–256/869–870
Yamakjūr al-Turkī	
Aṣram al-Turkī	

al-Mu'tamid	256–279/870–892
Amājūr al-Turkī	257/871

Aḥmad b. Ṭūlūn	264–270/877–884
'Alī b. Amājūr al-Turkī	
Aḥmad b. Yidaghbāsh	
Aḥmad b. Waṣīf	

APPENDIX B

Governors of the *jund* of Qinnasrīn (based on *ZḤ* I: 49–74)

al-Saffāḥ	132–136/749–754
‘Abd al-Ṣamad b. ‘Alī	132/750
al-Manṣūr	136–158/754–775
Zufar b. ‘Āṣim al-Hilālī	137/755
Abū Muslim al-Khurāsānī	137/755
Ṣāliḥ b. ‘Alī	137–152/755–769
al-Faḍl b. Ṣāliḥ	152–???/769–???
Mūsā b. Sulaymān al-Khurāsānī	??? –157/???–773
al-Mahdī	158–169/775–785
‘Alī b. Sulaymān b. ‘Alī	163/779
Hārūn b. Muḥammad al-Mahdī	167?/783?
Yaḥyā b. Khālid al-Barmakī	
al-Hādī	169–170/785–786
Hārūn b. Muḥammad al-Mahdī	
Yaḥyā b. Khālid al-Barmakī	
al-Rashīd	170–193/786–809
‘Abd al-Malik b. Ṣāliḥ	175/791
Mūsā b. ‘Īsā	176/792
Mūsā b. Yaḥyā b. Khālid	176/792
Ja‘far b. Yaḥyā b. Khālid	178/794

'Īsā b. al- 'Akkī	
'Abd Allāh b. Ṣāliḥ	
Ismā'īl b. Ṣāliḥ	182/798
'Abd al-Malik b. Ṣāliḥ	???–187/???–802
'Abd Allāh b. Ṣāliḥ	187/802
al-Qāsim b. Hārūn al-Rashīd	187/802
[Aḥmad b. Isḥāq b. Ismā'īl b. 'Alī	189?/804?]
Khuzayma b. Khāzim b. Khuzayma	193/809

al-Amīn	193–198/809–813
al-Qāsim b. Hārūn al-Rashīd	
Qumāma b. Abī Zayd al-Kātib	
Khuzayma b. Khāzim b. Khuzayma	194/809
'Abd al-Malik b. Ṣāliḥ	196/811
[Khuzayma b. Khāzim b. Khuzayma	197/812?]
Warqā' [b. 'Abd al-Malik b. Ṣāliḥ?]	
Yazīd b. Mazyad al-Shaybānī	

al-Ma'mūn	198–218/813–833
Yazīd b. Mazyad	
'Abd Allāh b. Ṭāhir	204–213/819–828
al-'Abbās b. al-Ma'mūn	213/828
Isḥāq b. Ibrāhīm b. Muṣ'ab b. Zurayq	214/829
al-'Abbās b. al-Ma'mūn	214–223/829–837
Waraqa al-Ṭarīfī	
'Īsā b. 'Alī b. Ṣāliḥ	
'Ubayd Allāh b. 'Abd al-'Azīz b. al-Faḍl b. Ṣāliḥ	218/833

al-Mu'taṣim	218–227/833–842
al-'Abbās b. al-Ma'mūn	214–223/829–837
'Ubayd Allāh b. 'Abd al-'Azīz b. al-Faḍl b. Ṣāliḥ	
Ashnās al-Turkī	225–230/839–844

al-Wāthiq	227–232/842–847
Ashnās al-Turkī	225–230/839–844
'Ubayd Allāh b. 'Abd al-'Azīz b. al-Faḍl b. Ṣāliḥ	
Muḥammad b. Ṣāliḥ b. 'Abd Allāh b. Ṣāliḥ	

al-Mutawakkil	232–247/847–861
al-Shārbāmiyān	
'Alī b. Ismā'īl b. Ṣāliḥ	
Muḥammad b. 'Alī b. Ismā'īl	
'Īsā b. 'Ubayd Allāh b. al-Faḍl b. Ṣāliḥ	

Ṭāhir b. Muḥammad b. Ismā'īl
al-Muntaṣir b. al-Mutawakkil 235/849
Bughā al-Kabīr

al-Muntaṣir	247–248/861–862
Waṣīf al-Khādim	

al-Musta'īn	248–252/862–866
Mūsā b. Bughā	250/864
Maymūn b. Sulaymān b. Ḥadaqa b. 'Abd al-Malik	

al-Mu'tazz	252–255/866–869
Aḥmad b. al-Muwallad	252/866
Ṣāliḥ b. 'Ubayd Allāh b. al-Faḍl b. Ṣāliḥ	
Maymūn b. Sulaymān b. Ḥadaqa b. 'Abd al-Malik	
Ṣāliḥ b. 'Ubayd Allāh b. al-Faḍl b. Ṣāliḥ	
Abū al-Sāj Dīwadādh	254/868

al-Muhtadī	255–256/869–870
Abū al-Sāj Dīwadādh	

al-Mu'tamid	256–279/870–892
al-Muwaffaq b. al-Mutawakkil	258/871
Ja'far b. al-Mu'tamid	261/874
Sīmā al-Ṭawīl	

Aḥmad b. Ṭūlūn	264–270/877–884

APPENDIX C

A Chronology of Contention in Syria

Reigning Caliph	Contentious Activity
al-Saffāḥ 132–136/749–754	• Abū al-Ward & Abū Muḥammad al-Sufyānī, 132/750 • Ḥabīb b. Murra & Ibn Surāqa, 132/750 • 'Abbās b. Muḥammad al-Sufyānī, 133/751? • Abān b. Mu'āwiya, 133/751 • 'Abd al-Ṣamad b. Muḥammad b. al-Ḥajjāj, 134/752? • Hāshim/Hishām b. Yazīd, 136/754
al-Manṣūr 136–158/754–775	• 'Abd Allāh b. 'Alī, 136/754 • Theodore/Bundār, 142/759
al-Mahdī 158–169/775–785	• Ma'yūf b. Yaḥyā & *ahl dimashq*, 160/776
al-Hādī 169–170/785–786	
al-Rashīd 170–193/786–809	• Triumvirate of bandits • Factionalism in Damascus, 175/791? • Abū al-Haydhām [w/Zawāqīl], 177/793 • Factionalism, various locales, 180/796 • Factionalism in Damascus, 187/803 • Factionalism in Homs, 190/806 • Abū al-Nidā', 192/807?

Reigning Caliph	Contentious Activity
al-Amīn 193–198/809–813	• Vase incident in Damascus, 193/809? • Abū al-ʻUmayṭir [w/Zawāqīl], 195/811 • Autonomous *ashrāf* during civil war • [Zawāqīl vs. Abnā' at al-Raqqa]
al-Ma'mūn 198–218/813–833	• al-Faddaynī, 198/813?
al-Muʻtaṣim 218–227/833–842	• Revolt in favor of al-ʻAbbās b. al-Ma'mūn, 218/833. • 2nd revolt for ʻAbbās, 223/838 • Abū Ḥarb al-Mubarqaʻ, 226/840 • Ibn Bayhas, 226/840
al-Wāthiq 227–232/842–847	
al-Mutawakkil 232–247/ 847–861	• Factionalism under Sālim b. Ḥāmid • Factionalism in Homs, 240/854
al-Muntaṣir 247–248/861–862	
al-Mustaʻīn 248–252/862–866	• Factionalism in Homs, 248/862 • ʻUṭayf al-Kalbī in Homs, 250/864 • ʻUṭayf & al-Fuṣayṣ, 252/866
al-Muʻtazz 252–255/866–869	• ʻIsā b. al-Shaykh, 252/866
al-Muhtadī 255–256/869–870	
al-Muʻtamid 256–279/870–892	
Aḥmad b. Ṭūlūn 264–270/ 877–884	• Ibn Ṭūlūn takes Damascus, 264/877

Notes

CHAPTER ONE

1. Balādhurī, *Futūh,* 137.

2. On the historical geography of Syria in the Islamic period, readers are still best served by Guy LeStrange, *Palestine under the Moslems* (London: Palestine Exploration Fund, 1890) and René Dussaud, *Topographie historique de la Syrie antique et médiévale* (Paris: Paul Geuthner, 1927). But see also Eugen Wirth, *Syrien. Eine geographische Landeskunde* (Darmstadt: Wissenschaftlische Buchgesellschaft, 1971).

3. A satisfactory survey of early Islamic Syrian history has yet to be written. For now, readers must rely on several older studies: Henri Lammens, *La Syrie. Précis historique,* 2 vols. (Beirut: Imprimerie Catholique, 1921); Muḥammad Kurd 'Alī, *Kitāb khiṭaṭ al-shām,* 6 vols. (Damascus: Maṭba'at al-ḥadīth, 1925); Phillip K. Hitti, *History of Syria. Including Lebanon and Palestine* (New York: MacMillan, 1951); Dominique Sourdel, "La Syrie au Temps des Premiers Califes Abbassides (132/750–264/878)," *Revue des études islamiques* 48 (1980): 155–75; Kamal S. Salibi, *Syria under Islam. Empire on Trial,* 634–1097 (Delmar, NY: Caravan Books, 1977); 'Abbās, *Bilād al-shām.*

4. The earliest occurence of this anecdote is, perhaps, Ṭabarī 3:1142.

5. See, e.g., the anecdote on *TMD* 61:326, which has the caliph al-Rashīd refer to Syria as a "domain of discord in which [dwells] tribal tension (*wa-huwa ma'wāt al-fitan wa-fīhi al-'aṣabiyya*)," or the account reported by Ibn al-Faqīh, *Mukhtaṣar,* 315, where Syrians are characterized as knowing only loyalty to the Umayyads, with inveterate antagonism toward, and wilful ignorance of, anything else (*wa-amma ahl al-shām falaysa ya'arifūna illā āl abī sufyān wa-ṭā'at banī marwān wa-'adāwa rāsikha wa-jahl mutarākim*).

6. Sourdel, "La Syrie," 169ff., was the first to stress the variety of causes behind Syrian revolts.

7. For the concept of contention, see Charles Tilly, *From Mobilization to Revolution* (Reading, MA: Addison-Wesley, 1978), 143–59; idem, *The Contentious French* (Cambridge, MA: Harvard University Press, 1986), 3–4; idem, *Popular Contention in Great Britain, 1758–1834* (Cambridge, MA: Harvard University Press, 1995), 16–17, 43; Michael P. Hanagan et al., eds., *Challenging Authority: The Historical Study of Contentious Politics* (Minneapolis: University of Minnesota Press, 1998), xv–xix.

8. Tilly, Great Britain, 37. On repertoires of contention, see Tilly, Mobilization, 151–59; Idem, *Contentious French,* 3–4; idem, *Great Britain,* 41–44; Hanagan et al., *Challenging Authority,* xvii–xviii.

9. Tilly, *Contentious French,* 5–12; idem, *Great Britain,* 16.

10. China and Latin America are two of the most notable new frontiers in contention studies. See the contributions by Wong, Pérez–Stable, and De Avalar in Hanagan et al., *Challenging Authority.*

11. Two exceptions to this European modernist trend are of some relevance to the present work: James Given, *State and Society in Medieval Europe. Gwynedd and Languedoc under Outside Rule* (Ithaca and London: Cornell University Press, 1990), analyzes medieval (and not early modern) state-making processes and the responses to them in Wales and southern France. Karen Barkey, *Bandits and Bureaucrats: The Ottoman Route to State Centralization* (Ithaca and London: Cornell University Press, 1994) is, like Tilly, primarily interested in early modern state-society relations, but in one part of the Islamic Middle East (rural Anatolia).

12. On the historiographical problem of ʿAbbāsid Syria, and a detailed assessment of Ibn ʿAsākir as a source for this period, see now Paul M. Cobb, "Community versus Contention: Ibn ʿAsākir and ʿAbbāsid Syria," in James E. Lindsay, ed., *Ibn ʿAsākir and Early Islamic History* (Princeton, NJ: Darwin Press, forthcoming). In addition to the complete edition of the *Taʾrīkh madīnat dimashq* by al-ʿAmrāwī (cited in this study as *TMD*), I have also consulted the magnificent (but incomplete) scholarly edition by al-Munajjid et al. published haphazardly since 1951 by the Majmaʿ al-lugha al-ʿarabiyya in Damascus. Some lacunae in the *TMD* are filled by the medieval abridgment compiled by Ibn Manẓūr, the *Mukhtaṣar taʾrīkh madīnat dimashq* (cited in this study as *MTMD*).

13. R. Stephen Humphreys, *Islamic History. A Framework for Inquiry,* rev. ed. (Princeton: Princeton University Press, 1991), 88.

14. For an excellent study of the bases upon which ties of loyalty in one early Islamic society were founded, see Roy P. Mottahedeh, *Loyalty and Leadership in an Early Islamic Society* (Princeton, NJ: Princeton University Press, 1980).

CHAPTER TWO

1. At some point in the early ʻAbbāsid period, the city of Aleppo gradually superseded the city of Qinnasrīn as the capital of the *jund* of Qinnasrīn, perhaps after al-Rashīd created the new district of the ʻAwāṣim. Later geographers noticed this development: compare the geographers that Ibn al-ʻAdīm quotes in *BṬ* 1:72.

2. See another designation, *bilād al-shām,* "the lands of Syria."

3. The actual origin of the Umayyad system of *ajnād* is still open to debate. The point here is that the system that the ʻAbbāsids used was that in use after the creation of the *jund* of Qinnasrīn, an innovation generally attributed to the Umayyad caliph Yazīd I (r. 60–64/680–83), although the attribution is not certain.

4. Frequently, though, several *ajnād* were grouped together under the control of one subgovernor.

5. Ṭabarī 3:604. On the development of the frontier region in the ʻAbbāsid perod, see Michael Bonner, *Aristocratic Violence and Holy War. Studies in the Jihad and the Arab-Byzantine Frontier* (New Haven: American Oriental Society, 1996).

6. Ibn al-Faqīh al-Hamadhānī (d. ca. 289–90/902–903), citing al-Madā'inī (d. ca. 228/842), lists these as: Sidon, Beirut, Tripoli, ʻArqah, and Tyre. Ibn al-Faqīh, *Mukhtaṣar,* 105.

7. Ya'qūbī, *Buldān,* 327. Religiously, i.e., with regard to Friday prayer, the coastal cities were subordinate to Dimashq. As al-Madā'inī put it: "their pulpit [is subordinated to] Dimashq, and their land tax to al-Urdunn (*minbaruhā ilā dimashq wa-kharājuhā ilā al-urdunn*)." See Ibn al-Faqīh, *Mukhtaṣar,* 105.

8. As under al-Manṣūr when ʻAlī b. Ṣāliḥ (or perhaps Ṣāliḥ b. ʻAlī) held both offices (*TMD* 41:529).

9. Ya'qūbī, *Buldān,* 327.

10. According to Ya'qūbī, *Buldān,* 329, they were: Lakhm, Judhām, ʻĀmila, Kinda (all of Yaman), and Qays and Kināna (of Qays). On the *ajnād* of Filasṭīn and al-Urdunn, and on southern Syria in general, see Alan G. Walmsley, "The Administrative Structure and Urban Geography of the Jund of Filastin and the Jund of al-Urdunn" (Ph.D. dissertation, University of Sydney, 1987).

11. The scope of the *jund* can be seen in the list that al-Madā'inī provides of the sub-districts (*kuwar*) subordinate to Dimashq: the Sanīr Mts., Jubayl, Beirut, Sidon, Bathaniyya, Ḥawrān, Jawlān, "the highlands of al-Balqā' (*ẓāhir al-balqā'*)," Jibrīn, al-Ghawr, Ma'āb, Jibāl al-Sharāt, Buṣrā,

'Ammān, Jābiya, Qaryatayn, al-Ḥūla, and al-Biqā' (Ibn al-Faqīh, *Mukhtaṣar,* 105). Khalid Yahya Blankinship, *The End of the Jihâd State* (Albany, NY: State University of New York Press, 1994), 48, n. 7 discusses the Umayyad precedent for this arrangement.

12. Ya'qūbī, *Buldān,* 326, says of the city of Damascus: "The majority in the city of Damascus are from Yaman, but there is also a group from Qays (*wa-al-aghlab 'alā madīnat dimashq ahl al-yaman wa-bi-hā qawm min qays*)." The gardens and pastureland of the Ghūṭa supported tribes from every confederation, including Ghassān (Yaman), Qays, and Rabī'a.

13. The tradition is attributed to Ka'b al-Aḥbar (d. 34/654), but appears among the corpus of later Umayyad/early 'Abbāsid *aḥādīth* collected by Nu'aym b. Ḥammād (*Kitāb al-fitan,* British Museum MS Or. 9449, fol. 67b).

14. Ya'qūbī, *Buldān,* 324. These tribes included Ṭayyi', Kinda, Ḥimyar, Kalb, Hamdān, and others.

15. On the tribal geography of the *ajnād* of Qinnasrīn and Ḥimṣ, see the detailed study based on Ibn al-'Adīm by Muṣṭafā 'Alī al-Ḥiyārī, "Tawaṭṭun al-qabā'il al-'arabiyya fī bilād jund qinnasrīn ḥattā nihāyat al-qarn al-rābi' al-hijrī," in I. As-Sa'āfīn, ed., *Fī miḥrāb al-ma'rifah: Festschrift for Iḥsān 'Abbās* (Beirut: Dār ṣādir, 1997), 417–31.

16. Muḥammad b. 'Abdūs al-Jahshiyārī, *Kitāb al-wuzarā' wa-al-kuttāb,* ed. Muṣṭafā al-Ṣafā et al. (Cairo: Muṣṭafā al-bābī al-ḥalabī, 1938), 286–87.

17. Balādhurī, *Futūḥ,* 203; John Haldon and Hugh Kennedy, "The Arab-Byzantine Frontier in the Eighth and Ninth Centuries: Military Organisation and Society in the Borderlands," In *Zbornik Radova Vizantoloskog Instituta XIX,* edited by Božidar Ferjančic (Belgrade: Srpska Akademija Nauka i Umetnosti, 1980), 112–13.

18. The classic study of 'Abbāsid provincial government, based on the examples of Mosul and Egypt, is Hugh Kennedy, "Central Government and Provincial Elites in the Early 'Abbasid Caliphate," *BSOAS* 44 (1981): 26–38. See also Jacob Lassner, *The Shaping of 'Abbāsid Rule* (Princeton: Princeton University Press, 1980), 58–90.

19. See examples from Egypt in Kennedy, "Central Government," 33; see also the clarifications in Alexander H. Morton, "Ḥisba and glass stamps in eighth and early ninth century Egypt," in Y. Rāġib, ed., *Documents de l'Islam Médiéval. Nouvelles Perspectives de Recherche* (Cairo: Institut Français d'Archéologie Orientale, 1991), 19–42, esp. 26, n. 32. Forand says that the literary sources use the terms *wālī, amīr,* and *'āmil* interchangeably to refer to the governor. See P. G. Forand, "The Governors of Mosul, according to al-Azdī's *Ta'rīkh al-Mawṣil,*" *JAOS* 89 (1969): 102.

20. Michael the Syrian, 538/3:104, quoting Dionysios of Tell Maḥrē (d. 230/845).

21. The latter two duties are usually specified in the sources with the formula *kāna 'alā al-ṣalāt* or *kāna 'alā al-ḥarb* or the like.

22. Kennedy, "Central Government," 28. Von Sievers rather overstresses the military responsibilities of Syrian governors, especially of those in the south. Peter von Sievers, "Military, Merchants and Nomads: The Social Evolution of the Syrian Cities and Countryside during the Classical Period, 780–969/164–358," *Der Islam* 56 (1979): 218–19

23. Kindī, *Wulāt,* 122–23; Ibn Taghribirdī, *Nujūm*, 2:44.

24. In 227/841, Al-Mu'taṣim sent Abū al-Mughīth al-Rāfiqī as governor of Damascus to act as supervisor (*nāẓir*) in the case of the previous governor, 'Alī b. Isḥāq, who had murdered his revenue official (*TMD* 67:250–52)

25. *MTMD* 5:30–3

26. In Syria, this is attested as early as 135/753 at Baysān by an inscription of 'Abd Allāh b. 'Alī, al-Saffāḥ's governor of al-Urdunn and all of Syria (Amikam Elad, "The Caliph Abū'l-'Abbās al-Saffāḥ, the First 'Abbāsid *Mahdī*: Implications of an Unknown Inscription from Bet-Shean (Baysān)", in E. Fleischer et al., eds., *Mas'at Moshe: Studies in Jewish and Islamic Culture Presented to Moshe Gil* (Jerusalem: Bialik Institute, 1998), 9–55 [Hebrew]; v–vi [English summary]. See also the inscription of al-Ramla, mentioning one Dīnār, al-Rashīd's *mawlā,* and governor of Filasṭīn (*Répertoire chronologique d'épigraphie arabe,* 17 vols. [Cairo: Institut Français d'Archéologie Orientale, 1931–], 5:89). At al-Ramla, both the Umayyad caliphs and the 'Abbāsid caliphs themselves customarily paid for the upkeep of the city's cisterns and waterways. Al-Mu'taṣim discontinued this practice and made it the express duty of the governor (Balādhurī, *Futūḥ,* 143–44). In Damascus, al-Faḍl b. Ṣāliḥ b. 'Alī replaced doors on the Umayyad mosque and "the dome in the courtyard known as the Treasury Dome (*al-qubba allatī fī al-ṣaḥn al-ma'rūf bi-qubbat al-māl*)," evidently the extant structure known by that name today (*MTMD* 20:277).

27. On these two, see the references in notes 38 and 98, respectively.

28. E.g., Yazīd b. Rawḥ al-Lakhmī, who was *'āmil* of Baalbek prior to 138/755 (*TMD* 65:176–77); compare with the *'āmil* of the region (*rub'*) of Apamea (*TMD* 67:251).

29. For an excellent analysis of the position of *qāḍī* of Damascus and the administrative hierarchy associated with it, see Gerhard Conrad, *Die Quḍāt Dimašq und der Madhab al-Auzā'ī. Materialen zur syrischen Rechtsgeschichte* (Beirut: In Kommission bei Franz Steiner Verlag

Stuttgart, 1994), esp. 612–48 and 759–62. On the judges of Egypt, see R. Guest's introduction to his edition of Kindī, *Wulāt*.

30. Dionysios of Tell Maḥrē lists a judge, an agent to gather taxes, another to pursue delinquents, another in charge of the post "to inform the king of the state of the land," another in charge of state lands, and another to redress the grievances of the people. Dionysios goes on to add indignantly that similar bodies of officials were appointed in every city. Michael the Syrian, 538/3:104–5.

31. Kennedy, "Central Government," 38.

32. *EAC,* 176–97.

33. Kennedy, "Central Government," 28. Examples of the use of largesse: 'Abd Allāh b. Ṭāhir, al-Ma'mūn's governor of the western provinces, distributed the revenues of Syria among his officers, the *ashrāf,* and, it is said, a few young destitute *'ulamā'* (TMD 29:234, 220; *BṬ* 3:1188). Mālik b. Ṭawq, governor of Dimashq for al-Wāthiq and al-Mutawakkil, made free food available to all during Ramaḍān, and is said to have been 30,000 dīnārs in debt to the local merchants when he left, having spent all of his own wealth on the people, rich and poor (*TMD* 56:462, 465). Then again, the overt use of bribery tarnished the reputation of Muḥammad b. Ṣāliḥ, governor of Qinnasrīn for al-Wāthiq (*ZḤ* 1:70).

34. The classic exposition of this phenomenon is Albert Hourani, "Ottoman Reform and the Politics of Notables," in W. R. Polk and R. L. Chambers, eds., *Beginnings of Modernization in the Middle East: The Nineteenth Century* (Chicago: University of Chicago Press, 1968), 41-68. See also Kennedy, "Central Government," and the comparative discussion of Boaz Shoshan, "The 'Politics of Notables' in Medieval Islam," *Asian and African Studies* 20 (1986): 179–215. For a detailed account of the notables of Syria, see chapter 5.

35. This dynamic is discussed in Hourani, "Ottoman Reform," 46. In the 'Abbāsid period, Syrian *ashrāf* openly courted the local governors. See, e.g., the case of Muḥammad b. 'Amr b. Ḥuwayy al-Saksakī, a wealthy Yamanī landowner from the Ghūṭa who frequently offered his hospitality to Samarran elites like 'Ubayd Allāh b. Yaḥyā b. Khāqān and Ibn al-Mudabbir (*TMD* 55:19–22).

36. For example, during the *miḥna* under al-Ma'mūn, local leaders negotiated with the *qāḍī* Yaḥyā b. Aktham for the release of one of their imprisoned comrades (*MTMD* 27:209).

37. Kennedy, "Central Government," 35. See also the task of the governor as described in *EAC* 176ff.

38. 'Abd Allāh b. Sulaymān: Ṭabarī 3:416; *TMD* 29:92. Ibrāhīm b. Ṣāliḥ was unable to put an end to the predations of an Umayyad rebel in

Upper Egypt while he was governor of Egypt from 165–67/781–83. He was sacked, and his and his agents' revenues were confiscated (Kindī, *Wulāt,* 123–25; Ibn Taghribirdī, *Nujūm,* 2:49). Despite Umayyad precedent, governors in the early 'Abbāsid period were not usually executed because so many governors were kinsmen of the caliphs.

39. E.g., 'Alī b. Sulaymān al-'Abbāsī, the governor of Egypt in 169/785. He was so popular with the Muslim populace that he attempted to claim the caliphate for himself after the death of al-Hādī (Kindī, *Wulāt,* 132-33; Ibn Taghribirdī, *Nujūm,* 2:62). For a Syrian example, see chapter 3, for the caliph al-Manṣūr's suspicions about the governor Ṣāliḥ b. 'Alī.

40. On tribal factionalism, see chapter 5. Ibrāhīm b. Muḥammad: *TMD* 7:159. Compare also Sindī b. Shāhak, governor of Dimashq for al-Rashīd, who adopted much the same policy. A factionally balanced, if tense, feast at which he presided served as the setting for an anecdote by al-Jāḥiẓ (*MTMD* 10:210; 'Amr b. Baḥr al-Jāḥiẓ, *Kitāb al-ḥayawān,* ed. 'Abd al-Salām Muḥammad Hārūn, 7 vols. [Cairo: Muṣṭafā al-bābī al-ḥalabī, 1948], 5:393–94).

41. *MTMD* 15:270–72. See also Moshe Gil, *A History of Palestine, 634–1099,* trans. Ethel Broido (Cambridge: Cambridge University Press, 1992), 281.

42. To my knowledge, the man is unknown, and is identified only as "al-Ghassānī." Because the Banū al-Ghassān were a prominent tribe in Filasṭīn, he was probably a local tribal *sharīf.*

43. *"yā ibn fulān taqtul al-ghassānī wa-tata'aṣṣaḅ fa-law annaka idh kharajta min dīnika 'ammamta wa-lakin ta'aṣṣabta fa-man ya'dil bayna al-nāṣ?"* *MTMD* 15:270–72. For the importance of concepts of "balance" in another political setting, see Mottahedeh, *Loyalty and Leadership,* 179ff.

CHAPTER THREE

1. On the prominence of the *ahl al-bayt* in provincial positions, see Lassner, *Shaping,* 58ff.; *EAC,* 52–53.

2. The most cogent discussion of the succession after al-Saffāḥ, the revolt of 'Abd Allāh b. 'Alī, and its historiographical repercussions, is Lassner, *Shaping,* 19–38, largely superseding the study by Fawwaz Ahmad Tuqan, " 'Abdallāh Ibn 'Alī: A Rebellious Uncle of Al-Manṣūr," *Studies in Islam* 6 (1969): 1–26. See also the speculations of Moshe Sharon regarding the succession in *Revolt. The Social and Military Aspects of the 'Abbāsid Revolution* (Jerusalem: Hebrew University, 1990), 234–42. A detailed account of 'Abd Allāh's revolt can be found in *EAC,* 58–61.

3. Ṭabarī 3:92–93; Balādhurī, *Ansāb,* 3:105; Abū Bakr Muḥammad b. Yaḥyā al-Ṣūlī, *Kitāb al-awrāq (Ash'ār awlād al-khulafā'),* ed. J. Heyworth Dunne (Cairo: Maṭba'at al-Ṣāwī, 1936), 297; Ya'qūbī, *Ta'rīkh,* 2:437–38; Mas'ūdī, *Murūj,* 6:176–77.

4. Ḥafṣ al-Umawī, an Umayyad court poet who later attached himself to 'Abd Allāh's retinue in Syria, identified 'Abd Allāh with this title in one of his verses (*MTMD* 7:212–13). See also *Ajbar Machmuâ,* ed. Emilio Lafuentes Alcántara (Madrid: M. Rivadeneyra, 1867), 46; Maqdisī, *Bad',* 6:74. In Balādhurī, *Ansāb,* 3:72, the title has been garbled as "al-Shammākh," "the Haughty." See also Farouk Omar, "A Note on the Laqabs [i.e., epithets] of the Early 'Abbāsids and Their Religio-Political Implications," in F. Omar, ed., *'Abbāsiyyāt. Studies in the History of the Early 'Abbāsids* (Baghdad: University of Baghdad, 1976), 141–47.

5. Agapius, *'Unwān,* 536.

6. Crone, *Slaves,* 71, generalizes the revolt as a "Syrian attempt at a come back." 'Abbās, *Bilād al-shām,* 23, rightly stresses that the revolt is a purely military one.

7. Compare the conditions for Byzantine field revolts analyzed in Walter E. Kaegi, Jr., *Byzantine Military Unrest, 471-843. An Interpretation* (Amsterdam: Adolf M. Hakkert, 1981), 293–95: a perceived threat from the center, especially in the initial reign of a new emperor, and the presence of a large number of troops already concentrated prior to campaigning.

8. Azdī, *Mawṣil,* 163.

9. 'Abd al-Ḥamīd b. Rib'ī: Ṭabarī 3:53, 93; *TMD* 34:66–67; Crone, *Slaves,* 174–75.

10. Ḥumayd b. Qaḥṭaba: Ṭabarī 3:93; *TMD* 15:289–90; *BṬ* 6:2973–75; Crone, *Slaves,* 188. Other Khurāsānī commanders mentioned among 'Abd Allāh's followers are listed in Ṭabarī 3:93, and Balādhurī, *Ansāb,* 3:105. See the annotations in Ṭabarī, *History,* 28:9–11, for full biographical details on these other figures. 'Abd al-Ṣamad: Ṭabarī 3:48; *ZḤ* 1:53.

11. *"inna balā'aka 'inda ahl al-shām ghayr jamīl fa-lan yanfa'aka illā mithlī mimman 'indahu balā' ḥasan wa-ayādī mutaẓāhira aw rajul ṣāḥib fitna yaltamis an yudrik fīhā sharafan."* Balādhurī, *Ansāb,* 3:105. Bakkār b. Muslim: Ṭabarī 3:96; Crone, *Slaves,* 106; al-Ḥakam b. Ḍa'bān: Ṭabarī 3:47; *TMD* 15:10; Crone, *Slaves,* 100; Zufar b. 'Āṣim: Ṭabarī 3:94; *BṬ* 8:3803–3805; Crone, *Slaves,* 166; 'Uthmān b. 'Abd al-A'lā: Ṭabarī 3:94; Azdī, *Mawṣil,* 164; *TMD* 60:100; Crone, *Slaves,* 129; Conrad, *Quḍāt,* 421–24, and chapter 5; Manṣūr b. Ja'wana: *TMD* 11:245–46; *MTMD* 6:108–9; Crone, *Slaves,* 168.

12. Balādhurī, *Ansāb,* 3:106.

13. *EAC*, 59, where it is suggested that, to the Khurāsāniyya, the revolt was "little more than a family dispute."

14. Ṭabarī 3:94–95; Balādhurī, *Ansāb*, 3:106; Ya'qūbī, *Ta'rīkh*, 2:439; *ZḤ* 1:58.

15. Ṭabarī 3:95–96; Balādhurī, *Ansāb*, 3:107–8.

16. Ṭabarī 3:94; Balādhurī, *Ansāb*, 3:108; Agapius, *'Unwān*, 534.

17. Ṭabarī 3:98–99; Balādhurī, *Ansāb*, 3:108; Ya'qūbī, *Ta'rīkh*, 2:439; Azdī, *Mawṣil*, 164. 'Abd al-Ṣamad even went on to govern Dimashq briefly for al-Rashīd (*TMD* 26:64, 36:240, 244, 246).

18. Ṭabarī 3:98; Balādhurī, *Ansāb*, 3:109. But compare Theophanes' statement that Abū Muslim was only prevented from exacting revenge on the Syrians by the intervention of al-Manṣūr (*Chronographia*, 429/593). According to Ibn A'tham al-Kūfī, it was the *ahl al-shām* themselves who sought amnesty: *Kitāb al-futūḥ*, ed. Muḥammad 'Abd al-Mu'īd Khān et al. (Hyderabad: Dā'irat al-ma'ārif al-'uthmāniyya, 1968–75), 7:216.

19. Ṭabarī 3: 419–20; Balạdhurī, *Ansāb*, 3:109; Azdī, *Mawṣil*, 167. Thus, Sharon's statement that the *ahl al-shām* were disbanded after the revolt is curious (Sharon, *Revolt*, 280–81).

20. 'Uthmān b. 'Umāra: *MTMD* 16:275–77; Crone, *Slaves*, 98. Al-Ḥārith b. 'Abd al-Raḥmān: *TMD* 11:448ff.

21. See below. There is some evidence that suggests that al-Manṣūr attempted to post Abū Muslim as governor-general of the western provinces (Ṭabarī 3:103; *ZḤ* 1:58; Ibn Taghribirdī, *Nujūm*, 1:333) in 136/754. But the rationale given in al-Ṭabarī, in which the caliph evinces a desire to have Abū Muslim reside in Syria, where he might readily consult him, seems absurd in light of 'Abd Allāh's recent revolt. Curiously, the otherwise thorough Ibn 'Asākir does not mention Abū Muslim in this capacity: see his entry in *TMD* 35:408–28.

22. Ṣāliḥ b. 'Alī: Ṭabarī 3:48–49, 73; Kindī, *Wulāt*, 96–100, 102–3. The campaign in Filasṭīn and al-Ḥakam b. Ḍab'ān: Balādhurī, *Ansāb* MS, 2:389; Kindī, *Wulāt*, 103–05; Agapius, *'Unwān*, 536; *TMD* 15:10, 65:176–77; Ibn Taghribirdī, *Nujūm*, 1:331–32; Crone, *Slaves*, 100.

23. Hugh Kennedy, *The Prophet and the Age of the Caliphates* (London and New York: Longman, 1986), 133–34, in speaking of Ṣāliḥ and his kin, notes that "The acceptance of 'Abbasid rule in the area was in part the consequence of there being a resident branch of the ruling dynasty with whose interests the Syrians could identify themselves."

24. Ya'qūbī, *Ta'rīkh*, 2:461.

25. Ṭabarī 3:124, 147; *ZḤ* 1:59.

26. Dimashq: *MTMD* 20:277; Qinnasrīn: *ZḤ* 1:60. However, al-Ṭabarī mentions al-Faḍl as governor of Qinnasrīn in the context of the death of the ʿAlid rebel Ibrāhīm b. ʿAbd Allāh in 145/762: Ṭabarī 3:283.

27. Al-Jazīra: Ṭabarī 3:466, 491. Al-Mahdī in Jerusalem: Ṭabarī 3:500; Yaʿqūbī, *Taʾrīkh* 2:480. While in Jerusalem, Al-Faḍl had a ruined church (*"al-kanīsa"*, the Holy Sepulchre?) rebuilt by order of al-Mahdī: Muḥammad b. Aḥmad al-Wāsiṭī, *Faḍāʾil al-bayt al-muqaddas,* ed. Isaac Hasson (Jerusalem: Hebrew University Press, 1979), 84.

28. Ibrāhīm: *MTMD* 4:63–64. On the *sulḥ,* and the delegation to al-Kūfa: *TMD* 26:64–65. On his governorate of Filasṭīn: Ṭabarī 3:500, Gil, *Palestine*, 284. Egypt: Ṭabarī 3:503.

29. Isḥāq b. Ibrāhīm: *TMD* 26:60; *MTMD* 4:266–67. Isḥāq retired to the family estate at Salamiyya near Homs, where he died. His sons established themselves in Aleppo: *BṬ* 3:1375–76, 1467–68. On the revolt of Abū al-Haydhām, see chapter 5.

30. *BṬ* 1:451. The move was made at al-Rashīd's expense, and stipends were given to Ibrāhīm's family. They remained in Aleppo until al-Rashīd's death in 193/809.

31. For a careful elucidation of the chronology of this stage of ʿAbd al-Malik's career, see Bonner, *Aristocratic Violence,* 88–93. On ʿAbd al-Malik b. Ṣāliḥ under al-Rashīd, see Ṭabarī 3:652–53, 688–94; Yaʿqūbī, *Taʾrīkh,* 2:424, 513–14; Masʿūdī, *Murūj,* 6:302–5; Azdī, *Mawṣil,* 262–66; *ZḤ* 1:62–63; *EAC* 74–75. ʿAbd Allāh b. Ṣāliḥ later moved to Baghdad and was governor of al-Jazīra for al-Mahdī. He died at his estate in Salamiyya in 186/802. ʿAẓīmī, *Ḥalab,* 232, lists him as governor of al-Shām in 175/791. On his career: *TMD* 29:178–82; *TMD* 37:23. On the confusion regarding the details of his career, see *ZḤ* 1:63–64. Ismāʿīl b. Ṣāliḥ, another brother, also governed Qinnasrīn in 182/798 after leaving his post as governor of Egypt. See *ZḤ* 1:63, where it is also said that he later governed Dimashq, a claim not verified elsewhere; *MTMD* 4:351–53; *BṬ* 4:1648–55.

32. According to Azdī, *Mawṣil,* 306, al-Rashīd also confiscated ʿAbd al-Malik's money and weapons. Accounts of ʿAbd al-Malik's arrest are many and various, and most of the medieval Arabic sources repeat them in one form or another. The most informative compilations of these accounts are: Ṭabarī 3:688–94; Muḥammad b. Maḥmūd b. al-Najjār al-Baghdādī, *Dhayl taʾrīkh baghdād,* 5 vols. (Hyderabad: Osmania Oriental Publications Bureau, 1978) 1:48–77; *MTMD* 15:194–98.

33. For his activities under al-Amīn, see: Ṭabarī 3:841–43; Yaʿqūbī, *Taʾrīkh,* 2:534; *MTMD* 15:194–98; *ZḤ* 1:64–65. On the revolt of the Syrians at al-Raqqa, see chapter 6. The degree to which the Syrian troops actually supported al-Amīn is in question. However, it may be significant that al-

Amīn's commanders advised him during the siege of Baghdad to flee to Syria and set himself up as caliph there (Ṭabarī 3:911–12).

34. E.g., Ṭabarī 3:689. There is some evidence to suggest that 'Abd al-Raḥmān's enmity toward his father was real and long-lived: while the father supported al-Amīn in the Jazīra, the son was leading troops in al-Ma'mūn's army in Marw (Ṭabarī 3:772).

35. Ya'qūbī, *Ta'rīkh,* 2:513.

36. For 'Abd al-Malik's close ties to al-Qāsim, one need only cite his support of al-Qāsim as al-Rashīd's third heir (Ṭabarī 3:652–53). It did not help that 'Abd al-Malik's mother was a concubine of Marwān II: rumors abounded that 'Abd al-Malik was, as it were, living testimony of the Umayyad legacy (Jahshiyārī, *Wuzarā',* 263). See also Bonner, *Aristocratic Violence,* 92–93. But Bonner suggests that 'Abd al-Malik's coup attempt was purely independent.

37. Lassner, *Shaping,* 39–57, notes that a complicated ruse that al-Manṣūr employed to kill 'Abd Allāh b. 'Alī was necessary to avoid charges of fratricide. Al-Rashīd was faced with the same problem. See Ṭabarī 3:692, where al-Rashīd says to 'Abd al-Malik: "By God, if it were not for sparing the blood of the Banū Hāshim, I would cut off your head!"

38. *EAC,* 74–75.

39. Bonner, *Aristocratic Violence,* 86, 87–93. Particularly problematic is Kennedy's assertion that 'Abd al-Malik was the "spokesman of the Syrian 'interest' in the reign of Harun," *EAC,* 74. This assertion assumes that 'Abd al-Malik's authority was widely respected outside of northern Syria and the frontier (which Bonner has contested) and never really clarifies what is meant by "Syrian": does it involve the whole populace or just the *ashrāf*?

40. See the Ṣāliḥī governors controlling Qinnasrīn until the reign of al-Mu'tazz (r. 252/866–255/869) in Appendix B.

41. Especially at al-Ramla: Balādhurī, *Futūḥ,* 143.

42. Al-Faḍl's house and private canals: *TMD* 2:371.

43. At Salamiyya, where 'Abd Allāh b. Ṣāliḥ built an estate and irrigation works: Balādhurī, *Futūḥ,* 134; in the mid-third/ninth century, Ya'qūbī noted that the family and its clients were prospering at Salamiyya: *Buldān,* 324.

44. Balādhurī, *Futūḥ,* 132; Ṭabarī 3:694; *ZḤ* 1:62.

45. The Fāṭimid geographer al-Muhallabī (d. 380/990) noted that the Banū Ṣāliḥ living in the city in his day were known as Banū al-Qalandar, and that the family grew rich off their holdings in Aleppo, and bought up

yet more property (*BṬ* 1:59). The basis for these holdings included important urban properties like Ismā'īl's holdings in the *sūq* (*ZḤ* 1:62), and land outside the city such as the family estate and stables at Qaṣr Biṭyās, northwest of Nayrab overlooking Aleppo. Ibn al-'Adīm notes that traces of marble and mosaic had been found at the ruins of the estate in his day (*BṬ* 1:451, 528–29; *ZḤ* 1:59). Note also the private estates of al-Faḍl at al-'Aqaba near Aleppo (*ZḤ* 1:60) or of Ismā'īl at Artāḥ (*MTMD* 4:351–53), or of Muḥammad b. 'Abd al-Malik b. Ṣāliḥ at Qaṣr al-Banāt in Aleppo proper (*BṬ* 1:65–66). Isma'īl b. Ṣāliḥ inherited all of his father's estate and *awqāf*, including a choice section of the *sūq* of the city (*BṬ* 4:1648–49).

46. Note also the grandson of 'Abd al-Malik b. Ṣāliḥ and his family at Antioch: *BṬ* 1:530. Al-Ya'qūbī likewise notes the presence of the descendants of Ṣāliḥ b. 'Alī at Antioch in his day (mid-third/ninth century). Ibn al-'Adīm cites this passage from the *Kitāb al-buldān,* but it is not present in the edition of al-Ya'qūbī's text as we now have it: *BṬ* 1:88. At the time, the Banū Ṣāliḥ were still prominent local leaders. Maymūn b. Sulaymān, a greatgreatgrandson of Ṣāliḥ, was the governor of the 'Awāṣim and was active during the revolt in Aleppo that occured upon al-Musta'īn's accession, as was his kinsman Ḥusayn b. Muḥammad b. Ṣāliḥ (*ZḤ* 1:73).

47. For a list of the prominent slaves of the Banū Ṣāliḥ, see: *BṬ* 1:529.

48. *BṬ* 1:529–530. Descendants of some of the *mawālī* of the Banū Ṣāliḥ held a *waqf* in Ayyūbid Aleppo (*BṬ* 10:4765).

49. Such as al-Aḥwaṣ, Dīk al-Jinn, and al-Buḥtūrī: *BṬ* 3:1322–23.

50. A lethal case of sibling rivalry among the grandsons of 'Abd al-Malik b. Ṣāliḥ: *BṬ* 3:1190.

51. *BṬ* 1:529. However, the *awqāf* of their clients remained under the control of the family only until 320/932. For a list of these inalienable holdings in Aleppo, Damascus, and elsewhere in Syria, see: *BṬ* 1:529–30.

52. *BṬ* 1:529.

53. On al-'Abbās generally, see *TMD* 26:394–401. For his early activities on the frontier, see: Ṭabarī 3:121, 141, 353. Another example of the older generation of 'Abbāsid nobles in Syria is al-'Abbās' cousin, Isḥāq b. 'Īsā b. 'Alī, who was governor of Medina for al-Mahdī, and who replaced 'Abd al-Malik b. Ṣāliḥ as governor of Dimashq in 177/793 (*TMD* 8:266–69; *MTMD* 4:307–8).

54. On the Imām Ibrāhīm, see Farouk Omar, *The 'Abbāsid Caliphate, 132/750–170/786* (Baghdad: National Printing and Publishing Co., 1969), 75ff.

55. Balādhurī, *Ansāb,* 3:127; *MTMD* 15:270–72. The exact date of his governorship in Filasṭīn is unknown, but Ibn 'Asākir places his dismissal

in the context of al-Manṣūr's second visit to Damascus in 154/771. On his reputation there, see chapter 2. In his list of governors of Dimashq appended to his edition of Ṣafadī, *Umarā'*, al-Munajjid has 'Abd al-Wahhāb listed as governor in 136/754, but there is no explicit reason for this. On the contrary, Ibn 'Asākir is quite clear in saying that 'Abd al-Wahhāb was governor of Dimashq when he died–that is, in 158/774 or 159/775.

56. There is confusion in the sources regarding Ibrāhīm b. 'Abd al-Wahhāb. Ibn 'Asākir names him as governor under al-Manṣūr, but he adds that actually only his father was governor for al-Manṣūr, and that Ibrāhīm was in fact governor much later, for al-Ma'mūn (*MTMD* 4:307–8; see also Ṣafadī, *'Umarā'*, 3). But Ibn 'Asākir himself may be confused here, for al-'Aẓīmī confirms that Ibrāhīm was ousted as governor in 160/776 ('Aẓīmī, *Ḥalab*, 228).

57. For a detailed analysis of the composition, rise, and demise of the Abnā' (with some reference to the Khurāsāniyya in general), see Patricia Crone, "The 'Abbāsid Abnā' and Sāsānid Cavalrymen," *JRAS, 3rd series,* 8 (1998): 1–19.

58. Abū 'Awn al-Azdī: Ṭabarī 2:2001ff., 3:49–50; Kindī, *Wulāt,* 101ff.; Crone, *Slaves,* 174.

59. On the Manṣūrid reorganization of power and the practice of using Khurāsānīs and 'Abbāsid *mawālī* to circumvent the influence of 'Abbāsid nobles, see Ya'qūbī, *Ta'rīkh,* 2:461–62; Lassner, *Shaping,* 11–13, 91ff.

60. According to the *Zuqnīn Chronicle*. See *Chronicum anonymum pseudo-Dionysianum vulgo dictum,* ed. J.-B. Chabot, 2 vols., *CSCO* 91, 104, *Scriptores Syri* 43, 53 (Louvain: E. Peeters, 1927 and 1933), 2:273/240.

61. Muḥammad b. al-Ash'ath: *TMD* 52:133–34; Crone, *Slaves,* 184–85. He remained in Syria until 141/758 when he was made governor of Egypt.

62. Yaḥyā b. Mu'ādh: Ṭabarī 3:711, 732; Crone, *Slaves,* 183–84. Yaḥyā's family already had a slim connection with Syria: Yaḥyā's grandfather had a house in Damascus assigned to him by the Umayyad caliph Mu'āwiya. His name, Muslim, was a convert's favorite and suggests that he was the source of the family's client status. On Abū al-Nidā', see chapter 6.

63. Isḥāq b. Yaḥyā: Ṭabarī 3:1133; *MTMD* 4:317.

64. On Rajā', see *MTMD* 6:335–36.

65. On the affair of 'Alī b. Isḥāq, see Ṭabarī 3:1313–14; *TMD* 18:122–24; *MTMD* 6:335–36, 17:198–201; Michael the Syrian,

540–41/3:107–8. Von Sievers, "Military," 223, is thus mistaken in seeing this "as a response to the appointment of Ashnās al-Turkī," and a revolt of a "Syrian head of the auxiliary force" against an "easterner." Even if one accepts that such social tensions existed, the accounts in Ibn 'Asākir suggest that 'Alī, who (despite his ancestry) considered himself a member of the Khurāsāniyya, and not a "Syrian," was motivated by small-scale personal motives and, in the end, may have only had a grudge against Rajā'. A fuller analysis can be found in 'Abbās, *Bilād al-shām,* 64–67.

66. Sindī: *MTMD* 10:210; Crone, *Slaves,* 194–95. On his handling of tribal factions, see al-Jāḥiẓ's anecdote cited in note 40, chapter 2. Other 'Abbāsid clients included members of the powerful Barmakī family like Mūsā b. Yaḥyā b. Khālid, who was governor of Dimashq briefly in 176/792 (*TMD* 61:233–39; Crone, Slaves, 176–77), and his brother Ja'far, who was governor-general of Syria in 188/803 (*MTMD* 6:98ff.; Crone, *Slaves,* 176–77).

67. On the course of the civil war and al-Ma'mūn's new order, see *EAC,* 135–74; Kennedy, *Prophet,* 148–57; A. Arazi and A. El'ad, " 'L'Épître à l'Armée.' Al-Ma'mūn et la seconde Da'wa," *SI* 66 (1987): 27–70, and 67 (1988): 29–74.

68. Ṭabarī 3:975, 1039ff.; *ZḤ* 1:65–66. On Ṭāhir's client status, see C. E. Bosworth, "The Ṭāhirids and the Ṣaffārids," in R. N. Frye, ed. *The Cambridge History of Iran, Volume IV: From the Arab Invasion to the Seljuqs* (Cambridge: Cambridge University Press, 1975), 91; Crone, *Slaves,* 78, n. 610. 'Abd Allāh: Ṭabarī 3:1045, 1086, 1094, 1098; *TMD* 29:216ff.; *ZḤ* 1:66–67. Ṭāhir's paternal nephew Isḥāq b. Ibrāhīm b. Muṣ'ab was governor of Qinnasrīn for al-Ma'mūn: *BṬ* 3:1409–12; *ZḤ* 1:67.

69. On Isḥāq, see note 29, above.

70. Ṭabarī 3:1099–1100. On al-'Abbās in Qinnasrīn: *ZḤ* 1:67.

71. Azdī, *Mawṣil,* 385; *ZḤ* 1:67.

72. Azdī, *Mawṣil,* 395, 412.

73. Ṭabarī 3:1133; Mas'ūdī, *Murūj* 7:102–3. That is to say, 'Abbāsid historical writing suggests that al-Ma'mūn explicitly made al-Mu'taṣim his heir shortly before his death. There is always the possibility, of course, that these accounts are the sort of back-projected legitimizing accounts that we have seen were generated concerning the succession to al-Saffāḥ. Indeed, there are fragments of a tradition favoring the succession to al-'Abbās (Ṭabarī 3:1469; Abū Ḥanīfa al-Dinawarī, *al-Akhbār al-ṭiwāl,* ed. V. Guirgass [Berlin: Weidman, 1910], 279).

74. Ṭabarī 3:1164; Mas'ūdī, *Murūj,* 7:103; Ya'qūbī, *Ta'rīkh,* 2:575; Azdī, *Mawṣil,* 427; *FHA* 1:395–98. The rebellion does not emerge as one of indigenous Arabs versus "easterners" as von Sievers interprets it ("Military," 222).

75. Ya'qūbī, *Ta'rīkh,* 2:575 suggests that the army held al-'Abbās' decision to give in to al-Mu'taṣim against him. On the plot to assassinate al-Mu'taṣim, see the detailed account in Ṭabarī 3:1256–67; Ya'qūbī, *Ta'rīkh,* 2:581–82; Mas'ūdī, *Murūj,* 7:136–37; Azdī, *Mawṣil,* 427–28, 430.

76. The background of the commanders involved in the plot is manifest from the accounts in the primary sources, especially that of al-Ṭabarī. See also M. A. Shaban, *Islamic History. A New Interpretation,* 2 vols. (Cambridge: Cambridge University Press, 1971), 2:61–62; Kennedy, *Prophet,* 167.

77. By "marginal," I am, of course, indicating these groups' political and cultural status vis-à-vis the incumbent ruling elite, composed of Hāshimī nobles, Khurāsānīs, and the Abnā'.

78. Matthew S. Gordon, "The Breaking of a Thousand Swords: A History of the Turkish Community of Sāmarrā (218–264 A.H./833–877 C.E.)" (Ph.D. diss., Columbia University, 1993), 283–98.

79. 'Ubayd Allāh b. 'Abd al-'Azīz b. al-Faḍl b. Ṣāliḥ: *ZḤ* 1:69.

80. Dīnār b. 'Abd Allāh: Ṭabarī 3:1030; *TMD* 17:319.

81. Abū Dulaf: *MTMD* 21:34–43; Ṣafadī, *Umarā',* 67; *Encyclopaedia Iranica,* ed. E. Yarshater (Boston: Routledge and Kegan Paul, 1983–), s.v. "Abū Dolaf al-Qasem b. 'Īsā" [F. M. Donner].

82. E.g., Abū al-Mughīth Mūsā b. Ibrāhīm al-Rāfiqī, who was governor of Dimashq and later of Ḥimṣ. He had been in charge of the *shurṭa* of Egypt for al-Mu'taṣim when the latter was governor-general of the western provinces for al-Ma'mūn (Ṭabarī 3:1420–21; Ya'qūbī, *Ta'rīkh* 2:599; Kindī, *Wulāt,* 190, 192; *TMD* 60:388–90). But see the more ambiguous Abū Ṣāliḥ Muslim b. Muḥammad, who was governor of Dimashq for al-Mu'taṣim. Ibn 'Asākir calls him *min quwwād surra man ra'a,* and he was evidently bilingual, as he is depicted playing a Persian song for the caliph. He later became governor of Isfahan (*TMD* 58:118–19).

83. Ashnās: Gordon, "Breaking," 151–63; *BṬ* 4:1919–20; according to Ya'qūbī, Ashnās' authority was renewed or expanded in 227/841, when the caliph al-Wāthiq made Ashnās governor of all the provinces "from his door to the farthest province of al-Maghrib" (*Ta'rīkh,* 2:585). Ṣūl Artikīn: Ṭabarī 3:1313. On this person, who was evidently once a rebellious Gurgānī prince, see Ṭabarī, *History,* 33:44, n. 148. On 'Alī b. Isḥāq b. Yaḥyā, see above.

84. On Ītākh, see Gordon, "Breaking," 176–89; On his responsibilities, see Ya'qūbī, Ta'rīkh, 2:587. He certainly succeeded Ashnās over Egypt: Kindī, *Wulāt,* 196. That he did so in Syria is further suggested by the fact that Harthama Shār Bāmiyān was made governor of Qinnasrīn shortly after 230/844: al-Ṭabarī considers Harthama as one of Ītākh's closest companions (*min wujūh aṣḥābihi*), Ṭabarī 3:1373.

85. Sālim b. Ḥāmid: *TMD* 20:38–39. On the factional revolt under him, see chapter 5. Another Arab commander in Damascus at this time was Mālik b. Ṭawq al-Taghlibī of Rabī'a/Qays, who was governor of al-Urdunn and Dimashq for al-Wāthiq in 232/846. He continued under al-Mutawakkil, and later established the city of al-Raḥba on the Euphrates. *TMD* 56:460ff.

86. Ṭabarī 3:1382. Canard's article in *EI2*, s.v., " 'Īsā b. al-Shaykh," is the most detailed discussion of 'Īsā and his progeny, available. On 'Īsā's revolt in Syria, see Gil, Palestine, 299–300; Ṣādiq Jawda, *Madīnat al-ramla mundhu nashā'ihā ḥattā 'ām 492 H / 1099 M* (Beirut: Dār 'Ammār, 1986), 59–64; 'Abbās, *Bilād al-shām,* 71–73.

87. Ṭabarī 3:1585. 'Īsā wrote to al-Musta'īn in 251/869, asking to have enough weapons sent to him so that his *jund* would be able to make a raid. He also requested that the *"ṣāḥib al-ṣūr [sic]"* ("the one in charge of Tyre," i.e., the governor of the *sawāḥil,* or coastal districts) send him four additional ships for the raid. The account only refers to 'Īsā's position as "the town," *al-balad,* but since it had Mediterranean access and troops preparing for a frontier raid, then it can only be a town in a Syrian district. Since 'Īsā had to ask Samarra to correspond with the shipyards in al-Urdunn, he could have been in any other district, probably, following Canard, on the frontier itself, although neither Ibn 'Asākir nor Ibn al-'Adīm mention him in this regard. Al-Muwaffaq al-Khārijī (not to be confused with the 'Abbāsid prince of that name) is otherwise unknown.

88. Ya'qūbī, *Ta'rīkh,* 2:611.

89. On the "Anarchy at Samarra" at this time and the factional politics in the capital surrounding the accession of al-Mu'tazz, see Kennedy, *Prophet*, 171–75, esp. 173; Gordon, "Breaking."

90. Ya'qūbī, *Ta'rīkh,* 2:611–12. The name of 'Īsā's stronghold is mentioned in 2:614.

91. Ṭabarī 3:1685; *MTMD* 20:73–74.

92. Mas'ūdī, *Murūj,* 7:395–96.

93. Ṭabarī 3:1685.

94. Ya'qūbī, *Ta'rīkh,* 2:613–14; *TMD* 48:311.

95. Ṭabarī 3:1840–41 (in the year 256/870); Ya'qūbī, *Ta'rīkh,* 2:617–18, 621, where it is said that he never returned all the money he had seized; *MTMD* 20:73–74; Ibn al-Athīr, *Kāmil,* 7:238; Ibn Taghribirdī, *Nujūm,* 3:7.

96. See Appendixes A and B.

97. And, most likely, examples of the group that Gordon identifies as the "steppe" Turks. Gordon, "Breaking," 310–62, esp. 334–44.

98. Amājūr al-Turkī: Ṭabarī 3:1840; *MTMD* 5:30–31.

99. 'Alī b. Amājūr: *TMD* 41:266. Aḥmad b. Yidghabāsh was the son of a Turkish slave given to al-Mu'taṣim by "the king of the Turks": *BṬ* 3:1241–42.

CHAPTER FOUR

1. On the discourse generated by this event, see Sabatino Moscati, "Le massacre des Umayyades dans l'histoire et dans les fragments poétiques," *Archiv Orientální* 18 (1950): 88–115; For a later accumulation, see Tāqī al-Dīn Aḥmad al-Maqrīzī, *Kitāb al-nizā' wa'l-takhaṣṣum fīmā bayna banī umayya wa-banī hāshim,* ed. Ḥusayn Mu'nis (Cairo: dār al-ma'ārif, 1988), and the introduction to the English translation of al-Maqrīzī's treatise: C. E. Bosworth, *Al-Maqrīzī's "Book of Contention and Strife Concerning the Relations Between the Banū Umayya and the Banū Hāshim,"* Journal of Semitic Studies Monographs, 3 (Manchester: University of Manchester, 1980).

2. To obtain a rough idea of the survival rate of the Umayyad nobility after 132/750, one only needs to consider the large number of Umayyads killed throughout the course of the 'Abbāsid period. For a ballpark estimate, see the accounts compiled (uncritically) in Muḥammad Ṭāhir Ḥusaynī, *Maqātil al-umawiyyīn* (Beirut: Mu'assasat al-balāgha, 1990), 289–364. For some particulars, see Amikam Elad, "Aspects of the Transition from the Umayyad to the 'Abbāsid Caliphate," *Jerusalem Studies in Arabic and Islam* 19 (1995): 92–95.

3. On the fate of 'Ubayd Allāh b. Marwān, see Ṭabarī 3:46; *TMD* 38:117–20. There is some confusion as to whether or not it was 'Abd Allāh b. Marwān who was captured. 'Abd Allāh's son al-Ḥakam was captured in Egypt in 132/750 and imprisoned until the reign of al-Rashīd (Ṣalāḥ al-Dīn al-Munajjid, *Mu'jam banī umayya* [Beirut: Dār al-kitāb al-jadīd, 1970], 26). Captured Umayyads seemed to have had a high entertainment value: Ibrāhīm b. Sulaymān b. 'Abd al-Malik was also made to recount his perils in avoiding the 'Abbāsid armies (al-Munajjid, *Mu'jam,* 8–9).

4. Some Umayyads who found a home in the court at Baghdad (selected at random from al-Munajjid, *Mu'jam*): 'Abd al-'Azīz b. 'Umar II was in the *ṣaḥāba* of al-Manṣūr (pages 103–5); Ādam b. 'Abd al-'Azīz b. 'Umar II, a poet/ascetic in the *ṣaḥāba* of al-Mahdī (pages 1–3) ; 'Abd al-Malik b. 'Abd Allāh b. Yazīd II was an adviser to al-Mahdī (page 109); and there are still others. As late as 250/864, Umayyads held positions of rank in the 'Abbāsid court (Ṭabarī 3:1533).

5. Umayyad wealth after 132/750 is still difficult to determine. Ibn 'Asākir frequently cites a now-lost 'Abbāsid-era work by a certain Ibn Abī al-'Ajā'iz entitled *Tasmiyat man kāna bi-dimashq wa-ghūṭatihā min banī umayya* [name-list of those Umayyads who lived in Damascus and its Ghūṭa]. Among other things, this work names many Umayyads who were alive and living on their estates in the vicinity of Damascus for generations after the 'Abbāsid revolution. On Ibn Abī al-'Ajā'iz's work, see Cobb, "Community versus Contention," 11–12.

6. Muḥammad b. al-Ḥasan b. Ḥamdūn, *Al-tadhkira al-ḥamdūniyya,* ed. Iḥsān 'Abbās and Bakr 'Abbās (Beirut: Dār ṣādir, 1996), 8:55–59. I owe this reference to Patricia Crone.

7. For example, for generations after the fall of the Umayyads, the families of Umayyad *mawālī* from the Filasṭīnī town of Ayla were active as transmitters of Prophetic tradition (Paul M. Cobb, "Scholars and Society at Early Islamic Ayla," *JESHO* 38 [1995]: 417–28).

8. 'Abd Allāh b. al-Muqaffa', *Risāla fī al-ṣaḥāba,* ed. Muḥammad Kurd 'Alī in *Rasā'il al-bulaghā'* (Cairo: n. p., 1913), 127. See also the translation and edition by Charles Pellat, *Ibn al-Muqaffa', "conseilleur" du calife* (Paris: G. P. Maisonneuve et Larose, 1976), 46–49 (§§41–43). For a novel interpretation of this work and its author, see Said Amir Arjomand, "'Abd Allāh Ibn al-Muqaffa' and the 'Abbasid Revolution," *Iranian Studies* 27 (1994): 9–36.

9. Unless otherwise noted, the following discussion of the revolt of Abū al-Ward and Abū Muḥammad al-Sufyānī is based on Ṭabarī 3:52–5; Balādhurī, *Ansāb,* 3:169–70; *TMD* 19:153–55, 57:46–48; *BṬ* 9:3927–32. See also Omar, *Caliphate,* 270–73; 'Abbās, *Bilād al-shām,* 17–19.

10. On the Euphrates outpost of Bālis, see the descriptions collected in *BṬ* 1:119–21. On Nā'ūra, see *ZḤ* 1:45. Za'ārat Banī Zufar is also called Khusāf (Ṭabarī 3:52). On the history of the relationship of the Banū Zufar with the Banū Maslama, see Crone, *Slaves,* 108–9.

11. *TMD* 57:46–48; Ṭabarī 3:52. Other examples: the revolts of Mulabbad b. Ḥarmala (Balādhurī, *Ansāb,* 3:248), and of al-Ḍiḥḍāḥ al-Shaybānī (Balādhurī, *Ansāb,* 3:252), and the revolt of al-Mubarqa' (see chapter 6). The precise nature of the "insult" is unknown. The earliest account appears to be that of al-Haytham b. 'Adī (d. 206/821) in his now lost *Kitāb al-dawla al-'abbāsiyya,* but preserved in *BṬ* 9:3928–30. Here, matters are more specific: the Khurāsānī commander actually proposes marriage to "a woman of the descendants of Abū Sufyān" at Bālis. Trapped between a chaste death or a shameful marriage, she and her kin call in Abū al-Ward. This is more or less the same story found in Balādhurī, *Ansāb,* 3:169, where the Khurāsānī is specified as 'Abd Allāh b. 'Alī's *'āmil.* On al-Haytham b. 'Adī's work, see Stefan Leder, *Das Korpus al-Haitam ibn 'Adī*

(st. 207/822). Herkunft, Überlieferung, Gestalt früher Texte der Aḥbār Literatur (Frankfurt am Main: Vittorio Klostermann, 1991).

12. In Balādhurī, *Ansāb,* 3:169, it is Abū al-Ward's brother Abū al-Wāzi' who kills the Khurāsānī in his bath at Bālis. In al-Madā'inī's account in Ṭabarī 3:52 and *TMD* 57:46–48, it is Abū al-Ward who does the dirty work.

13. Ṭabarī 3:52: *"wa-aẓhara al-tabyīḍ wa-al-khal' li-'abd allāh ibn 'alī."*

14. On Abū Muḥammad's imprisonment and release, see Ṭabarī 3:43.

15. Azdī, *Mawṣil,* 142: "In this year [133/751, *sic*] Abū Muḥammad al-Sufyānī revolted, and he and his troops donned red garments (*wa-fīhā kharaja abū muḥammad al-sufyānī fa-labisa al-ḥumra huwa wa-junduhu*)." The color red may be a Qaysī symbol as 'Abbās, *Bilād al-shām,* 59, suggests in connection with the caliphate of Maslama b. Ya'qūb (on whom, see below), but given Abū Muḥammad's Yamanī following, this seems strange. Nor was red exclusively Sufyānid or Marwānid, as both Abū Muḥammad (a Sufyānid) and, later, Maslama b. Ya'qūb (a Marwānid) made use of it. Perhaps it was a specifically Umayyad color, as opposed to a simple anti-'Abbāsid white (which non-Umayyads also used). On the political content of colors, see Farouk Omar, "The Significance of the Colours of Banners in the Early 'Abbāsid Period," in his *'Abbāsiyyāt,* 148–54.

16. However, in the field, it seems that Abū al-Ward commanded the Qaysiyya while the Palmyrene warlord Aṣbagh b. Dhu'āla al-Kalbī commanded the Yamaniyya (on him, see Crone, *Slaves,* 156): see Ṭabarī 3:55. Strangely, al-Maqdisī, *Bad',* 6:73–74 makes no mention of Abū al-Ward in this revolt at all. With regard to other Umayyads in the revolt, in Balādhurī, *Ansāb,* 3:170, Abū Muḥammad received at Dayr Ḥanīnā the allegiance of an "al-Walīd" and "the army (*al-nās*)," who are otherwise unidentified. He also wrote to the Umayyad Hishām b. al-Walīd b. 'Uqba, but he did not get involved. For Hishām's lineage, see Balādhurī, *Ansāb,* 3:311. Note that he is most likely a Qinnasrīnī *sharīf,* as this is the setting of the revolt; moreover, a "Walīd b. Hishām b. Walīd b. 'Uqba"—who must be related—was governor of Qinnasrīn for 'Umar II (Crone, *Slaves,* 127).

17. On the development of the figure of the Sufyānī in early Islamic apocalyptic, see the magisterial study of Wilfred Madelung, "The Sufyānī Between Tradition and History," *SI* 68 (1984): 5–48, which elegantly overturns earlier Orientalist depictions of the Sufyānī as a "Syrian national hero" and the like. The *locus classicus* of the older interpretation of the Sufyānī is Henri Lammens, "Le «Sofiānī,» héros national des Arabes syriens," in his *Études sur le siècle des Omayyades* (Beirut: Imprimerie Catholique, 1930), 391–408.

18. Ṭabarī 3:53: *huwa al-sufyānī alladhī kāna yudhkar*. See Balādhurī, *Ansāb*, 3:170: *anā al-sufyānī alladhī yurwā annahu yarudd dawlat banī umayya*.

19. On the joint revolt of Ibn Surāqa and Ḥabīb, see chapter 5. Bassām b. Ibrāhīm: Balādhurī, *Ansāb*, 3:171. Note that Bassām himself later rebelled against 'Abd Allāh b. 'Alī.

20. On the influence of Abū Muḥammad's revolt on Qaysī pro-Umayyad unrest in the Jazīra, see Ṭabarī 3:56–58; Ya'qūbī, *Ta'rīkh*, 2:425; Maqdisī, *Bad'*, 6:73–74; *BṬ* 9:3929, where Abū Muḥammad's sphere of influence is said to have included Diyār Muḍar. See also Omar, *Caliphate*, 273–74.

21. Balādhurī, *Ansāb*, 3:170; Maqdisī, *Bad'*, 6:73–74; Ibn al-Athīr, *al-Kāmil*, 5:434–35; *BṬ* 9:3929.

22. The revolt of al-'Abbās b. Muḥammad al-Sufyānī is known to us only by the unique account in *ZḤ* 1:56. On the Jazīran revolt, see the sources listed in note 20.

23. Abān b. Mu'āwiya: Balādhurī, *Ansāb*, 3:109; idem, *Ansāb* MS, 2:392; *Ajbar Machmuâ*, 46–47; *BṬ* 6:2974; *ZḤ* 1:55–56.

24. On 'Abd Allāh b. 'Alī's revolt, see chapter 3. 'Abd al-Ṣamad b. Muḥammad b. al-Ḥajjāj b. Yūsuf and *sayf al-ḥajjāj*: Balādhurī, *Ansāb* MS, 2:392. Note also that in his discussion of the revolt of Abū al-Ward in his lost work, the *Kitāb al-awsaṭ*, al-Mas'ūdī discussed an otherwise unknown Bishr b. 'Abd Allāh al-Wāḥidī, who, given the context, may also have been a Syrian rebel under al-Saffāḥ (Mas'ūdī, *Murūj*, 4:91).

25. On Ibn Surāqa's background, see chapter 3. On the revolt of Hāshim/Hishām b.Yazīd: Shams al-Dīn al-Dhahabī, *Ta'rīkh al-islām wa-wafayāt al-mashāhīr wa-al-a'lām*, ed. 'Umar 'Abd al-Salām Tadmurī (Beirut: Dār al-kitāb al-'arabī, 1991), 8:353. The account of the revolt presents some problems, as Ṭabarī mentions that Ibn Surāqa was with 'Abd Allāh fighting Abū Muslim at Naṣībīn, and Dhahabī's account does not make clear exactly when Ibn Surāqa was at Damascus, nor precisely when the revolt started. Perhaps he returned to Damascus *after* 'Abd Allāh's defeat in Jumāda II 137/November 754, as Crone, *Slaves*, 129, seems to suggest.

26. For a study of the ways in which 'Abbāsid historiography transmuted the history of the prerevolutionary and revolutionary periods to legitimize its patrons, see Jacob Lassner, *Islamic Revolution and Historical Memory: An Inquiry into the Art of 'Abbāsid Apologetics* (New Haven: American Oriental Society, 1986).

27. On the integration of the Umayyad elite, see Omar, *Caliphate*,

280–83; Irit Bligh-Abramski, "Evolution versus Revolution: Umayyad Elements in the 'Abbāsid Regime 133/750–320/932," *Der Islam* 65 (1988): 226–243; Elad, "Aspects."

28. The account probably dates from the Umayyad period, as its *isnād* suggests: Abū Bakr b. Abī al-Dunyā>Aḥmad b. Jamīl al-Marwazī>'Abd Allāh b. al-Mubārak>'Umar b. Sa'īd>Ibn Sābiṭ al-Jumaḥī (d. 118/736): *TMD* 34:377; *BṬ* 10:4681. Elsewhere, Syrians could be smeared for venerating al-Ḥajjāj, and not even knowing who 'Alī was (*TMD* I:366).

29. The source is Yāqūt al-Ḥamawī, *Mu'jam al-udabā'*, ed. A. F. al-Rifā'ī, 20 vols. (Cairo: Dār al-ma'mūn, 1936–38), 14:128–29, citing al-Madā'inī. The passage is cited in Ḥabīb Zayyāt, "Al-Tashayyu' li-mu'āwiya fī 'ahd al-'abbāsiyyīn," *Al-Mašriq* 26 (1928): 410–15, and translated in Charles Pellat, "Le Culte de Mu'āwiya au IIIe siècle de l'hégire." *SI* 7(1956): 54. Note the reference to the title of *khalīfat allāh*.

30. See, e.g., the accounts collected in Ṣalāḥ al-Dīn al-Munajjid, *Madīnat dimashq 'ind al-jughrāfiyyīn wa-al-raḥḥālīn al-muslimīn* (Beirut: Dār al-kitāb al-jadīd, 1967). For examples of *aḥādīth*, see, e.g., Ibn Ḥanbal, *Musnad*, 6 vols. (Beirut: Dār ṣādir, 1969), 4:110, 160; 5:184ff.; 6:457.

31. On the *faḍā'il* genre, see E. A. Gruber, *Verdienst und Rang. Die Faḍā'il als literarisches und gesellschaftliches Problem im Islam*, Islamkundliche Untersuchungen, B. 15 (Freiburg: Klaus Schwarz, 1975). On the *faḍā'il* of Jerusalem in particular, see Amikam Elad, *Medieval Jerusalem and Islamic Worship* (Leiden: E. J. Brill, 1995), esp. 6–22.

32. M. J. Kister, "A Comment on the Antiquity of Traditions Praising Jerusalem," *The Jerusalem Cathedra* 1 (1981): 185–86; Elad, *Jerusalem*, 13–22.

33. Al-Raba'ī, *Faḍā'il*. Al-Raba'ī's work was later used by Ibn 'Asākir in the topographical introduction to his history of Damascus, which Nikita Elisséeff translated as *La description de Damas d'Ibn 'Asākir* (Damascus: Institut Français de Damas, 1959). Earlier collections of *faḍā'il al-shām* traditions are known to have existed, but al-Raba'ī's is the earliest complete collection to survive. A *Kitāb madīḥ ahl al-shām* ["The Book of Praise of the People of Syria"] is attributed to Haytham b. 'Adī (d. 206/821; see al-Raba'ī, *Faḍā'il*, introduction, page 7), and Abū al-Ḥusayn al-Rāzī (d. 347/958), among others, is also known to have written a *Kitāb faḍā'il dimashq* (Gerhard Conrad, *Abū'l-Ḥusain al-Rāzī [-347/958] und seine Schriften. Untersuchungen zur frühen damaszener Geschichtsschreibung* [Stuttgart: Franz Steiner, 1991], 69–80).

34. Al-Raba'ī, *Faḍā'il*, passim. For specific examples, see, e.g., 4, 8, 10 (angel's wings); 11 ("Verily God has blessed Syria from the Euphrates to al-'Arīsh."); 5, 14–16 (Syria as choice land). On the Umayyad background

of these latter traditions, see Wilfred Madelung, "Has the *Hijra* Come to an End?" *Revue des Études Islamiques* 54 1986: 225–37. For clear evidence of the impact of *faḍā'il al-shām* traditions in 'Abbāsid Syria, note the frequent allusions to them in the late Umayyad/early 'Abbāsid traditions from Ḥimṣ collected in Nu'aym b. Ḥammād, *Kitāb al-fitan*, e.g., fol. 66b, 82b:1–7, 82a7–13.

35. Al-Raba'ī, *Faḍā'il,* 15–16 (*ahl al-shām* are one of the swords of God, which He uses to smite those who rebel against Him.); 3 (Syria is God's quiver, if He grows angry with a people, He will hurl upon them an arrow-shaft from it); 10 (The *umma* will continue to be victorious until the day of judgment, and most of them are *ahl al-shām*).

36. Al-Raba'ī, *Faḍā'il,* 12 (the Prophet silently, but eloquently, refuses to call for blessings on Iraq as he has done for Syria), and also *TMD* 1:130ff. for variants.

37. On early Syrian-Iraqi antipathy, see, e.g., the complaints that led to the building of Wāsiṭ (Ṭabarī 2:1125–26); see the speech attributed to al-Saffāḥ upon his accesion to the caliphate in al-Kūfa in 132/749 (Ṭabarī 3:29–30).

38. E.g., the speech attributed to Dāwud b. 'Alī upon al-Saffāḥ's accession (Ṭabarī 3:32–33): "Men of Kūfa . . . [God] has made manifest among you a Caliph of the clan of Hāshim, brightening thereby your faces and making you prevail over the army of Syria, and transferring the sovereignty and the glory of Islam to you." A similar Syria/Umayyad-Iraq/'Abbāsid equation is expressed in Ya'qūbī, *Buldān,* 236. The Ḥimṣī traditionist Ḥarīz b. 'Uthmān al-Raḥabī (d. 163/779) was considered a "Sufyānī" in the sense of an anti-'Alid. He is said to have said to an Iraqi scholar, "We have our Commander of the Faithful, and you have yours (*lanā amīr wa-laka amīr*)." On him, see *TMD* 12:336ff.; *BṬ* 5:2201–21; Madelung, "Sufyānī," 29.

39. *TMD* 33:437.

40. On Umayyad religious authority, see Patricia Crone and Martin Hinds, *God's Caliph. Religious Authority in the First Centuries of Islam* (Cambridge: Cambridge University Press, 1986); Wadād al-Qāḍī, "The Religious Foundation of Late Umayyad Ideology and Practice," in *Saber Religioso y Poder Político en el Islam. Actas del Simposio Internacional (Granada, 15–18 octubre 1991)* (Madrid: Agencia Española de Cooperación Internacional, 1994), 231–73.

41. Crone and Hinds, *God's Caliph.* On the "sifting out" of pro-Umayyad traditions from the corpus of religio-legal traditions as it crystalized under the 'Abbāsids, see Ignaz Goldziher, *Muslim Studies* (London: Allen and Unwin, 1967–71), 2:52–54, 105–108.

42. Al-Manṣūr's plan: *BṬ* 4:1601–2. The Damascene family: *TMD* 58:181. Pro-Umayyad sentiment might also imply anti-ʿAlid tendencies: it is said that traditions evoking the virtues of ʿAlī were unknown in Syria until the time of Ismaʿīl b. ʿAyyāsh al-Ḥimṣī (d. 181–2/797–8); on him, see Madelung, "Sufyānī," 17. It is said that even in the third century, anyone overheard discussing *faḍā'il ʿalī* in the Umayyad mosque was likely to be attacked (*MTMD* 3:88–89).

43. Al-Rabaʿī, *Faḍā'il,* 42. The account is attributed to Abū Ḥāritha Aḥmad b. Ibrāhīm b. Hishām al-Ghassānī, about whom little is known save that his father lived from 150–233/767–847. As Abū Ḥāritha also related an account in which al-Ma'mūn praised the Umayyad mosque while in Damascus (*ibid.,* 43), one can presume that he was active sometime after the caliph's death in 218/833.

44. The phrase is Norman Cohn's. See his *Cosmos, Chaos and the World to Come: the Ancient Roots of Apocalyptic Faith* (New Haven: Yale University Press, 1993).

45. A point made long ago by Paul Casanova, but well worth repeating. See his *Mohammed et la fin du monde: étude critique sur l'Islam primitif* (Paris: P. Geuthner, 1911–24). See now Fred M. Donner, "From Believers to Muslims: Confessional Self-Identity in the Early Islamic Community," in *The Byzantine and Early Islamic Near East, IV: Patterns of Communal Identity,* ed. Lawrence I. Conrad (Princeton: Darwin Press, forthcoming).

46. See the tradition where the intellectual strengths of various regions are enumerated in *TMD* 1:330: ". . . and if [a man in search of knowledge] is looking for apocalyptic traditions, then [I say to him] 'Go to the people of Syria (*wa-in aradta al-malāḥim fa-ʿalayka bi-ahl al-shām*).' " On Syria and Damascus as the arena for the apocalypse in Islamic tradition, see al-Rabaʿī, *Faḍā'il,* 20, 27 (Damascus is *fusṭāṭ al-muslimīn* on the day of judgment); Wilferd Madelung, "Apocalyptic Prophecies in Ḥimṣ in the Umayyad Age," *Journal of Semitic Studies* 31 (1986): 155ff.

47. On the apocalyptic background to the ʿAbbāsid revolution, see the classic study by Gerlof van Vloten, "Recherches sur la domination arabe, le chiitisme, et les croyances messianiques sous le Khalifat des Omayades," *Verhandelingen der Koninlijke Akademie van wetenschappen te Amsterdam; Afdeeling Letterkunde*. Deel I:3 (Amsterdam: J. Muller, 1894) and also Moshe Sharon, *Black Banners from the East: The Establishment of the ʿAbbāsid State—Incubation of a Revolt* (Jerusalem: Magnes Press, 1983), 187–88.

48. Azdī, *Mawṣil,* 66. On Thābit's revolt, see chapter 5. On the Qaḥṭānī, see Madelung, "Apocalyptic Prophecies," 149–55. Other sources predict that a Qaḥṭānī was expected to emerge in the ʿAbbāsid period,

though without legitimate claims to rule (*MTMD* 7:162). Qaḥṭānid expectations might be used to other ends, as well, as in an account where a Yamanī *sharīf,* in response to taunts about his belief in the expected Qaḥṭānī, allegedly claimed that he had already appeared, and was none other than al-Mahdī, the infant son of al-Manṣūr. Not surprisingly, the *sharīf* was given the governorship of Mosul upon al-Mahdī's accession (Azdī, *Mawṣil,* 214).

49. That this (predominantly Ḥimṣī) discourse has survived at all is due to its presence in the remarkable *Kitāb al-fitan* of Nu'aym b. Ḥammād (al-Raba'ī cites only one [rather apolitical] tradition about the Sufyānī, and even it is a Ḥimṣī tradition: *Faḍā'il,* 43). On this work, see esp. Madelung, "Sufyānī," "Apocalyptic Prophecies." One would dearly like to have at hand the now-lost Andalusī *Kitāb al-barahīn fī imāmat al-umawiyyīn* ["The book of proofs of the Imamate of the Umayyads"] that al-Mas'ūdī mentioned having examined in the library of an Umayyad *mawlā* in Tiberias in 324/935–36, which, while late, implies a preexisting corpus of pro-Umayyad literary material (see the description of the work in his *Kitāb al-tanbīh wa-al-ishrāf,* ed. M. J. de Goeje [Leiden: E. J. Brill, 1894] 336–37).

50. E.g., Ṭabarī 3:830; Ya'qūbī, *Ta'rīkh,* 2:532. See also Gil, *Palestine,* 293–94. 'Abbās, *Bilād al-shām,* 53–61 has by far the most complete account and was the first to examine the information in Ibn 'Asākir; but note that he identifies a dubious "united Arab sentiment" in opposition to the 'Abbāsids (page 60).

51. See Ibn al-Athīr, *Kāmil,* 6:249–50; Ibn Taghribirdī, *Nujūm,* 2:159; Khalīl b. Aybak al-Ṣafadī, *Al-Wāfī bi-al-wafayāt,* ed. Helmut Ritter et al., 22 vols. (Istanbul and Wiesbaden: F. Steiner for the Deutsche Morgenländische Gesellschaft, 1931–), 21:197.

52. Others dupe him into revolt: *MTMD* 18:110–11. His holdings at al-Mizza and at Damascus, where his *dār* was located west of Raḥbat al-Zabīb (*TMD* 43:25, 27). His reputation for learning, and his *riwāya: MTMD* 18:109–10, 112. His 'Alid descent (his mother was Nafīsa bt. 'Abd Allāh b. al-'Abbās b. 'Alī): *MTMD* 18:110. Other prophecies mentioned in connection with his revolt: *MTMD* 18:112, 113.

53. Nu'aym b. Ḥammād, *Kitāb al-fitan,* fol. 81a:5–9. This and other traditions clearly circulated by supporters of Abū al-'Umayṭir are discussed in Madelung, "Sufyānī," 42–44; Tilman Nagel, *Rechtleitung und Kalifat. Versuch über eine Grundfrage der islamischen Geschichte,* vol. 2 of *Studien zum Minderheitenproblem im Islam,* Bonner orientalistische Studien, n.s. 27 (Bonn: Orientalische Seminar der Universität Bonn, 1975), 253–56. In addition to these, note also the "prediction" attributed to none other than Marwān II, who is alleged to have taken comfort in the face of his imminent defeat at the hands of the 'Abbāsids from the expectation that after the reign of the fifth 'Abbāsid, a Sufyānī would rule once more in

195/810–11 (*MTMD* 15:243).

54. Ya'qūbī, *Ta'rīkh,* 2:534.

55. On the decline of central authority in Syria during the Fourth Civil War, see chapter 5. On Ibn Wajh al-Fals, see Ṭabarī 3:830; *MTMD* 18:110–11, where it is mentioned that Ibn Wajh al-Fals later surrendered to 'Abd Allāh b. Ṭāhir, along with another rebel from the coast named Mikraz b. Ḥafṣ al-'Āmirī, who appears to be the same mentioned in Werner Caskel, *Ǧamharat an-Nasab. Das genealogische Werk des Hišam Ibn Muḥammad al-Kalbī,* 2 vols. (Leiden: E. J. Brill, 1966), 2:407. 'Abd Allāh brought these two with him (probably as members of his army) to Khurāsān, where they both died. This is corroborated by al-Ṭabarī, who provides a short notice of Ibn Wajh al-Fals' death in 231/845 (Ṭabarī 3:1357).

56. *MTMD* 18:111–12. The *'aṣabiyya*-precursor to the revolt is not known to the narrative sources, but is attested in the "prophecy" of Marwān II mentioned in note 53, where an outbreak of *'aṣabiyya* in 194/809 is mentioned as one of the portents of the coming of the Sufyānī. Note that the Umayyads disparage the Qays as "these Zawāqīl" (*hādhihi al-zawāqīl*), even though, after taking power they "sent for their Zawāqīl (*ba'athū ilā zawāqīlihim*)."

57. Kinsmen support: in addition to those mentioned earlier, see *TMD* 26:268 (his brother, al-'Abbās), *TMD* 40:18 ('Uthmān b. 'Anbasa, a nephew). Yamanī support: in addition to those mentioned earlier, see *MTMD* 18:112 (Damascene notable Muḥammad b. Ma'yūf b. Yaḥyā, whose family had fought against Abū al-Haydhām [see chapter 5]). His domain specified: Ṣafadī, *Wāfī,* 21:197. Some supporters from Ḥimṣ: *TMD* 43:32. However, the people of Ṭarābulus on the coast rejected his overtures (*TMD* 43:31). Ṣafadī, *Wāfī,* 21:197 states that, although the faction of the Qaysiyya did not support the rebels, tribesmen of Muḍar did.

58. His followers systematically hunt down Qaysīs in the city: *MTMD* 18:113. 'Abbās, *Bilād al-shām,* 57 refers to his reliance on Yaman as a "weak spot," and (58) discusses on the basis of some poetry his attempts to broaden his base of support.

59. *TMD* 43:31; *BṬ* 1:564. Isḥāq was the grandfather of the errant notable al-Fuṣays, on whom see chapter 5. Isḥāq's son joined Abū al-'Umayṭir's cause with a group of other Tanūkhīs from Qinnasrīn.

60. "Commander of the Faithful": *TMD* 37:346. "The Chosen One": *MTMD* 18:114. His guard and their refrain: *MTMD* 18:114. The flight of the Banū Hāshim and the fate of their property: *TMD* 54:121. But some Hāshimī *mawālī* were found to be useful in winning the support of others and were allowed to stay on despite the suspicion in which they were regarded: *TMD* 43:32–33.

61. Fleeing Damascenes: *TMD* 43:32–33. Attempts to dissuade him: *MTMD* 18:112. Door-to-door *bay'a: MTMD* 18:114. Calls to allegiance: *MTMD* 18:114. His introduction before the congregation: *MTMD* 16:353–54. A listing in the *dīwān* and promise of cash was of course a traditional way of assembling a *qawm* in early Islamic times: see Bonner, *Aristocratic Violence,* 6.

62. The Khaḍrā' and his Syrian version of the Khurāsāniyya : *TMD* 43:32. His scribes: *TMD* 57:313 (Marwān b. 'Anbasa b. al-Fayḍ, an Umayyad), *TMD* 21:45 (Sa'īd b. Khālid al-Azdī, Ibn al-'Ajā'iz, a Yamanī). His *wazīr*: *TMD* 63:318 (al-Walīd b. Hishām, *mawlā* of Umayyads). Abū Mushir (of the Yamanī tribe of Ghassān): *TMD* 33:435. Unflattering accounts of his judgment: *TMD* 21:36–37 (when a slave-girl engaged to a Khurāsānī is brought before him by a gang of followers, Abū al-'Umayṭir states that the blood and property of the Khurāsāniyya are *ḥalāl* for his followers); *MTMD* 17:212 (After ordering an opponent to leave his domains, the man replies "The world in its entirety belongs to you, O Commander of the Faithful," and is reprieved), 18:113 (A shopowner complains that his shops have been looted. Upon learning that the man is not of Quraysh, Abū al-'Umayṭir replies that sometimes those who say "my shops" do not really own them. After a pious reminder of the equity of caliphs from Abū Mushir, though, he promises to return the shopkeeper's property).

63. The phrase should perhaps be read *ahl al-bawādī,* i.e., nomads from the desert.

64. On the intervention of Ibn Bayhas, see *TMD* 53:257–65. On the flight of Qaysīs to other cities, see *TMD* 68:254.

65. On the "accession" of Maslama b. Ya'qūb, see *TMD* 53:263. His name given there is Maslama b. Ya'qūb b. 'Alī b. Muḥammad b. Sa'īd b. Maslama b. 'Abd al-Malik.

66. The return of Ibn Bayhas: *TMD* 53:264. The final end of Maslama and Abū al-'Umayṭir: *TMD* 53:264–65, 58:70–71.

67. The war-cries: *TMD* 53:260 (*"yā 'alī! yā mukhtār!"* and *"yā ma'mūn! yā manṣūr!"* respectively). Narrative statements about his appointment: *TMD* 53:258, 55: 31–32, 68:254 (he sends a messenger to al-Ma'mūn for help); Ṣafadī, *Wāfī,* 2:156. Coinage: Tayeb El-Hibri, "Coinage Reform Under the 'Abbāsid Caliph al-Ma'mūn," *JESHO* 36 (1993): 58–83. Ibn 'Asākir probably expresses the situation best when he refers to Ibn Bayhas as having stayed at Damascus "as governor, having taken it over (*wa-huwa muqīm bi-dimashq amīran mutaghalliban 'alayhā*)." *TMD* 53:265.

68. On the revolt of al-Faddaynī, see the account from Abū al-Ḥusayn al-Rāzī in *TMD* 21:56–57, and the same text in Yāqūt al-Ḥamawī, *Mu'jam al-buldān,* ed. F. Wüstenfeld (Leipzig: F. A. Brockhaus for the Deutsche

Morgenländische Gesellschaft, 1866–73), 3:858–59. On Yaḥyā b. Ṣāliḥ, see *TMD* 64:272–73. See also Oleg Grabar, "A Small Episode of Early 'Abbāsid Times and Some Consequences," *Eretz-Israel* 7 (1964): 44–47; 'Abbās, *Bilād al-shām,* 61–62. Note that Grabar's study was made without knowledge of related events in Syria and Damascus, and on the sole basis of the text in Yāqūt, which is full of errors (in particular confusing Yaḥyā b. al-Ḥakam with Yaḥyā b. Ṣāliḥ). Grabar was right, however, to stress that this revolt found much of its support in the area of former Umayyad "desert castles," which probably points to the presence of Umayyad clients and kinsmen in the area.

69. Returned property: *TMD* 54:121. The interrogation at al-Mizza: *MTMD* 3:61 Elsewhere, 'Abd Allāh compared the feats of Ibn Bayhas to those of his father Ṭāhir b. al-Ḥusayn (*MTMD* 3:320). Ṣadaqa b. 'Uthmān: chapter 5. His advice: *TMD* 24:28, 37:374.

70. The last time was in 294/906, when a man claimed to be the Sufyānī, but he was quickly subdued. It was alleged that he had gone insane (Ṭabarī 3:2277).

71. Despite Salibi, *Syria,* 38–39, they do not appear to have been supported by Andalusī agents.

72. Ibn Ṭūlūn at Mu'āwiya's tomb: *BṬ* 2:829.

CHAPTER FIVE

1. E.g., R. Dozy, *Histoire des musulmans d'Espagne* (Leiden: E. J. Brill, 1861), 1:70–84.

2. Shaban, *Islamic History,* 1: passim, esp. 120–22. See Patricia Crone, "Were the Qays and Yemen of the Umayyad Period Political Parties?" *Der Islam* 71 (1994): 2–5, for the various explanations that have been posited for Umayyad tribal conflict.

3. Crone, *Slaves,* an interpretation that has informed most of the following discussion. A more "user-friendly" restatement of her fundamental points can be found in Crone, "Qays and Yemen," 1–57, esp. 42–57. On the confusing course of Umayyad tribal politics, see also the clarifying statement of Ella Landau-Tasseron, "The Waning of the Umayyads: Notes on Ṭabarī's History Translated, vol. XXVI," *Der Islam* 59 (1992): 81–109, esp. 81–84; Bonner, *Aristocratic Violence,* 3–6.

4. Crone, *Slaves,* 40. See especially Crone's list of the Marwānid subgovernors of Syria, 124–29.

5. On the crisscrossing of genealogical categories in the formation of

factions, see Landau-Tasseron, "Waning," 82–83. Note especially the case of the "northern" confederation of Rabī'a, which joined with Yaman in the eastern provinces, yet sided with Qays in the Jazīra.

6. Crone, *Slaves,* 30–32, cites the clearest example of this situation, during the Third Civil War, when the tribally Yamanī *ashrāf* of Syria appeared as opponents of Yazīd III's Yamaniyya faction, and became instead legitimist supporters of the reigning Umayyad caliph, Walīd II.

7. Unless otherwise noted, the following discussion of the Third Civil War is based on Ṭabarī 2:1825–34; Julius Wellhausen, *The Arab Kingdom and Its Fall,* trans. M. G. Weir (Calcutta: University of Calcutta, 1927), 350–69; Crone, *Slaves,* 46–48; G. R. Hawting, *The First Dynasty of Islam,* (Carbondale: Southern Illinois University Press, 1987), 90–103.

8. Crone, *Slaves,* 45.

9. On the varying relationships of the old *ashrāf* of Syria to the Third Civil War and factional politics in general, see the family histories encapsulated in Crone, *Slaves,* Appendix I, and below.

10. Especially those of Damascus and the villages of the Ghūṭa. On the precise makeup of Yazīd III's Yamaniyya, which included a few "northerners" and plenty of non-Syrians, see Josef van Ess, "Les Qadarites et la Ġailānīya de Yazīd III," *SI* 41 (1970): 269–86; and especially Crone, *Slaves,* 154–64. Ṭabarī 2:1791–92 mentions the following villages in the vicinity of Damascus as supplying men for the Yamaniyya: al-Mizza, Dārayyā, Dūma, Ḥarastā, Dayr al-Murrān, al-Arza, Saṭrā, al-Ḥadītha, and Dayr Zakkā.

11. On the rebellion in Ḥimṣ, see Ṭabarī 2:1826–31; see Balādhurī, *Ansāb* MS, 2:342 with differences in details. The rebels' preoccupation with stipends shows that with the *ahl Ḥimṣ* of the sources we are dealing here with the local *jund* and not just the "populace," as Crone renders it in *Slaves,* 97, or the "people" as Carole Hillebrand renders it in Ṭabarī, *History,* 26:184–89. On Abū Muḥammad al-Sufyānī, see chapter 4. On the *ashrāf,* see Crone, *Slaves,* 97, 99, 101–2.

12. Ṭabarī 2:1831–34. In the case of the troops of Filasṭīn, they chose a son of the Umayyad caliph Sulaymān, whose family had extensive properties in the *jund,* and had founded the city of al-Ramla. Here, as elsewhere, patronage ties are at issue: according to Ṭabarī 2:1831, "the troops of Filasṭīn liked them because of the protection that they extended to them (*li-jiwārihim*)." On the *ashrāf,* see Crone, *Slaves,* 99–101.

13. On the delinquent career of Thābit (an "unprincipled scoundrel," according to D. C. Dennett, "Marwān ibn Muḥammad: The Passing of the Umayyad Caliphate" [Ph.D. diss., Harvard University, 1939], 225), see Ṭabarī 2:1716, 1871; Crone, *Slaves,* 161. But note that, despite Crone,

Thābit is in fact a descendant of the Yamanī Filasṭīnī *sharīf* Rawḥ b. Zinbā‘: see his genealogy in Balādhurī, Ansāb MS, 2:352. On the family of Rawḥ b. Zinbā‘, see Crone, Slaves, 99–101.

14. On Thābit's mutiny, see Ṭabarī 2:1872–73; Ya‘qūbī, *Ta'rīkh,* 2:403; Balādhurī, *Ansāb* MS, 2:347–48; Ibn al-Athīr, *Kāmil,* 5:309–10; Dennett, "Marwān ibn Muḥammad," 224–26.

15. On the family of these two, see Crone, Slaves, 108–9. On the *wujūh Qays* that join Marwān, see Khalīfa, *Ta'rīkh,* 2:391, where Abū al-Ward is incorrectly made a son of al-Hudhayl b. Zufar, like al-Wathīq.

16. On Marwān's march into Syria in general, see Ṭabarī 2:1876–79; Balādhurī, *Ansāb* MS, 2:348; Ya‘qūbī, *Ta'rīkh,* 2:403; Khalīfa, *Ta'rīkh,* 2:391–93; Agapius, *'Unwān,* 513–15; Dennett, "Marwān ibn Muḥammad," 226–29. On the battle at ‘Ayn al-Jarr, or ‘Anjar, and the death of the sons of al-Walīd II, see Ṭabarī 2:1876–79; Balādhurī, *Ansāb* MS, 2:348–49; Hawting, *First Dynasty,* 97. On Marwān's accession: Ṭabarī 2:1890–92, where the *ru'ūs ahl Ḥimṣ* give allegiance; Balādhurī, *Ansāb* MS, 2:350; Azdī, *Mawṣil,* 62–63 (where the *wujūh ahl Dimashq* do the same), 64–65; Ya‘qūbī, *Ta'rīkh,* 2:404–5; Agapius, *'Unwān,* 514–15, stresses Marwān's retributions against the murderers of al-Walīd, as does Theophanes, *Chronographia,* 419/580, and Dīnawarī, *Akhbār,* 350; Dennett, "Marwān ibn Muḥammad," 230–37.

17. Kawthar b. al-Aswad al-Ghanawī was the head of Marwān's *shurṭa,* and acted as Marwān's governor of *jund* Dimashq: Ṭabarī 2:1910; *TMD* 50:263–64. His son, ‘Abd al-Malik b. Kawthar, governed *jund* Qinnasrīn, the traditional enclave of the Qaysiyya: *ZḤ* 1:50.

18. Crone, "Qays and Yemen," passim.

19. Ṭabarī 2:1892; Balādhurī, *Ansāb* MS, 2:350.

20. Following Crone, *Slaves,* 172; note also the corrected form of his *nisba* given there. Crone refers to him as "enigmatic": although tribally Yamanī, he appears to be factionally Qaysī, supporting Marwān II against Yamanī revolts later in his reign (see below). Then again, he is also said to have sided against Marwān. He may (or may not) have been a member of the Damascene sharīfal (and Yamanī) family of Ziml al-Saksakī as well: Crone, *Slaves,* 103–4.

21. Psuedo-Dionysios, 190/176 and (perhaps using the same source) Michael the Syrian, 464/2:505, explicitly link the subsequent unrest in Syria to Marwān's move to Ḥarrān. See also Dennett, "Marwān ibn Muḥammad," 235–39.

22. On the revolts in Syria under Marwān II, see Ṭabarī 2:1892–97; Khalīfa, *Ta'rīkh,* 2:393–94; Balādhurī, *Ansāb* MS, 2:351–52; Ya‘qūbī, *Ta'rīkh,* 2:404–7; Agapius, *'Unwān,* 515–17; Ibn al-Athīr, *Kāmil,* 5:328–30;

Dennett, "Marwān ibn Muḥammad," 239–42; Hawting, *First Dynasty,* 98–99.

23. Rumāḥis b. 'Abd al-'Azīz al-Kinānī: Ṭabarī 2:1895; Crone, *Slaves,* 170–71.

24. On Sulaymān's revolt, see Ṭabarī 2:1907–12; Agapius, *'Unwān,* 517–19; Balādhurī, *Ansāb* MS, 2:353–55; *FHA* 1:158–59; Dennett, "Marwān ibn Muḥammad," 242–46; Hawting, *First Dynasty,* 99. Agapius, *'Unwān,* 518, states that "the army of Homs revolted against Marwān, killing 'Abd Allāh, their governor, and they blocked up the breach that Marwān had made in their citadel." This 'Abd Allāh must be the (probably Yamanī) 'Abd Allāh b. Shajara al-Kindī, whom the *jund* had elected as their governor in 127/745 (see above). Evidently, the army now found fault with him, despite his previous relationship with them. Agapius is the only source that mentions the activities in Filasṭīn and Dimashq associated with Sulaymān's revolt. Theophanes, *Chronographia,* 422/584, also alludes to revolts and retribution at Heliopolis (Baalbek) and Jerusalem.

25. Ṭabarī 3:45–46; Agapius, *'Unwān,* 527; Azdī, *Mawṣil,* 134–35; *FHA* 1:203; *TMD* 37:423–25, where the population of Damascus is described as divided between Yaman and Qays, and between partisans of the Banū Umayya and the Banū Hāshim.

26. On the importance of Abū Muslim's early factional policies in Khurāsān and their implications, see Khalid Yahya Blankinship, "The Tribal Factor in the 'Abbāsid Revolution: The Betrayal of the Imam Ibrāhīm b. Muḥammad," *JAOS* 100 (1988): 589–603.

27. Ṭabarī 3:52: *fa-bāya'ahu abū al-ward wa-dakhala fīmā dakhala fīhi junduhu*. Of course, Abū al-Ward would himself later be involved in an Umayyad legitimist revolt (see chapter 4).

28. On these early alternatives to 'Abbāsid rule, see chapter 4.

29. On this event, see Moscati, "Massacre"; 'Abbās, *Bilād al-shām,* 12–14.

30. On Ḥabīb and the initial stages of his revolt, see Ṭabarī 3:55–56; Ibn al-Athīr, *Kāmil,* 5:432; Crone, *Slaves,* 167. It is most likely Ḥabīb's activities that Theophanes describes when he mentions a rebellion of "Kaisinoi in Arabia" (Theophanes, *Chronographia,* 427/590). The statement in Ya'qūbī, *Ta'rīkh,* 2:428, that Ḥabīb supported an Umayyad pretender (*wa-naṣṣaba rajulan min banī umayya*), while plausible given the pattern of other revolts at this time (see chapter 4), is otherwise unattested.

31. Ṭabarī 3:56 states: *wa-kāna sabab tabyīḍihi al-khawf 'alā nafsihi wa-qawmihi*. 'Abbās, *Bilād al-shām,* 117 does not understand what the source of Ḥabīb's fear is.

32. On the revolt of Abū Muḥammad al-Sufyānī, see chapter 4.

33. On Ibn Surāqa, see chapter 3.

34. Balādhurī, *Ansāb* MS, 2:394–95, where Ibn Surāqa is explicitly named as a commander sent with 'Abd al-Ḥamīd b. Ribʿī; *TMD* 34:66–67. Note the speech attributed to the deserting Yamanī troops in the *Ansāb*: "We are not about to kill our brothers (*lam nakun li-nuqātil ikhwatanā*)!" 'Abbās, *Bilād al-shām,* 17, 19 does not discuss this Yaman-Qays cooperation.

35. The fullest account of the joint revolt of Ḥabīb and Ibn Surāqa is Balādhurī, *Ansāb* MS 2:394–95. Condensed accounts with added detail can be found in Ṭabarī 3:53, 54; Azdī, *Mawṣil,* 144; *Chronicon ad annum Christi 1234 pertinens,* ed. J.-B. Chabot, 2 vols. *CSCO* 18, 32, Scriptores Syri 36, 37 (Paris: L. Durbecq, 1920), 333/260.

36. Azdī, *Mawṣil,* 144: *innakum wa-ikhwatakum min rabīʿa kuntum bi-khurāsān shīʿatanā wa-anṣāranā wa-antum dafaʿatum ilaynā madīnat dimashq wa-qataltum al-walīd ibn muʿāwiya wa-antum minnā wa-bikum qawām amrinā.* This is echoed in the wording of 'Abd Allāh's appeal in Balādhurī, *Ansāb* MS, 2:395 (*innakum anṣārunā mudh kānat hādhihi al-daʿwa*).

37. In *TMD* 26:79, however, an allusion is made to Ḥabīb's later arrest and capture at the hands of his fellow tribesman Riyāḥ b. 'Uthmān al-Murrī, then governor of the *jund* of Dimashq for Ṣāliḥ b. 'Alī.

38. On 'Abd Allāh b. 'Alī's revolt, and the role of Syrian *ashrāf* and factional leaders in it, see chapter 3.

39. However, the threat of rebellion was still there, most notably in the 'Alid revolt of Muḥammad b. 'Abd Allāh al-Nafs al-Zakiyya. Riyāḥ b. 'Uthmān al-Murrī, onetime governor of Dimashq, is said to have warned al-Manṣūr of the risks if the Syrian troops took up Muḥammad b. 'Abd Allāh's cause (Ṭabarī 3:178). Muḥammad is also said to have tried to raise support in Syria, but to no avail (Ṭabarī 3:215–16; but see 231, where Muḥammad claims that "the troops of Syria, Iraq, and Khurāsān have already put on white [for my cause]"). References to Syrian rebels in the reign of al-Manṣūr (Ṭabarī 3:436–37) and al-Mahdī (Ṭabarī 3:536) appear to be didactic tales. See also the litany of Qaysī complaints against al-Manṣūr, including a Yamanī vision of early Islamic history, in Azdī, *Mawṣil,* 218–19.

40. The statement in Theophanes, *Chronographia,* 451/660, that "Thumamas established himself at Dabekon (i.e., Dābiq, in north Syria) and raised a rebellion" in 777 makes no sense in light of his subsequent depiction of Thumāma as leading campaigns on the frontier in cooperation with al-Mahdī, and would seem to be a misunderstanding, as Mango sug-

gests. This "Thumamas, son of Baka" is no doubt the Qinnasrīnī *sharīf* Thumāma b. al-Walīd b. al-Qa'qā', on whom see Crone, *Slaves,* 105–6.

41. The source is Ṭabarī; the context, the revolt of al-Nafs al-Zakiyya: Ṭabarī 3:215–16.

42. On the rise of the Banū Ṣāliḥ in Syria, see chapter 3.

43. 'Aẓīmī, *Ḥalab,* 228: *wa-aḥraqa ahl dimashq al-dafātir wa-waliyahā ma'yūf wa-'azala 'anhā ibrāhīm ibn 'abd al-wahhāb.* On Ibrāhīm, the ousted governor, see chapter 3. On Ma'yūf: Ṭabarī 3:371 385, 568; Azdī, *Mawṣil,* 62; 'Aẓīmī, *Ḥalab,* 226, 227, 228; *TMD* 59:444–46. His name is often misread, compare al-Azdī's Ma'tūq (*Mawṣil,* 216) and Michael the Syrian's Malshūf (483/III:8).

44. See Salibi, *Syria,* 38, who has Syrians united against the 'Abbāsids.

45. Crone, "Qays and Yemen," 52.

46. For the assumption that it did, see Omar, *Caliphate,* 94; yet elsewhere, Omar is careful to note the mixed tribal background of the Khurāsānī following of the Hāshimiyya. See also M. A. Shaban, in *The 'Abbāsid Revolution* (Cambridge: Cambridge University Press, 1970), 135–37, and *Islamic History,* 1:165–79.

47. See Appendixes A and B.

48. On the revolt of Abū al-Haydhām, see below. On his family history, see Crone, *Slaves,* 98. Other Syrians: 'Īsā b. 'Amr al-Sakūnī (al-Baṣra in 143/760 and 152/769: Crone, *Slaves,* 99); Riyāḥ b. 'Uthmān al-Murrī (Medina in 144/761: Ya'qūbī, *Ta'rīkh,* 2:451; Ṭabarī 3:143); Rajā' b. Sallām b. Rawḥ al-Judhāmī (Yemen for al-Mahdī: Ya'qūbī, *Ta'rīkh,* 2:481); Mālik b. Dalham al-Kalbī (Egypt in 192/807: Kindī, *Wulāt,* 144ff.) certainly sounds Syrian. The head of his guard was Ḥimṣī, at least.

49. Yazīd in north Africa: Ya'qūbī, *Ta'rīkh,* 2:465; Abū Bakr b. al-Qūṭiyya al-Qurṭubī, *Ta'rīkh iftitāḥ al-andalus,* ed. A. al-Ṭabāṭabā' (Beirut: n.p., 1958), 41. Tammām b. Murra: Ya'qūbī, *Ta'rīkh,* 2:497; Aḥmad b. 'Idhārī al-Marākushī, *Kitāb al-bayān al-mughrib,* ed. G. S. Colin and E. Lévi-Provençal (Leiden: E. J. Brill, 1948–1951), 1:190.

50. Syrian troops outside Syria: some fought in Armenia and Azerbaijan, but this is just an extension of their role on the Syro-Jazīran frontier. Al-Manṣūr used them (Ya'qūbī, *Ta'rīkh,* 2:446) and so did al-Rashīd (ibid, 2:516). Other Syrian troops were used in al-Baṣra, fighting against the 'Alid rebel Ibrāhīm b. 'Abd Allāh in 145/762 (Ṭabarī, 3:292, 305) and in Egypt, fighting against, of all things, an Umayyad legitimist. But they arrived in the retinue of the governor al-Faḍl b. Ṣāliḥ, whom one would expect to find amid Syrians anyway (Kindī, *Wulāt,* 129).

51. Dimashq: under al-Saffāh, there were three Syrian deputy governors. They were: ʻUmar b. Shurayḥ al-Ḥaḍramī (*TMD* 45:79), Ibn Surāqa (Crone, *Slaves,* 129), and Riyāḥ b. ʻUthmān al-Murrī (see note 39 above); al-Manṣūr appointed one Syrian as governor of Dimashq, Yazīd b. Rawḥ al-Lakhmī (*TMD* 65:176–77). The de facto Syrian governors during the Fourth Civil War were Ibn Bayhas and Ṣadaqa b. ʻUthmān. On Ibn Bayhas, see chapter 4. On Ṣadaqa, see *TMD* 37:374. The two Syrian governors of 160/776 were Maʻyūf b. Yaḥyā (see above) and al-Ḥārith b. ʻAbd al-Raḥmān (see below), both Yamanīs. It is perhaps noteworthy that in the very same year of 160/776, a member of the Yamanī *ashrāf* of Ḥimṣ was named governor there. This was Abū Thawr b. ʻĪsā b. ʻAmr al-Sakūnī, who was replaced in 161/777 (ʻAẓīmī, *Ḥalab,* 228; Crone, *Slaves,* 99). Qinnasrīn: Al-Manṣūr appointed Zufar b. ʻĀṣim (Crone, *Slaves,* 166), but he was the only Syrian except for Yazīd b. Mazyad al-Shaybānī (Crone, *Slaves,* 169), a creature of the Fourth Civil War.

52. Campaign of 136/753: see chapter 3; campaign of 190/806: Ṭabarī 3:708ff., Azdī, *Mawṣil,* 309. Others: 138/755 (Yaʻqūbī, *Ta'rīkh,* 2:470), 141/758 or 142/759 (Balādhurī, *Futūḥ,* 168); 162/778 (ibid., 169); 169/785 (ibid., 190); 218/833 (Ṭabarī 3:1164). Occasionally, the *ahl al-thughūr* are specified: Azdī, *Mawṣil,* 274; Khalīfa, *Ta'rīkh,* 732.

53. Al-Ḥārith: Yaʻqūb b. Sufyān al-Fasawī, *Kitāb al-maʻrifa wa-al-ta'rīkh,* ed. Akram Ḍiyā' al-ʻUmarī, 3 vols. (Baghdad: Ri'āsat dīwān al-awqāf, 1974–76), 1:116; *TMD* 11:450. Ibn Hubayra: Ṭabarī 3:709. Other Syrian commanders: Naḍr b. Yarīm in 133/751 (Khalīfa, *Ta'rīkh,* 626; Crone, *Slaves,* 94–95); Mālik b. Adham al-Bāhilī in 142/759 (Balādhurī, *Futūḥ,* 168; Crone, *Slaves,* 168–69); Maʻyūf b. Yaḥyā al-Ḥajūrī in 153/770, 158/774, 169/785 (Ṭabarī 3:371); Zufar b. ʻĀṣim al-Hilālī in 156–57/772 (Azdī, *Mawṣil,* 225; Yaʻqūbī, *Ta'rīkh,* 2:570; Crone, *Slaves,* 166); Thumāma b. al-Walīd al-ʻAbsī in 160 or 161/777 and 166/782 (Yaʻqūbī, *Ta'rīkh,* 2:486; *TMD* 11:450); Ḥumayd b. Maʻyūf in 189/805 and 190/806 by sea (ibid., 2:523).

54. Bligh-Abramski, "Evolution," 226–43, esp. 230–32. But many of Bligh-Abramski's *ashrāf* are Iraqis. See the more thorough study by Elad, "Aspects," 89–132. Other examples of Marwānid generals among the *ṣaḥāba*: Crone, *Slaves,* 67 n. 489, citing a few of "old" sharīfal descent, too.

55. On the demilitarization of the Syrian armies and the end of the *ashrāf,* see below.

56. For a contemporary ʻAbbāsid-era example of Syrian families that included administrators, soldiers, and scholars in their ranks, see Cobb, "Scholars and Society". For a yet more relevant example, one might note the Qaysī *sharīf* Abū al-Haydhām al-Murrī (see below), whose sons included young men who fought side by side with him in his revolt, but also Mūsā b. ʻĀmir (*TMD* 60:436–40), a scholar of some minor importance.

57. Various sources place Abū al-Haydhām's revolt at different times. Ṭabarī 3:624–27, and Michael the Syrian 483/3:8, for example, place it in the year 176/792 (=Michael's A. G. 1104). Yet the account of al-Madā'inī described below is very explicit about the course of events, all of which take place within the year 177/793. Perhaps al-Ṭabarī and Michael are referring to the "prelude" to Abū al-Haydhām's revolt proper, eventually settled by Ibrāhīm b. Sāliḥ. On this prelude, see below.

58. A good idea of the geographical range of the revolt can be obtained from the list of toponyms that occur in Madā'inī's account, compiled by 'Abbās in *Bilād al-shām,* appendix 4, 228–29.

59. *TMD* 26:62–87. Ibn 'Asākir's entry also includes some Damascene accounts of the revolt excerpted by Abū al-Ḥusayn al-Rāzī. Ibn al-Athīr, *Kāmil,* 6:127–33 merely summarizes Madā'inī's account. See also Thierry Bianquis, "Deux révoltes bédouines en Syrie méridionale au Moyen-Age," in *The Third International Conference on Bilad al-Sham* . . . (Amman: Lajnat ta'rīkh bilād al-shām, 1984). The most thorough discussion of the revolt to date is 'Abbās, *Bilād al-shām,* 41–48, but for an illuminating study of the topographical data that emerge from the accounts of this revolt, see Alexandrine Guérin, "Les territoires de la ville de Damas à la période abbasside," to be published in the proceedings of the "Table Ronde:Villes syriennes," held at the Institut Français des Études Arabes in 1999. For a detailed consideration of the historiographical value of Ibn 'Asākir's accounts of this revolt, see Cobb, "Community versus Contention."

60. *TMD* 26:65–66. See 64–65, where it is stated that the revolt began with the theft of a melon from a Judhāmī/Yamanī in the Ḥawrān. 'Abbās, *Bilād al-shām,* 42, is uncritical of Madā'inī's account, except in noting its Qaysī bias. This prelude may be reflected in the other sources that place the revolt in the year 176/792; the *'aṣabiyya* in Syria reported for 174/790 may also be related (Ṭabarī 3:609).

61. *TMD* 26:66. Contrary to Sourdel's hypothesis, the revolt was not religiously motivated (Sourdel, "La Syrie," 170–71).

62. *TMD* 40:4.

63. *TMD* 26:66. In al-Madā'inī's account, Abū al-Haydhām's murdered relative is Kulayb b. 'Umar b. al-Junayd b. 'Abd al-Raḥmān, a second paternal cousin once removed.

64. On Ibrāhim and his ancestors, see Crone, *Slaves,* 175. Strangely, no real motive is given for Isḥāq's desire to see (arrest?) Abū al-Haydhām, nor is his reason for ignoring Abū al-Haydhām when he finally did arrive.

65. *TMD* 26:67–68. Ibn Ghawth is earlier (*TMD* 26:66) called "al-Haytham b. 'Awf," from Kinda, and is referred to as the governor's *kātib.* However, elsewhere (*TMD* 26:81), Ibn Ghawth is described as *'alā*

shurṭatihi, i.e., in charge of the governor's guard. This makes sense in light of his connection with the local *jund.*

66. 'Āṣim b. Muḥammad b. Sa'īd b. Baḥdal al-Kalbī was a confidant of al-Faḍl b. Ṣāliḥ when he served as governor of Dimashq, and was a member of a family whose glory began with Mu'āwiya: *TMD* 26:69; Crone, *Slaves,* 93–94. Of the "Banū Ma'yūf" that appear frequently here, only two are named explicitly, namely Aḥmad and Yazīd: *TMD* 26:70; their father was the hero of the revolt of 160/776 (see above), and a prominent commander in the Syrian army under the early 'Abbāsids. On the family of Ziml al-Saksakī, see Crone, *Slaves,* 103–4. The person described in the revolt is a daughter of al-Ḍaḥḥāk b. Ziml (*TMD* 26:72, where "Riml" should be "Ziml").

67. The tribal affiliation of al-Ḥārith b. 'Abd al-Raḥman and his kin is a source of confusion: is it Ḥarashī/Qays, or Jurashī/Yaman? While most editors make it Ḥarashī, it makes better sense as Jurashī, a more common Syrian *nisba,* especially given the presence of the family here among the Yamaniyya: *TMD* 26:70 (where it is Ḥarashī). Al-Ḥārith's behavior in the chronicles certainly sounds Yamanī: in 132/749, he attacked Marwān II from Damascus as the latter fled the battle of the Zāb, and he was one of the first Damascenes to take up the 'Abbāsid colors (Azdī, *Mawṣil,* 136). He led the summer campaign against the Byzantines in 135/752 (al-Fasawī, 116), and was the spokesman in the delegation of Syrians in 136/753 that sought Manṣūr's clemency after 'Abd Allāh b. 'Alī's revolt failed (Ṭabarī 3:419; Balādhurī, *Ansāb,* 3:193; *TMD* 11:448–50). One last encounters him as governor of Dimashq in 160/776 ('Aẓīmī, *Ḥalab,* 228).

68. *TMD* 26:70.

69. On Ḥabīb b. Murra, see above. The bulk of Abū al-Haydhām's companions are named in *TMD* 26:69. Note also the presence of a "Bayhas" on page 70, who is no doubt a member of the Kilābī/Qaysī family of Kardam b. Bayhas, and probably the father of the Ibn Bayhas al-Kilābī mentioned in events during and after the Fourth Civil War. On this family, see Crone, *Slaves,* 151.

70. On the first phase of the revolt, see *TMD* 26:64–73. The putative text of Abū al-Haydhām's *amān*-guarantee is given on page 73 of the volume.

71. *TMD* 26:73–75. The Umayyad notable was 'Abd al-'Azīz al-'Umarī, a descendant of the caliph 'Umar II.

72. *TMD* 26:75–77. On Sindī b. Shāhak, see chapter 2.

73. *TMD* 26:77. On the Khurāsānī commander Harthama b. A'yan, see chapter 2. Once replaced, Isḥāq b. Ibrāhīm left for Ḥimṣ (*MTMD* 4:266–67).

74. *TMD* 26:77–78. Ibn Riyāḥ was the son of the Qaysī general Riyāḥ b. 'Uthmān b. Ḥayyān al-Murrī who was an adviser to al-Manṣūr and had served as governor of Dimashq under Ṣāliḥ b. 'Alī. He was governor of Medina during the revolt of Muḥammad b. 'Abd Allāh al-Nafs al-Zakiyya, and was killed there in 145 (Ṭabarī 3:143, 162–67, 242). Ya'qūbī, *Ta'rīkh,* 2:495 states that al-Rashīd was planning to march against Abū al-Haydhām himself, but when it was reported that he had been killed, he campaigned on the frontier instead. Note that al-Madā'inī's account mentions that Ibn Riyāḥ's forces sought refuge in the Roman amphitheatre of Bostra (*mal'ab al-rūm*), which is described as "a fortress in the city of Bostra (*ḥiṣn fī madīnat buṣrā*)."

75. *TMD* 26:78–80. The act of treachery that Abū al-Haydhām ascribes to Ibn Riyāḥ's father is of some relevance to this study: while serving as governor of the *jund* of Dimashq for Ṣāliḥ b. 'Alī, Riyāḥ b. 'Uthmān had evidently turned in the rebel (and fellow Murrī) Ḥabīb b. Murra, who had gone into hiding in 132/750 (see above), just as Ibn Riyāḥ tried to do to Abū al-Haydhām (*TMD* 26:79). The exact circumstances of the end of Abū al-Haydhām is a subject of some confusion. See the various contradictory statements assembled and discussed in 'Abbās, *Bilād al-shām,* 47. His date of death: *TMD* 26:87.

76. *TMD* 26:62–63.

77. Al-Marzubānī pointed out that some people attributed the verses to someone other than Abū al-Haydhām (although he himself preferred to think of them as Abū al-Haydhām's): *TMD* 26:63.

78. Lewond (Ghevond), *History of Lewond the Eminent Vardapet of the Armenians,* trans. Zaven Arzoumanian (Wynnewood, PA: SS Sahag & Mesrob Armenian Church, 1982), 142–44; Balādhurī, *Ansāb* MS, 2:1092; *Ta'rīkh-i sīstān,* ed. Malik al-Shu'arā' Bahār (Tehran: Muḥammad Ramāānī, 1935), 152–53; *MTMD* 16:275–77. For the context of 'Uthmān's career in Sīstān, see C. E. Bosworth, Sīstān *Under the Arabs, From the Islamic Conquest to the Rise of the Ṣaffārids (30–250/651–864)* (Rome: Istituto Italiano per il Medio ed Estremo Oriente, 1968), 85–86.

79. Muhammad b. 'Imrān al-Mārzubānī, *Mu'jam al-shu'arā',* ed. Fritz Krenkow (Cairo: Maktabat al-Quds, 1926), 256.

80. 'Abbās, *Bilād al-shām,* 45, n. 1, was not aware of the dating of 'Uthmān's removal of office, nor that the man who was responsible for his downfall was Yamanī.

81. As did Abū al-Haydhām himself, according to *TMD* 26:62. On Abū al-Haydhām's family history, see Crone, *Slaves,* 98. Note that according to *Ta'rīkh-i sīstān,* 152–53, 'Uthmān's son Ṣadaqa (a future governor of Dimashq, see chapter 4) served as a commander under his father.

82. *TMD* 43:28. On the revolt of Abū al-'Umayṭir al-Sufyānī, see chapter 4.

83. A *da'wā jāhiliyya* is predicted for the reign of the fifth 'Abbāsid caliph in *TMD* 43:28, 62:204–5. Other topographical references in the "prophecy" (to Mizza, to a breach in the city wall) make it clear that Abū al-Haydhām's revolt is intended. Another account tells of an anonymous Damascene ascetic who, during Abū al-Haydhām's revolt, had a dream that he saw three spears imbedded in the wall of the Umayyad mosque bearing messages which urged the populace to repent (*TMD* 68:235).

84. He is 'Abd al-Raḥmān b. Bishr b. 'Abd al-Waḥīd al-Naṣrī, of the Banū Naṣr b. Mu'āwiya: *TMD* 34:239–40.

85. On the arrival of Mūsā b. Yaḥyā and the end of the revolt, see Ṭabarī 3:624–26; *ZḤ* 1:62.

86. Ṭabarī 3:639–41; Ya'qūbī, *Ta'rīkh,* 2:495; Azdī, *Mawṣil,* 289; Jahshiyārī, *Wuzarā',* 208–9. The contemporary account is that of Stephen of Mar Saba (d. 807), *Exēgēsis ētoi Martyrion tōn Hagiōn Paterōn* . . . ed. A. Papadopoulou-Kerameos in *Pravoslavnĭ Palestinskĭ sbornik,* vol. 19 (St. Petersburg, 1907), 1–41, esp. 1–4. Latin translation in *Acta Sanctorum Bollandiana,* Martii, 3:167–71. See also Robert Schick, *The Christian Communities of Palestine from Byzantine to Islamic Rule* (Princeton: Darwin Press, 1995), 92–93. 'Abbās, *Bilād al-shām,* 48–49, was not aware of the Palestinian connection of this conflict, but he also sees this as a continuation of Abū al-Haydhām's revolt, and even muses that he may have taken part. On the Zawāqīl and the Ṣa'ālīk, see chapter 6.

87. Ṭabarī 3:688; *TMD* 23:88–89.

88. Ya'qūbī, *Ta'rīkh,* 2:519. Of course, al-Rashīd might have already been on his way to the frontier when the revolt in Ḥimṣ broke out: the text is not specific.

89. On 'Abd al-Malik's mission, see chapter 3.

90. Theophanes, *Chronographia,* 484/665: "For this reason [i.e., al-Amīn's war with al-Ma'mūn] the inhabitants of Syria, Egypt, and Libya were divided into different principalities and destroyed the common weal as well as each other."

91. On Abū al-'Umayṭir's rebellion, see chapter 4.

92. Ya'qūbī, *Ta'rīkh,* 2:541; Crone, *Slaves,* 181–83.

93. 'Abbās: Ya'qūbī, *Ta'rīkh,* 2:541; *FHA* 1:363 (where he is at Qinnasrīn); Michael the Syrian, 495/3:27, 499/3:36, 38; Crone, *Slaves,* 166.

94. 'Uthmān b. Thumāma: Ya'qūbī, *Ta'rīkh,* 2:541 ("al-Ḥiyār and its dependent territories in the subdistricts of Qinnasrīn." Note that this is

the preferred reading over "the Ḥijāz" as suggested in al-Ya'qūbī, *Mushākalat al-nās li-zamānihim,* ed. William Millward [Beirut: Dār al-kitāb al-jadīd, 1962], 29); *FHA* 1:363 (Ḥimṣ); Michael the Syrian, 494/3:27 (Qinnasrīn, Antioch, Apamea), 500/3:36 (his friendship with Dionysios of Tell Mahrē), 507/3:49 (Coele-Syria, Ḥimṣ, Phonecia), 510/3:53 (his surrender); Crone, *Slaves*, 105–6.

95. Aleppo and the Banū Tanūkh: Ya'qūbī, *Ta'rīkh,* 2:541 (where the Ṣāliḥī notable is Ya'qūb b. Ṣāliḥ); Balādhurī, Futūḥ, 145–46; Michael the Syrian, 497/3:31; *BṬ* 1:563. Al-Ḥawārī: Ya'qūbī, *Ta'rīkh*, 2:541 (where he is in control of Ma'arat al-Nu'mān and Tall Mannas); Ya'qūbī, *Mushākalat,* 29 (where he is a rebel at Aleppo, and pardoned). His full genealogy: *BṬ* 6:2987.

96. Ḥimṣ: Ṭabarī 3:776, 795; 'Aẓīmī, *Ḥalab, 238; BṬ* 3:1467. 'Abd Allāh b. al-Simṭ and kin: *MTMD* 10:207–208; Crone, *Slaves,* 101–2. 'Abbās, *Bilād al-shām,* 51, suggests that Isḥāq's bad government is involved in the revolt, but he was unaware of the presence of local notables among the leaders of the revolt.

97. Ya'qūbī, *Ta'rīkh,* 2:541. Some areas of the larger district of Ḥimṣ may have been under the control of 'Uthmān b. Thumāma (see note 94).

98. Theophanes, *Chronographia,* 499/683; on 497/680 he states: "Damascus was occupied by a usurper [this is Abū al-'Umayṭir], Egypt and Africa were divided by two rulers, and another devastated Palestine like a robber." This latter is no doubt a reference to the Zawāqīl chieftain 'Amr b. 'Abd al-'Azīz al-Sulamī, whose activities in Palestine had first attracted Naṣr b. Shabath's notice (Michael the Syrian, 491/3:21). Ibn Sarḥ: Ya'qūbī, *Ta'rīkh,* 2:528, *FHA* 1:363; Gil, *Palestine,* 293; *Sylloge Numorum Arabicorum Tübingen. Palästina IV (Bilād aš-Šām I),* ed. Lutz Ilisch (Berlin: Ernst Wasmuth, 1993), 14, 24 (coins struck in his name, dated AH 200).

99. Other, more obscure local leaders appeared in other areas of Syria. In Shayzar, the Banū Bisṭām; at Hama, Ḥarrāq (?) al-Bahrānī (Ya'qūbī, *Ta'rīkh,* 2:541). Michael the Syrian, 513/3:61, mentions a rebel Ḥasan at Tyre.

100. On the Banū Bayhas, see Crone, *Slaves,* 151. They had also played a role with the Qaysiyya during Abū al-Haydhām's revolt (see above). For details of the revolt of Abū al-'Umayṭir and the role of Ibn Bayhas, see chapter 4.

101. *Chronicum ad annum Domini 846 pertinens,* ed. E. W. Brooks in *Chronica Minora,* II, *CSCO* 3, Scriptores Syri 3 (Louvain: E. J. Peeters, 1903), 238.

102. Ṣadaqa b. 'Uthmān al-Murrī: *TMD* 24:28; Caskel, *Gamharat,* 2:388. Naṣr b. Ḥamza: *TMD* 62:33–34; Crone, *Slaves,* 181–83. He was later

sent as governor of the *thughūr* and *al-'awāṣim* in 231/845 (Ṭabarī 3:1357; *BṬ* 2:759). Al-Ḥasan b. Wahb: *TMD* 56:283ff. He is a mysterious figure, known best in his context as chief scribe and right-hand man for al-Mu'taṣim's vizier, Muḥammad b. al-Zayyāt (Dominique Sourdel, *Le vizirat abbaside de 749 à 936 (132 à 324 de l'Hégire),* 2 vols. [Damascus: Institut Français de Damas, 1960], 1:256 n. 3). 'Abd Allāh b. Ṭāhir's arrival in 210/825 is referred to as *madkhal al-sulṭān* in Abū Zur'a al-Dimashqī, *Ta'rīkh* ed. Shukr Allāh al-Qujānī, 2 vols. (Damascus: Majma' al-lugha al-'arabiyya, 1980), 1:284–85. Some of the rebels in 'Abd Allāh's custody are named in Ṭabarī 3:1098, where "Ibn al-Sarj" is surely the Filasṭīnī *sharīf* Ibn Sarḥ (see above). 'Abd Allāh's activities in Syria are referred to in *BṬ* 3:1187–88.

103. Aḥmad b. Yazīd and Ma'yūf b. Yaḥyā: *TMD* 59:446–47; Ṣafadī, *'Umarā',* 86.

104. On Ma'yūf b. Yaḥyā (the Elder), see above, note 43. Ḥumayd b. Ma'yūf: Ṭabarī 3:709; *TMD* 15:304. The above sequence differs markedly from that of al-Munajjid in Ṣafadī, *'Umarā',* 204. There, Ma'yūf and Ḥumayd fall between Ibn Bayhas and Ṣadaqa. However, Ibn 'Asākir is quite explicit that, although Ibn Bayhas never left Syria until he went to Baghdad with 'Abd Allāh in 210/825, the latter had named Ṣadaqa before leaving for Egypt in 208, and he also replaced Ṣadaqa with Naṣr upon returning to Syria en route to Baghdad. This sequence leaves no room for Ma'yūf and his son, since we are told that they were named by the amīr who came to Syria after Ibn Bayhas' absence (i.e., after he had left with 'Abd Allāh in 210/825). This *amīr* must surely be Naṣr, who may well have needed a local deputy, if he was needed elsewhere.

105. On the details of 'Alī's activities in Damascus, see chapter 3.

106. *TMD* 18:94–96, 67:250; Ibn al-Athīr, *Kāmil,* 6:528. See also 'Abbās, *Bilād al-shām,* 66–67.

107. On the factionalism under Sālim b. Ḥāmid, see *TMD* 20:38–39 (with an identical account in Ibn Taghribirdī, *Nujūm,* 2:286). The event is not precisely dated in any of the medieval sources, yet, oddly, Hitti, citing Ibn 'Asākir, provides it the specific date of 854/5 (*History of Syria,* 542). Note that among the notables fighting with the Yamaniyya against Sālim b. Ḥāmid is an Ibn Bayhas, who is probably of the lesser-known Yamanī family of Bayhas, and not that of the more prominent Qaysī Bayhas. On the confusion bewteen the Qaysī and Yamanī Bayhases, see Crone, *Slaves,* 151.

108. *Ayalon,* "Military Reforms," 22–25. Garrisoning Ṭuwāna: Ṭabarī 3:1111–12.

109. On the revolt of al-Mubarqa', see chapter 6.

110. Dīk al-Jinn al-Ḥimṣī (d. ca. 235/850), *Dīwān,* ed. Aḥmad Maṭlūb and 'Abd Allāh al-Jabūrī (Beirut: Dār al-thiqāfa, 1964), 110–11. The ambiguity of the term *wajh* (meaning "face" as well as "tribal leader") in this poem may not be accidental. Abū al-Faraj al-Iṣfahānī, *Kitāb al-aghānī,* various editors (Cairo: Dār al-kutub al-miṣriyya, 1927–1961), 14:67, citing an earlier work, provides the following unlikely explanation for these verses: "The preacher of the people of Ḥimṣ used to invoke prayers for the Prophet three times [in succession] in his sermon. The people of Ḥimṣ were all of them of Yaman, and none of them was of Muḍar except for three families. So, they broke out in factional fighting over the imām and removed him." The implication here is that the imām's blessing of the Prophet, a Qurashī/Qaysī, did not sit well with the Yamanī majority in the city. Then again, there is evidence for anti-Quraysh sentiment in Ḥimṣ in late Umayyad times: Madelung, "Apocalyptic Prophecies," 151–58.

111. Compare Von Sievers, "Military," 224.

112. On the revolt of al-Mubarqa', see chapter 6. The revolt of 240/854: Ṭabarī 3:1420–21. Note that, once expelled, Abū al-Mughīth went to Hama; the second phase: Ṭabarī 3:1422–24; Ya'qūbī, *Ta'rīkh,* 2:599; 'Aẓīmī, *Ḥalab,* 258. On Abū al-Mughīth's background, see *TMD* 60:388–90, Ibn Taghribirdī, *Nujūm,* 2:215–16. The leaders (*ru'asā'*) of the revolt all appear to be unknowns, and their tribal affiliation is uncertain; they are: Muḥammad b. 'Abd al-Ḥamīd al-Ḥamīdī, al-Qāsim b. Mūsā b. Fū'ūs, and 'Abd al-Malik b. Isḥāq b. 'Umāra. Shaban, *Islamic History,* 2:73, 78 and Gil, *Palestine,* 297, link Christian participation in this revolt to al-Mutawakkil's recent sumptuary laws against religious minorities, but 'Abbās, *Bilād al-shām,* 68 is right to be wary of drawing too direct a link.

113. Ṭabarī 3:1508; Ya'qūbī, *Ta'rīkh,* 2:605. Note that, as in the revolt of 240/854, the expelled governor sought shelter in Hama. Al-Faḍl b. Qārin was the brother of al-Māzār b. Qārin, the Persian prince of Ṭabaristān who capitulated to 'Abbāsid forces in the reign of al-Ma'mūn (Ya'qūbī, *Ta'rīkh,* 2:582; Balādhurī, *Futūḥ,* 339). See also chapter 6.

114. Ṭabarī 3:1533–34; Balādhurī, *Futūḥ,* 134; Ya'qūbī, *Ta'rīkh,* 2:607; 'Aẓīmī, *Ḥalab,* 278.

115. Ya'qūbī, *Ta'rīkh,* 2:607–8. Compare with the account of Ibn al-Muwallad's march through northern Syria in *BṬ* 3:1297. On al-Fuṣayṣ's background, see *BṬ* 1:137, where it is mentioned that a brother of al-Fuṣayṣ al-Tanūkhī controlled the extramural settlement adjacent to Qinnasrīn as late as 271/884. His ancestors had been prominent Qinnasrīnī supporters of the Sufyānid rebel Abū al-'Umayṭir in 195/811 (see chapter 4).

116. 'Abbās, *Bilād al-shām,* 71, speculates that Abū al-Sāj may have conciliated Kalbī leaders with positions as well, but there is no evidence to

actually support this. This was not the last of the conflict at Ḥimṣ: it is most likely the Banū Kalb who were the "nomads (*al-a'rāb*)" who killed Manjūr, the governor of Ḥimṣ, in 260/873 (Ṭabarī 3:1885), and six years later when most of Syria was a Ṭulūnid province, there was probably more than mere murder involved when the populace killed their governor, 'Īsā al-Karkhī (Ṭabarī 3:1939).

CHAPTER SIX

1. On the lower strata of Baghdad during the Fourth Civil War, see Ṭabarī 3:885–89, 895–98; Mas'ūdī, *Murūj,* 6:452–53. See also Simha Sabari, *Mouvements populaires à Bagdad à l'époque 'abbasside, IXe-XIe siècles* (Paris: Librairie d'Amérique et d'Orient, 1981).

2. Ya'qūbī, *Ta'rīkh* 2:494–95 erroneously places the event in the reign of al-Rashīd. See *TMD* 2:278–79; *TMD* 60:351–53; 'Abbās, *Bilād al-shām,* 52–53.

3. *TMD* 60:351: "*wa-qad kāna ahl dimashq thārū bi-manṣūr ibn al-mahdī* [the governor] *marratan ba'da marratin.*"

4. On the Ḥimsī revolts of 248/862 and after, see chapter 5. Most of the information on the crowd's sentiments comes from Ya'qūbī, *Ta'rīkh,* 2:605. Note that the crowd explained their behavior to the new governor by complaining "of the foul way in which [the old governor] treated them (*wa-shakaw qubḥa mā kāna yu'āmiluhum bihi*)." On crucifixion, see Qur'ān 5:33, and Otto Spies, "*Über die Kreuzigung im Islam,*" in *Religion und Religionen. Festschrift für Gustav Mensching zu seinem 65. Geburtstag* (Bonn: Ludwig Röhrscheid, 1967), 143–56.

5. See chapter 5, and especially Ya'qūbī, *Ta'rīkh,* 2:607, and Balādhurī, *Futūḥ,* 134. Von Sievers, 227, has utterly misunderstood this revolt, somehow understanding it to involve an alliance of the governor with the crowd.

6. On rural rebellion in early medieval Europe, see Rodney H. Hilton, *Bond men made free; medieval peasant movements and the English rising of 1381* (New York: Viking Press, 1973); Coptic revolts: Michael C. Dunn, "The Struggle for 'Abbasid Egypt" (Ph.D. diss., Georgetown University, 1975), 163–68; Jazīran Khārijites: Chase F. Robinson, "The Early Islamic History of Mosul" (Ph.D. diss., Harvard University, 1992), 406–14. For other examples of 'Abbāsid rural unrest, see Crone, *Slaves,* 71–72.

7. These are the three papyri from near Lake Hula associated with a tax-survey of Syria in 241/855–56. See Nabia Abbot, "Arabic Papyri of the Reign of Ga'far al-Mutawakkil 'ala-llāh (AH 232–47/AD 847–61), *ZDMG* 92 (1938): 88–135.

8. André Latron, *La vie rurale en Syrie et au Liban: étude d'économie rurale* (Beirut: Institut Français de Damas, 1936); Jacques Weulersse, *Paysans de Syrie et du Proche-Orient* (Paris: Gallimard, 1946); see also the comments of R. Stephen Humphreys in *Islamic History,* 297, 306–307.

9. Crusader Palestine: Joshua Prawer, *Crusader Institutions* (Oxford: Clarendon Press, 1980), 169–87; the Roman Ḥawrān: Pierre Gentelle, "Élements pour une histoire des paysages et du peuplement du Djebel Hauran septentrional," in *Hauran I. Recherches archéologiques sur la Syrie du sud a l'époque hellénistique et romaine, deuxième partie,* edited by J.-M. Dentzer. Bibliothèque Archéologique et Historique, v. 124 (Paris: Paul Geuthner, 1986), 19–62, and François Villeneuve, "L'économie rurale et la vie des campagnes dans le Hauran antique (Ier siècle avant J.-C.-VIe siècle après J.-C." in *ibid.*, 63–136.

10. Most of these regional surveys can be examined in the form of periodic reports published in the *Annual of the Department of Antiquities of Jordan* (most prominently). Some recent syntheses of the findings of various surveys are Pierre-Louis Gatier, "Villages du Proche-Orient protobyzantin (4ème-7ème s.). Étude régionale," in *The Byzantine and Early Islamic Near East II: Land Use and Settlement Patterns,* edited by G. R. D. King and Averil Cameron (Princeton: Darwin Press, 1994), 17–48, and Henry Innes MacAdam, "Settlements and Settlement Patterns in Northern and Central Transjordania, *ca* 550-*ca* 750," in the same volume, 49–94.

11. The Khirbet al-Fâris Project has produced two reports to date: Jeremy Johns, A. M. McQuitty, and R. Falkner, "The Fâris Project: Preliminary Report upon the 1986 and 1988 Seasons," *Levant* 21 (1989): 63–95; A. McQuitty and R. Falkner, "The Fâris Project: Preliminary Report on the 1989, 1990, and 1991 Seasons," *Levant* 25 (1993): 37–62. See also a recent synthetic article by W. Lancaster and F. Lancaster, "Land Use and Population in the Area North of Karak," *Levant* 27 (1995): 103–24. Mention should also be made here of the important ethnoarcheological work of Alexandrine Guérin in the villages and badlands of the Lajā': "Terroirs, territoire et peuplement en Syrie méridionale à la période islamique (VIIe siècle-XVIe siècle)" (Ph.D. thesis, Université Lumière, Lyon 2, 1998).

12. Humphreys, *Islamic History,* 308.

13. On these preconditions discussed in another historical context, see most recently Barkey, *Bandits and Bureaucrats,* 85–90, a discussion of the constraints on peasant rebellion that has greatly informed my own. See also Tilly, *Mobilization,* 125–26. For more on the crucial role of peasant-elite alliances, see also William Brustein, "Class Conflict and Class Collaboration in Regional Rebellions, 1500–1700," *Theory and Society* 14 (1985): 445–68. However, Hilton, *Bond Men Made Free,* 122–25, downplays the importance of peasant-elite alliances.

14. George Rudé, *Ideology and Popular Protest* (New York: Pantheon Books, 1980), 41–54; Hilton, *Bond Men Made Free,* 40–44; Barkey, *Bandits and Bureaucrats,* 91.

15. According to Bulliet's estimates (such as they are), Muslims did not begin to become a statistical majority in Syria until the late third/ninth century, and it was not until the Fāṭimid period that Muslims formed an overwhelming majority of the population. Richard W. Bulliet, *Conversion to Islam in the Medieval Period. An Essay in Quantitative History* (Cambridge, MA: Harvard University Press, 1979), 104–13. For southern Syria, the conclusions of Schick, *Christian Communties,* 139–59, 220–25 tend to corroborate Bulliet's estimates.

16. Many Umayyad estates went to absentee 'Abbāsid princes, and others: Alexandretta (to the family of al-Mahdī, Balādhurī, *Futūḥ,* 148), some *iqṭā'*s allotted to the Banū Rabī' in northern Syria (to al-Ma'mūn, Balādhurī, Futūḥ, 148), Bālis (to Sulaymān b. 'Alī and others, Balādhurī, *Futūḥ,* 151), Qubbāsh, in the Balqā' (to the family of al-Mahdī and others, Balādhurī, *Futūḥ,* 129).

17. Claude Cahen, "Fiscalité, propriété, antagonismes sociaux en Haute-Mésopotamie au temps des premiers Abbassides, d'après Denys de Tell Mahré," *Arabica* 1 (1954): 149–50 notes these abuses in connection with the Jazīran peasantry, and the possible violent results.

18. Of course, not all the *'ulamā'* of Syria were hostile to the 'Abbāsid regime, even the popular ones. See, for example 'Alī b. 'Ayyāsh al-Ḥimṣī (d. 219/834), who was a local holy man (considered to be one of the *abdāl,* the immortal pious heroes of Syria) and was made *qāḍī* of Ḥimṣ by al-Ma'mūn (*MTMD* 7:329), or the cooperative *muḥaddith* Sulaymān b. 'Utba al-Sulamī (d. 185/801), of whom a later scholar said "[He is] trustworthy; he has no faults other than his adherence to the government" (*MTMD* 10:182).

19. It is said, for example, that his funeral procession in Beirut was attended by "Muslims, Jews, Nazarenes, and Copts," *TMD* 20:81.

20. Whether or not he was successful is unknown. The surviving epistles of al-Awzā'ī are conveniently collected in 'Abbās, *Bilād al-shām,* 201–23. See also the discussion of the revolt of Theodore, below.

21. Such was the case in 244/858 when al-Mutawakkil visited Damascus, and the populace (*al-nās*) from all over Syria (*min aqṭār al-ajnād*) complained of the the recent tax-survey, in which the officials involved were accused of pocketing part of the revenues for themselves and of oppressing the weak (*al-ḍu'afā'*). The caliph was moved by their plight and ordered an investigation into the affair (*TMD* 55:19–22. On the visit itself, see now Paul M. Cobb, "Al-Mutawakkil's Damascus: A New 'Abbāsid Capital?" *Journal of Near Eastern Studies,* 58 [1999]: 241–57). In 246/860, the

peasant cultivators of caliphal estates near Nābulus complained (to the caliph's local agent, presumably) of their inability to pay the new *kharāj* of five *dīnārs* a head, and so al-Mutawakkil agreed to let them pay at the old rate of three *dīnārs* (Balādhurī, *Futūḥ*, 158).

22. This would have been true earlier than later in our period. Following Umayyad practice, the *qāḍīs* of Damascus and Syria were almost exclusively local men who would be expected to have some ties to the local populace. But starting in the reign of al-Muʿtaṣim, the *qāḍīs* of Damascus at least were appointed by the caliph from men trained in Iraq, usually in Mālikī or Ḥanafī *fiqh*. Conrad, *Quḍāt,* 759–62.

23. Abū al-Fatḥ, *Annales,* 183–86. The conflict between the Muslims, in which two factions are involved, is plainly a reference to tribal factionalism, and the pillaging of the countryside is almost certainly that associated with the factionalism of 180/796–97, on which, see chapter 5.

24. On the general problems confronting peasants, see Eric R. Wolf, *Peasants* (Englewood Cliffs: Prentice-Hall, 1966), 4–17, and E. J. Hobsbawm, "Peasants and Politics," *Journal of Peasant Studies* 1 (1973): 3–22, esp. 12–13, which is highly critical of the ability of peasants to lead substantive movements alone. See also Patricia Crone, *Pre-Industrial Societies* (Oxford: Blackwell, 1989), 74–77. On peasant flight under al-Rashīd, Abū al-Fatḥ is the most graphic, but see also Balādhurī, *Futūḥ*, 144, 158; *Chronicon 1234,* 2:3/1.

25. Cahen, "Fiscalité," 149–50, shows that, according to the *Zuqnīn Chronicle,* local elites in the Jazīra were expected as a rule to pay the collective taxes of a village to the authorities, and they could also extend "protection" to needy peasants.

26. In the sixth/thirteenth century, that peasant labor could have been largely communal is suggested by Ibn Ḥajjāj's advice *against* allowing peasants to work in large groups, but this may not be applicable to earlier periods (from Ibn Ḥajjāj's *Kitāb al-filāḥa,* cited in Fāliḥ Ḥusayn, *al-Ḥayāt al-zirāʿiyya fī bilād al-shām fī al-ʿaṣr al-umawī,* [Amman: al-jāmiʿa al-urdunniyya, 1978], 76, n. 123).

27. Gil, *Palestine,* 241–42, mentions early Islamic market fairs at Ramla (April 23), Bostra (July 14), ʿAmmān (August 10), Jerusalem (September 15, associated with the *ʿīd al-ṣalīb*), and Adhraʿāt (October 13).

28. Hobsbawm, "Peasants and Politics," 13–14; On millenarianism and peasant revolts, see E. J. Hobsbawm, *Primitive Rebels. Studies in Archaic Forms of Social Movement in the 19th and 20th Centuries* (Manchester: University of Manchester Press, 1959), 57–107, esp. 57–65; Crone, *Pre-Industrial Societies,* 75–76.

29. That the Lebanon Mountains served throughout the ages as a

place of refuge has become something of a truism thanks to the work of Henri Lammens. For a deconstruction of Lammens' idea of the *asile du Liban* and its avatars, see Kamal Salibi, *A House of Many Mansions. The History of Lebanon Reconsidered* (Berkeley and Los Angeles: University of California Press, 1988), 130–50.

30. On the Jarājima in general, see *EI2,* s.v. "Djarādjima" [M. Canard]. To the bibliography listed there should be added Hratz Bartikjan, "Hē lusē tou ainigmatos tōn Mardaitōn," in *Byzantion. Aphieroma stōn Andrea N. Strato / Byzance. Hommage à Andreas Stratos / Byzantium. Tribute to Andreas Stratos,* edited by Zia Stratos (Athens: N. A. Stratou, 1986), 1:17–39, which argues for an Armenian origin for the Mardaites, and Mohsen Zakeri, *Sāsānid Soldiers in Early Muslim Society* (Wiesbaden: Harrassowitz, 1995), 151–64, which argues (unpersuasively) for a Persian origin. On collusion with the Byzantines, see, among others, Balādhurī, *Futūḥ,* 160, 161–62. Their privileges revoked: Balādhurī, *Futūḥ,* 161.

31. The following discussion of the revolt of Bundār/Theodore is based on the accounts in Balādhurī, *Futūḥ,* 162; Theophanes, *Chronographia,* 431/597; *TMD* 18:267–68. Theophanes refers to this rebel as Theodore, and, as 'Abbās, *Bilād al-shām,* 137 notes, it is almost certainly his correct name, as "Bundār" in Arabic might easily be a scribal mistake for an Arabic approximation of the name, e.g., "Taydār" or the like.

32. The most complete version of al-Awzā'ī's letter can be found in the appendix to 'Abbās, *Bilād al-shām,* 219. An extract of the letter, with some variations, is also cited by al-Balādhurī, *Futūḥ,* 162.

33. Secondary accounts of the revolt can be found in Kurd 'Alī, *Khiṭaṭ,* 1:51; Omar, *Caliphate,* 316–17; Salibi, *Syria,* 35–37; Crone, *Slaves,* 71. 'Abbās, *Bilād al-shām,* 136–38, has by far the most complete account to date.

34. On popular kingship and rebellion in Roman Judea, see Richard A. Horsley and John S. Hanson, *Bandits, Prophets, and Messiahs. Popular Movements in the Time of Jesus* (San Francisco: Harper and Row, 1988), 88–135. A more recent point of comparison is the Samaritan revolt of 529, led by the bandit "king" Julian. On this event see Irfan Shahid, *Byzantium and the Arabs in the Sixth Century,* 2 vols. (Washington, DC: Dumbarton Oaks, 1995), 1:82–95, with recent bibliography.

35. Theophanes, *Chronographia,* 430/594 notes that in AM 6248 (756–57 CE), Ṣāliḥ b. 'Alī ordered that no new churches were to be built, and that the cross should not be displayed in Syria. Mango suggests, furthermore, that these actions should be properly dated to 758–59 CE, yet closer to Theodore's revolt.

36. It is worth pointing out that, as Hobsbawm has noted with regard to millenarian bandit movements, the revolt of Theodore may also have

spawned long-lived folk tales. Compare the tale cited by Salibi, *Syria,* 36 (though the passage cited does not explicitly refer to Theodore/Bundār) to the nostalgia mentioned in E. J. Hobsbawm, *Bandits,* rev. ed. (New York: Pantheon Books, 1981), 127–34.

37. On the social context of pseudo-Methodius' *Apocalypse,* see G. J. Reinink, "Ps.-Methodius: A Concept of History in Response to the Rise of Islam," in *Byzantine and Early Islamic Near East,* I, edited by A. Cameron and L. I. Conrad, 149–88. On the "Emperor of the Last Days," see P. J. Alexander, "The Medieval Legend of the Last Roman Emperor and Its Messianic Origin," *Journal of the Warburg and Courtauld Institutes,* 41 (1978): 1–15; G. J. Reinink, "Pseudo-Methodius und die Legende vom römischen Endkaiser," in Werner Verbeke et al., eds., *The Use and Abuse of Eschatology in the Middle Ages* (Leuven: Leuven University Press, 1988): 82–110. On traditions of messianic kingship in Europe, see especially Norman Cohn, *The Pursuit of the Millenium,* revised and expanded ed. (Oxford: Oxford University Press, 1970), 31–35, 71–74, 108–26.

38. According to Ya'qūbī, *Ta'rīkh,* 2:586, his name was Abū Ḥarb Tamīm al-Lakhmī and almost all the sources refer to him as "al-Yamanī," Lakhm being a Yamanī tribe. On the revolt of al-Mubarqa', see Ṭabarī 3:1319–22; Ya'qūbī, *Ta'rīkh,* 2:586; *FHA* 1:408, 2:526–27; *TMD* 18:94–95, 66:135–38; Ibn al-Athīr, *Kāmil,* 6:522; Michael the Syrian 541–42/3:103; Abū al-Fatḥ, *Annales,* lxxxii. See also Herbert Eisenstein, "Die Erhebung des Mubarqa' in Palästina," *Orientalia* 55 (1986): 454–58; *EI2,* s.v. "al-Mubarḳa'" [H. Eisenstein]; Jawda, *Madīnat al-ramla,* 55–58; Gil, *Palestine,* 295–96; Ṣāliḥ al-Ḥamārna, "Thawrat al-fallāḥīn fī filasṭīn wa-al-urdunn ayyām al-mu'taṣim sanat 227 H/842 M," in his *al-Nās wa-al-Arḍ* (Amman: Dār al-Yanābī', 1991), 129–47; 'Abbās, *Bilād al-shām,* 64–67. On the revolt of al-Faddaynī, see chapter 4.

39. On "commanding and forbidding" as part of rebellion, see *Encyclopaedia Iranica,* s.v. "Amr be ma'rūf" [W. Madelung] at least until Michael Cook's much awaited study appears. Al-Maqdisī, *Bad',* 6:119 also ascribes to Abū Ḥarb belief in the transmigration of souls, but this is evidently later heresiographical slander.

40. My dating of the revolt follows the chronological observations made by Eisenstein, "Erhebung," 457. Michael the Syrian does not comment on Abū Ḥarb's Sufyānid claims, stating merely that he "named himself king." Ya'qūbī, *Ta'rīkh,* 2:586, notes that his followers came from Lakhm, Judhām, 'Āmila, and Balqayn (all Yamanī tribes). There is some confusion about one of the local notables (*ru'asā'*) involved in the revolt. Ṭabarī 3:1320 names him as Ibn Bayhas, "who commanded the obedience of the Yamaniyya." Most interpreters of this revolt (following Eisentstein) have confused this Yamanī Ibn Bayhas with the Kilābī/Qaysī Ibn Bayhas involved in the factionalism occuring at just this time in Damascus following the abortive revolt of the governor, 'Alī b. Isḥāq (see chapter 3). Howev-

er, as Crone has rightly noted (*Slaves,* 151) there was also a Yamanī Banū Bayhas clan in Syria, entirely unrelated to the Qaysī clan of the same name. Moreover, a Yamanī Ibn Bayhas was later involved in factional fighting in Damascus against the governor Sālim b. Ḥāmid (see chapter 5).

41. Admittedly, there is great chronological uncertainty. While Michael makes very clear that the year in which Abū Ḥarb revolted was a very bad one for the peasantry, the date he assigns to this year (1153 of the Seleucid era) begins in autumn of 228 AH, more than two years after the most likely date of the date as Eisenstein has established. On the description of Abū Ḥarb's followers and their tax break, see Michael the Syrian 541–42/3:103. On the natural disasters of 1153, see Michael the Syrian 541–42/3:108.

42. The looting in Filasṭīn: Ṭabarī: 3:1322 (al-Ramla); Michael the Syrian 541–42/3:103 (Jerusalem); Abū al-Fatḥ, *Annales,* lxxxii (Nābulus); Gil, *Palestine,* 296.

43. On the contemporary revolt of the Qaysī Ibn Bayhas in Damascus, see chapter 5. But as Eisenstein notes, the sequence of events is not certain. To the evidence that Eisenstein cites, it should also be noted that Ibn 'Asākir is at least clear on the dating of the confrontation between Rajā' and the Qaysiyya in Damascus: on 4 Jumāda I, 227/19 February 842 (*TMD* 18:95, Fasawī, *Ma'rifa,* 207). Perhaps, as 'Abbās, *Bilād al-shām,* 64–68 suggests, Abū Ḥarb rose up in 226, when al-Mu'taṣim sent Rajā' against him, who then interrupted his campaign in Filasṭīn to deal with the Qaysiyya in Damascus, before returning to Filasṭīn to decisively subdue Abū Ḥarb. The Ibn Bayhas who was put in prison may also be the Yamanī Ibn Bayhas who was one of his followers, but contextually it seems that the Qaysī rebel of Damascus is intended. On the confusion between these two, see chapter 5, n. 69.

44. Rajā' was also accompanied by 'Abd Allāh b. Dīnār, a commander from a prominent Khurāsānī military family in Baghdād. Al-Buḥturī, *Dīwān,* 1:104–7 (no. 34) composed an ode to 'Abd Allāh in which he mentions (ll. 20–21) his role in fighting Abū Ḥarb and the people of the Ghawr, i.e., the Wādī 'Araba in al-Urdunn.

45. Eliyahu Ashtor, in his *A Social and Economic History of the Near East in the Middle Ages* (London: William Collins, 1976), 69–70, hyperbolically calls the revolt "[t]he greatest peasant revolt in the first two hundred years of Moslem rule in the Near East."

46. David Ayalon, "The Military Reforms of Caliph Al-Mu'taṣim: Their Background and Consequences," in his *Islam and the Abode of War* (Aldershot: Variorum, 1994), 14–20. Robinson, "Mosul," 381–83, in his discussion of the Ṣa'ālīk of the 'Abbāsid era, suggests that, with the Zawāqīl, the two groups may be analogs, the Ṣa'ālīk representing a Yamanī group of

paramilitary marginals, and the Zawāqīl representing Qaysīs. This is an attractive suggestion, if only for its symmetry, and is, perhaps, supported by the frequent apposition (or opposition?) of the two terms. But note that the Zawāqīl *may* have included some Yamanīs as well (see below).

47. The first appearance of the Zawāqīl is on *TMD* 26:66. On their role in the revolt of Abū al-Haydhām, see chapter 5.

48. Medieval lexicographers: Ayalon, "Military Reforms," 20, n. 30, citing Ibn Manẓūr's *Lisān al-'arab*. 'Amr b. 'Abd al- 'Azīz's origins: Michael the Syrian 491/3:21. Di'āma (or Du'āma): *TMD* 26:66; *TMD* 7:160–63 (Yaḥyā b. Irimiyā). Al-Ma'mūn's letter to Naṣr: Ṭabarī 3:1071. If there is any truth behind the invective in this letter, it may be that the Zawāqīl were in fact a pariah group, a common source of bandits. See Hobsbawm, *Bandits,* 39–40.

49. The tribesman who first approached the Zawāqīl in Abū al-Haydhām's revolt is identified only as the brother of the murdered Qaysī man, who was simply identified as "a descendant of al-Miswar," suggesting, perhaps, a family of some notability (*TMD* 26:66). The account of Ibrāhīm and the three bandits: *TMD* 7:160–63; Gil, *Palestine,* 282–83, misconstrues this account as one relating a Jewish uprising. His attempt to connect the bandit activity with the factionalism of 180/796 is likewise untenable.

50. On the role of the Zawāqīl in Abū al-Haydhām's revolt, see chapter 5. On their role in the revolt of Abū al-'Umayṭir, see chapter 4. It is possible that the Zawāqīl are not as monolithically Qaysī as Ayalon has stated. That Abū al-'Umayṭir was able to find support among the Zawāqīl may indicate that some of them were Yamanī. Certainly some of them at least were clients of the Umayyads, like Di'āma b. 'Abd Allāh.

51. On bandits and the military, see Hobsbawm, *Bandits*, 33–34; Barkey, *Bandits and Bureaucrats,* 152–75. On the Zawāqīl under Naṣr b. Shabath, see chapter 5. On the Zawāqīl in the 'Abbāsid army: 'Aẓīmī, *Ḥalab,* 247 ('Abd Allāh brings them to Khurāsān); Gordon, "Breaking," 88 (al-Mutawakkil's new army). The final fate of the Zawāqīl is unknown, but it is possible that, over time, they identified themselves as a separate tribe despite the diverse origins of their original members: Ibn al-'Adīm, writing ca. 640/1240, discusses the longstanding enmity between two tribes in the vicinity of Aleppo, the Ḥabbāliyyūn of Asad, and the Qaysī Zawāqila of Kilāb (*BṬ* 1:536–37). On the propensity of tribal groups to coalesce like this, see Ignaz Goldziher, *Muslim Studies,* 2 vols. (London: Allen and Unwin, 1967–71), 2:65–70; *EI2*, s.v. "Ḥilf [E. Tyan]."

52. Abū al-Nidā': Ṭabarī 3:711, 732; Kindī, *Wulāt,* 143–44. Ibn Taghribirdī, *Nujūm,* 2:135; Dunn, "Abbasid Egypt," 44; Gil, *Palestine,* 292, suggests that the destruction of Samaritan synagogues at this time may have been connected with Abū al-Nidā's activities.

CHAPTER SEVEN

1. The following is just a sample of the most explicit scholarly statements of Syrian decline under the 'Abbāsids. The full genealogy of this historical truism is worth further study: L. A. Sédillot, *Histoire générale des arabes*. 2d ed., 2 vols. (Paris: Maisonneuve, 1877), 1:220–21; Wellhausen, *Kingdom,* 556–57; Lammens, *La Syrie,* 2:105–106; P. K. Hitti, *History of the Arabs,* 3rd ed. (London: Macmillan, 1943), 286; E. A. Belyaev, *Arabs, Islam, and the Arab Caliphate in the Early Middle Ages* (New York: Praeger, 1969), 130, 205; P. M. Holt et al., *Cambridge History of Islam,* 2 vols. (Cambridge: Cambridge University Press, 1970), 1A:77, 175; Salibi, Syria, 33, 35; Gil, *Palestine,* 279.

2. Indeed, there is mounting archeological evidence of demographic growth and continued economic vitality in 'Abbāsid Syria, at least in some places. See, e.g., Donald Whitcomb, "Archaeology of the 'Abbāsid Period: The Example of Jordan," *Archéologie islamique* 1 (1990): 75–85.

3. Elton Daniel, *The Social and Political History of Khurasan under Abbasid Rule, 747–820* (Minneapolis and Chicago: Bibliotheca Islamica, 1979), 157.

4. Daniel, *Khurasan*, 125–47 (rural revolts); 157–82 (local governors, the army).

5. Pro-Umayyad revolts: Dunn, "Struggle," 13–15, 27–31; Hugh Kennedy, "Egypt as a province in the Islamic caliphate, 641–868," in Carl F. Petry, ed., *The Cambridge History of Egypt. Volume I: Islamic Egypt, 640–1517* (Cambridge: Cambridge University Press, 1998), 78–79. Ḥawfī factionalism: Dunn, "Struggle," 190ff.

6. Dunn, "Struggle," 163–73; Kennedy, "Egypt," passim.

7. Robinson, "Mosul," 360–74 (*'aṣabiyya*), 406–14 (Khārijīs).

8. Robinson, "Mosul," 317–336.

9. Kennedy, "Egypt," 77.

10. Daniel, *Khurasan*, 111–12, 159–62.

11. Khurāsān: Daniel, *Khurasan,* 181–82. Jazīra: Robinson, "Mosul," 364–74. Egypt: Kennedy, "Egypt," 80–82.

12. As noted by Sourdel, "La Syrie," 170.

13. Kennedy, "Egypt," 76, 77.

14. On Aḥmad b. Ṭūlūn, see *MTMD* 3:122–26; *BṬ* 2:826–29; *EI2,* s.v. [Z. M. Hassan]; Thierry Bianquis, "Autonomous Egypt from Ibn Ṭūlūn to Kāfūr, 868–969," in Petry, *Cambridge History of Egypt,* 91ff.

15. An important exception being the 'Abbāsid interlude of 292–324/904–935, when control of the region was returned to Baghdād.

16. The history of Syrian contention *after* the 'Abbāsid period remains to be written, but for now the politics and society of post-'Abbāsid Syria are best surveyed in Von Sievers, "Military," 228–44 and especially Kennedy, *Prophet*, 200ff.

Works Cited

I. Primary Sources

A. Arabic Sources

Abū al-Fatḥ b. Abū al-Ḥasan al-Sāmirī. *Annales Samaritani*. Edited by E. Vilmar. Gotha: F. A. Perthes, 1865.

Abū Zur'a al-Dimashqī. *Ta'rīkh*. Edited by Shukr Allāh al-Qujānī. 2 vols. Damascus: Majma' al-lugha al-'arabiyya, 1980.

Agapius [Maḥbūb] of Manbij. *Kitāb al-'unwān. Part II*. Edited and translated by Alexandre Vasiliev as *Kitāb al-'unvān (histoire universelle)* in *Patrologia Orientalis* 8 (1911): 399–550.

Ajbar Machmuâ. Edited by Emilio Lafuentes y Alcántara. Madrid: M. Rivadeneyra, 1867.

al-Azdī, Yazīd b. Muḥammad. *Ta'rīkh al-mawṣil*. Edited by 'Alī Ḥabība. Cairo: al-Majlis al-a'lā li-al-shu'ūn al-islāmiyya, 1967.

al-'Aẓīmī, Muḥammad b. 'Alī. *Ta'rīkh ḥalab*. Edited by Ibrāhīm Za'rūr. Damascus: n.p., 1984.

al-Balādhurī, Aḥmad b. Yaḥyā b. Jābir. *Ansāb al-ashrāf*.

MS Istanbul, Süleymaniye Kütüphanesi (Reisülkuttap Mustafa Efendi) 597 (vol. I) and 598 (vol. II).

Volume III. Edited by 'Abd al-'Azīz al-Dūrī. Wiesbaden: Franz Steiner, 1978.

Volume IV/1. Edited by Iḥsān 'Abbās. Wiesbaden: Franz Steiner, 1979.

——. *Kitāb futūḥ al-buldān*. Edited by M. J. de Goeje. Leiden: E. J. Brill, 1866. Translated by Philip Hitti and Francis Murgotten as *The Origins of the Islamic State*. 2 vols. New York: Columbia University Press, 1916–24.

al-Buḥturī, al-Walīd b. 'Ubayd. *Dīwān*. Edited by Ḥasan Kāmil al-Ṣayrafī. 4 vols. Cairo: Dār al-ma'ārif, 1964.

al-Dhahabī, Shams al-Dīn. *Ta'rīkh al-islām wa-wafayāt al-mashāhīr wa-al-a'lām*. Edited by 'Umar 'Abd al-Salām Tadmurī. 31 vols. Beirut: Dār al-kitāb al-'arabī, 1991.

Dīk al-Jinn al-Ḥimṣī. *Dīwān*. Edited by Aḥmad Maṭlūb and 'Abd Allāh al-Jabūrī. Beirut: Dār al-thiqāfa, 1964.

al-Dinawarī, Abū Ḥanīfa. *al-Akhbār al-ṭiwāl*. Edited by V. Guirgass. Leiden: E. J. Brill, 1910.

al-Fasawī, Ya'qūb b. Sufyān. *Kitāb al-ma'rifa wa-al-ta'rīkh*. Edited by Akram Ḍiyā' al-'Umarī. 3 vols. Baghdad: Ri'āsat dīwān al-awqāf, 1974–76.

Fragmenta Historicorum Arabicorum. Edited by M. J. de Goeje. 2 vols. Leiden: E.J. Brill, 1869.

Ibn al-'Adīm, Kamāl al-Dīn 'Umar. *Bughyat al-ṭalab min ta'rīkh ḥalab*. Edited by Suhayl Zakkār. 11 vols. Damascus: n.p., 1988.

——. *Zubdat al-ḥalab min ta'rīkh ḥalab*. Edited by Sāmī al-Dahhān. 3 vols. Damascus: Institut Français de Damas, 1951–68.

Ibn 'Asākir, Abū al-Qāsim 'Alī. *Ta'rīkh madīnat dimashq*. Edited by 'Umar al-'Amrāwī. 70 vols. Beirut: Dār al-fikr, 1995–98.

Concurrent edition by Ṣalāḥ al-Dīn al-Munajjid et al. Damascus: Majma' al-lugha al-'arabiyya, 1951–.

Volume II translated by Nikita Elisséeff as *La description de Damas d'Ibn 'Asākir*. Damascus: Institut Français de Damas, 1959.

Ibn A'tham al-Kūfī, Abū Muḥammad Aḥmad. *Kitāb al-futūḥ*. Edited by Muḥammad 'Abd al-Mu'īd Khān et al. 8 vols. Hyderabad: Dā'irat al-ma'ārif al-'uthmāniyya, 1968–75.

Ibn al-Athīr, 'Izz al-Dīn 'Alī. *al-Kāmil fī al-ta'rīkh*. Edited by C. J. Tornberg. 13 vols. Beirut: Dār ṣādir and Dār bayrūt, 1965–67.

Ibn al-Faqīh al-Hamadhānī. *Mukhtaṣar kitāb al-buldān*. Edited by M. J. de Goeje. Leiden: E. J. Brill, 1885.

Ibn Ḥamdūn, Muḥammad b. al-Ḥasan. *al-Tadhkira al-ḥamdūniyya*. Edited by Iḥsān 'Abbās and Bakr 'Abbās. Beirut: Dār ṣādir, 1996.

Ibn Ḥanbal, Aḥmad. *Musnad*. 6 vols. Beirut: Dār ṣādir, 1969.

Ibn 'Idhārī, Aḥmad b. Muḥammad al-Marākushī. *Kitāb al-bayān al-mughrib*. Edited by G. S. Colin and E. Lévi-Provençal. 2 vols. Leiden: E. J. Brill, 1948–51.

Ibn Manẓūr, Jamāl al-Dīn Muḥammad. *Mukhtaṣar ta'rīkh dimashq li-ibn 'asākir*. Edited by 'Abd al-Ḥamīd Murād. 29 vols. Damascus: Dār al-fikr, 1984–.

Ibn al-Muqaffa', 'Abd Allāh. *Risāla fī al-ṣaḥāba*. Edited by Muḥammad Kurd 'Alī in his *Rasā'il al-bulaghā'*, 120–31. Cairo: n. p., 1913. Edited and translated by Charles Pellat as *Ibn al-Muqaffa', "conseilleur" du calife*. Paris: G. P. Maisonneuve et Larose, 1976.

Ibn al-Najjār al-Baghdādī, Muḥammad b. Maḥmūd. *Dhayl ta'rīkh baghdād*. 5 vols. Hyderabad: Osmania Oriental Publications Bureau, 1978.

Ibn Qūṭiyya, Abū Bakr al-Qurṭubī. *Ta'rīkh iftitāḥ al-andalus*. Edited by A. al-Ṭabbā'. Beirut: n.p., 1958.

Ibn Taghribirdī, Abū al-Maḥāsin Yūsuf. *al-Nujūm al-ẓāhira fī mulūk miṣr wa-al-qāhira*. 16 vols. Cairo: Dār al-kutub al-miṣriyya, 1963–72.

al-Iṣfahānī, Abū al-Faraj. *Kitāb al-aghānī*. Various editors. 16 vols. Cairo: Dār al-kutub al-miṣriyya, 1927–61.

al-Jāḥiẓ, 'Amr b. Baḥr. *Kitāb al-ḥayawān*. Edited by 'A. M. Hārūn. 7 vols. Cairo: Muṣṭafā al-Bābī al-Ḥalabī, 1948.

al-Jahshiyārī, Muḥammad b. 'Abdūs. *Kitāb al-wuzarā' wa al-kuttāb*. Edited by Muṣṭafā al-Ṣafā et al. Cairo: Muṣṭafā al-Bābī al-Ḥalabī, 1938.

Khalīfa b. Khayyāṭ al-'Uṣfūrī. *al-Ta'rīkh*. Edited by Akram Ḍiyā' al-'Umarī. 2 vols. Najaf: Maṭba'at al-ādāb, 1967.

al-Kindī, Abū 'Umar Muḥammad b. Yūsuf. *Kitāb al-wulāt wa-kitāb al-quḍāt*. Edited by Rueven Guest. Gibb Memorial Series, no. 19. Leiden : E. J. Brill, 1912.

al-Maqdisī, Muṭahhir b. Ṭāhir. *Kitāb al-bad' wa-al-ta'rīkh*. Edited by Clément Huart. 6 vols. Paris: Ernest Leroux, 1899–1919.

al-Maqrīzī, Tāqī al-Dīn Aḥmad. *Kitāb al-nizā' wa-al-takhaṣṣum fīmā bayna banī umayya wa-banī hāshim*. Edited by Ḥusayn Mu'nis. Cairo: Dār al-ma'ārif, 1988. Translated by C. E. Bosworth as *Al-Maqrīzī's "Book of Contention and Strife Concerning the Relations Between the Banū Umayya and the Banū Hāshim."* Journal of Semitic Studies Monographs, 3. Manchester: University of Manchester, 1980.

al-Mārzubānī, Muhammad b. 'Imrān. *Mu'jam al-shu'arā'*. Edited by Fritz Krenkow. Cairo: Maktabat al-quds, 1926.

al-Mas'ūdī, 'Alī b. al-Ḥusayn. *Kitāb al-tanbīh wa-al-ashrāf*. Edited by M. J. de Goeje. Leiden: E. J. Brill, 1894. Translated by B. Carra de Vaux as *Le Livre de l'avertissement et de la révision*. Paris: Imprimerie Nationale, 1896.

——. *Murūj al-dhahab wa-ma'ādin al-jawhar*. Edited by Charles Pellat. 7 vols. Beirut: al-Jāmi'a al-lubnāniyya, 1965–79. Translated by Charles Pellat as *Les prairies d'or*. 5 vols. Paris: Société Asiatique, 1965–74.

Nu'aym b. Ḥammād al-Marwazī. *Kitāb al-fitan*. MS London, British Museum Or. 9449. Edition by Suhayl Zakkār. Mecca: al-Maktaba al-tijāriyya, 1991.

al-Raba'ī, 'Alī b. Muḥammad. *Faḍā'il al-shām wa-dimashq*. Edited by Ṣalāḥ al-Dīn al-Munajjid. Damascus: Maṭba'at al-taraqqī, 1950.

al-Ṣafadī, Khalīl b. Aybak. *Kitāb umarā' dimashq fī al-islām*. Edited by Ṣalāḥ al-Dīn al-Munajjid. Damascus: al-Majma' al-'ilmī al-'arabī, 1955.

——. *al-Wāfī bi-al-wafayāt*. Edited by Helmut Ritter et al. 22 vols. Istanbul and Wiesbaden: F. Steiner for the Deutsche Morgenländische Gesellschaft, 1931–.

al-Ṣūlī, Muḥammad b. Yaḥyā. *Kitāb al-awrāq [Ash'ar awlād al-khulafā' wa-akhbāruhum]*. Edited by J. Heyworth Dunne. Cairo: Maṭba'at al-ṣāwī, 1936.

al-Ṭabarī, Muḥammad b. Jarīr. *Ta'rīkh al-rusul wa-al-mulūk*. Edited by M. J. de Goeje et al. 15 vols. Leiden: E. J. Brill, 1879–1901. Translated as *The History of al-Ṭabarī*. General editor Ehsan Yarshater. 38 vols. Albany: State University of New York Press, 1985–.

al-Wāsiṭī, Muḥammad b. Aḥmad. *Faḍā'il al-bayt al-muqaddas*. Edited by Isaac Hasson. Jerusalem: Hebrew University, 1979.

al-Ya'qūbī, Aḥmad b. Abī Ya'qūb. *Kitāb al-buldān*. Edited by M. J. de Goeje. Leiden: E. J. Brill, 1892.

——. *Mushākalat al-nās li-zamānihim*. Edited by William Millward. Beirut: Dār al-kitāb al-jadīd, 1962.

——. *Ta'rīkh al-ya'qūbī*. Edited by M. T. Houtsma. 2 vols. Leiden: E. J. Brill, 1883.

Yāqūt al-Ḥamawī. *Mu'jam al-buldān*. Edited by F. Wüstenfeld. 6 vols. Leipzig: F. A. Brockhaus for the Deutsche Morgenländische Gesellschaft, 1866–73.

——. *Mu'jam al-udabā' [Irshād al-arīb ilā ma'rifat al-adīb]*. Edited by A. F. Rifā'ī. 20 vols. Cairo: Dār al-ma'mūn, 1936–38.

B. Non-Arabic Sources

Acta Sanctorum Bollandiana. Paris: Société des Bollandistes, 1863–1940.

Chronicum ad annum Domini 846 pertinens. Edited by E. W. Brooks in *Chronica Minora,* II. *CSCO* 3, *Scriptores Syri* 3, 157–238. Louvain: E. J. Peeters, 1903. Translated by E. W. Brooks in *ZDMG* 51 (1897): 569–88.

Chronicum ad annum Christi 1234 pertinens. Edited by J.-B. Chabot. 2 vols. *CSCO* 18, 32, *Scriptores Syri* 36, 37. Paris: L. Durbecq, 1920. Volume II translated by Albert Abouna in *CSCO* 354, *Scriptores Syri* 154.

[pseudo-]Dionysios of Tel-Maḥrē. *Chronicum anonymum pseudo-Dionysianum vulgo dictum.* Edited by J.-B. Chabot. *CSCO* 91, 104, *Scriptores Syri* 43, 53. Louvain: E. Peeters, 1927 and 1933. Parts III and IV translated by Amir Harrak as *The Chronicle of Zuqnīn. Parts III and IV, A.D. 488–775.* Toronto: Pontifical Institute of Medieval Studies, 1999.

Exēgēsis ētoi Martyrion tōn Hagiōn Paterōn ... Edited by A. Papadopoulou-Kerameos. In *Pravoslavnī Palestinskiī sbornik,* vol. 19, 1–41. St. Petersburg, 1907.

Lewond (Ghevond). *History of Lewond the Eminent Vardapet of the Armenians.* Translated by Zaven Arzoumanian. Wynnewood, PA: SS Sahag & Mesrob Armenian Church, 1982.

Michael the Syrian. *Chronique de Michel le Syrien.* Edited and translated by J.-B. Chabot. 4 vols. Paris: Academie de Inscriptions et Belles-Lettres, 1924.

Ta'rīkh-i sīstān. Edited by Malik al-Shu'arā' Bahār. Tehran: Muḥammad Ramaẓānī, 1935.

Theophanes Confessor. *Theophanis chronographia.* Edited by Carolus de Boor. Leipzig: B. G. Teubner, 1883. Translated by C. Mango and R. Scott as *The Chronicle of Theophanes Confessor.* Oxford: Oxford University Press, 1997.

II. Secondary Sources

'Abbās, Iḥsān. *Ta'rīkh bilād al-shām fī al-'aṣr al-'abbāsī, 132–255 H/750–870 M.* Amman: Lajnat ta'rīkh bilād al-shām, 1993.

Abbott, Nabia. "Arabic Papyri of the Reign of Ǧa'far al-Mutawakkil 'ala-llāh (AH 232–47/AD 847–61)." *ZDMG* 92 (1938): 88–135.

Alexander, P. J. "The Medieval Legend of the Last Roman Emperor and its Messianic Origin." *Journal of the Warburg and Courtauld Institutes,* 41 (1978): 1–15.

Arazi, A., and A. El'ad. " 'L'Épître à l'Armée.' Al-Ma'mūn et la seconde Da'wa." *SI* 66 (1987): 27–70, and 67 (1988): 29–74.

Arjomand, Said Amir. "'Abd Allāh Ibn al-Muqaffa' and the 'Abbāsid Revolution." *Iranian Studies* 27 (1994): 9–36.

Ashtor, Eliyahu. *A Social and Economic History of the Near East in the Middle Ages.* London: William Collins, 1976.

Ayalon, David. "The Military Reforms of Caliph Al-Mu'taṣim: Their Background and Consequences." Unpublished paper reprinted in David Ayalon, *Islam and the Abode of War.* Aldershot: Variorum, 1994.

Barkey, Karen. *Bandits and Bureaucrats. The Ottoman Route to State Centralization.* Ithaca and London: Cornell University Press, 1994.

Bartikjan, Hratz. "Hē lusē tou ainigmatos tōn Mardaitōn." In *Byzantion. Aphieroma stōn Andrea N. Strato/Byzance. Hommage à Andreas Stratos/Byzantium. Tribute to Andreas Stratos,* edited by Zia Stratos, 17–39. Athens: N. A. Stratou, 1986.

Belyaev, E. A. *Arabs, Islam and the Arab Caliphate in the Early Middle Ages.* Translated by Adolphe Gourevitch. Jerusalem: Israel Universities Press, 1969.

Bianquis, Thierry. "Deux révoltes bédouines en Syrie méridionale au Moyen-Age." In *The Third International Conference on Bilad al-Sham: Palestine 19–24 April 1980. Volume 3: History of Palestine.* Amman: Lajnat ta'rīkh bilād al-shām, 1984.

——. "Autonomous Egypt from Ibn Ṭūlūn to Kāfūr, 868–969." In *The Cambridge History of Egypt. Vol. II: Islamic Egypt, 640–1517,* edited by Carl F. Petry, 86–119. Cambridge and New York: Cambridge University Press, 1998.

Blankinship, Khalid Yahya. "The Tribal Factor in the 'Abbāsid Revolution: The Betrayal of the Imam Ibrāhīm b. Muḥammad." *JAOS* 108 (1988): 589–603.

——. *The End of the Jihâd State. The Reign of Hishām Ibn 'Abd al-Malik and the Collapse of the Umayyads.* Albany: State University of New York Press, 1994.

Bligh-Abramski, Irit. "Evolution Versus Revolution: Umayyad Elements in the 'Abbāsid Regime 133/750–320/932." *Der Islam* 65 (1988): 226–43.

Bonner, Michael. *Aristocratic Violence and Holy War. Studies in the Jihad and The Arab-Byzantine Frontier*. American Oriental Series, vol. 81. New Haven, CT: American Oriental Society, 1996.

Bosworth, Clifford Edmund. *Sīstān Under the Arabs, From the Islamic Conquest to the Rise of the Ṣaffārids (30–250/651–864)*. Rome: Istituto Italiano per il Medio ed Estremo Oriente, 1968.

——. "The Ṭāhirids and the Ṣaffārids." In *The Cambridge History of Iran, Volume IV: From the Arab Invasion to the Seljuqs,* edited by R. N. Frye, 90–135. Cambridge: Cambridge University Press, 1975.

Brustein, William. "Class Conflict and Class Collaboration in Regional Rebellions, 1500–1700." *Theory and Society* 14 (1985): 445–68.

Bulliet, Richard W. *Conversion to Islam in the Medieval Period. An Essay in Quantitative History*. Cambridge, MA: Harvard University Press, 1979.

Cahen, Claude. "Fiscalité, propriété, antagonismes sociaux en Haute-Mésopotamie au temps des premiers Abbassides, d'après Denys de Tell Mahré." Arabica 1 (1954): 136–52.

The Cambridge History of Islam. Edited by P. M. Holt et al. 2 vols. Cambridge: Cambridge University Press, 1970.

Casanova, Paul. *Mohammed et la fin du monde: étude critique sur l'Islam primitif.* Paris: Paul Geuthner, 1911–24.

Caskel, Werner. *Ǧamharat an-Nasab. Das genealogische Werk des Hišam ibn Muḥammad al-Kalbī*. 2 vols. Leiden: E.J. Brill, 1966.

Cobb, Paul M. "Scholars and Society at Early Islamic Ayla." *JESHO* 38 (1995): 417–28.

——. "Al-Mutawakkil's Damascus: A New 'Abbāsid Capital?" *Journal of Near Eastern Studies* 58 (1999): 241–57.

——. "Community Versus Contention: Ibn 'Asākir and 'Abbāsid Syria." In *Ibn 'Asākir and Early Islamic History,* edited by James E. Lindsay. Princeton: Darwin Press, forthcoming.

Cohn, Norman. *The Pursuit of the Millenium*. Rev. ed. New York: Oxford University Press, 1970.

——. *Cosmos, Chaos and the World to Come. The Ancient Roots of Apocalyptic Faith*. New Haven: Yale University Press, 1993.

Conrad, Gerhard. *Abū'l-Ḥusain al-Rāzī (347/958) und seine Schriften. Untersuchungen zur frühen damaszener Geschichtsschreibung*. Stuttgart: Franz Steiner, 1991.

——. *Die Quḍāt Dimašq und der Madhab al-Auzāʿī. Materialen zur syrischen Rechtsgeschichte*. Beirut: In Kommission bei Franz Steiner Verlag Stuttgart, 1994.

Crone, Patricia. *Slaves on Horses. The Evolution of the Islamic Polity.* Cambridge: Cambridge University Press, 1980.

—. *Pre-Industrial Societies*. Oxford: Blackwell, 1989.

—. "Were the Qays and Yemen of the Umayyad Period Political Parties?" *Der Islam* 71 (1994): 1–57.

—. "The 'Abbāsid Abnā' and Sāsānid Cavalrymen," *Journal of the Royal Asiatic Society, 3rd Series* 8 (1998): 1–19.

— and Martin Hinds. *God's Caliph. Religious Authority in the First Centuries of Islam.* Cambridge: Cambridge University Press, 1986.

Daniel, Elton L. *The Political and Social History of Khurasan under Abbasid Rule, 747–820*. Minneapolis and Chicago: Bibiotheca Islamica, 1979.

Dennett, Daniel C. "Marwān b. Muḥammad and the Passing of the Umayyad Caliphate." Ph.D. diss., Harvard University, 1939.

Donner, Fred M. "From Believers to Muslims: Confessional Self-Identity in the Early Islamic Community." In *The Byzantine and Early Islamic Near East, IV: Patterns of Communal Identity,* edited by Lawrence I. Conrad. Princeton: Darwin Press, forthcoming.

Dozy, R. P. A. *Histoire des musulmans d'Espagne.* 2 vols. Leiden: E. J. Brill, 1861.

Dunn, Michael C. "The Struggle for 'Abbasid Egypt." Ph.D. diss., Georgetown University, 1975.

Dussaud, René. *Topographie historique de la Syrie antique et médiévale.* Paris: Paul Geuthner, 1927.

Eisenstein, Herbert. "Die Erhebung des Mubarqa' in Palästina." *Orientalia* 55 (1986): 454–58.

Elad, Amikam. *Medieval Jerusalem and Islamic Worship.* Leiden: E. J. Brill, 1995.

—. "Aspects of the Transition from the Umayyad to the 'Abbāsid Caliphate." *Jerusalem Studies in Arabic and Islam* 19 (1995): 89–132.

—. "The Caliph Abū'l-'Abbās al-Saffāḥ, The First 'Abbāsid *Mahdī*: Implications of an Unknown Inscription from Bet-Shean (Baysān)." In *Mas'at Moshe: Studies in Jewish and Islamic Culture Presented to Moshe Gil,* edited by E. Fleischer et al., 9–55. Jerusalem: Bialik Institute, 1998.

El-Hibri, Tayeb. "Coinage Reform Under the 'Abbāsid Caliph al-Ma'mūn." *JESHO* 36 (1993): 58–83.

Encyclopaedia Iranica. Edited by E. Yarshater. Boston: Routledge and Kegan Paul, 1983–.

Encyclopaedia of Islam, New Edition. Leiden: E. J. Brill, 1958–.

Forand, P. G. "The Governors of Mosul According to al-Azdī's Ta'rīkh al-Mawṣil." *JAOS* 89 (1969): 88–105.

Gatier, Pierre-Louis. "Villages du Proche-Orient protobyzantin (4ème-7ème s.). Étude régionale." In *The Byzantine and Early Islamic Near East II: Land Use and Settlement Patterns,* edited by G. R. D. King and Averil Cameron, 17–48. Princeton: Darwin Press, 1994.

Gentelle, Pierre. "Élements pour une histoire des paysages et du peuplement du Djebel Hauran septentrional." In *Hauran I. Recherches archéologiques sur la Syrie du sud à l'époque hellénistique et romaine, deuxième partie,* edited by J.-M. Dentzer, 19–62. Bibliothéque Archéologique et Historique, v. 124. Paris: Paul Geuthner, 1986.

Gil, Moshe. *A History of Palestine, 634–1099*. Translated by Ethel Broido. Cambridge: Cambridge University Press, 1992.

Given, James. *State and Society in Medieval Europe. Gwynedd and Languedoc under Outside Rule*. Ithaca and London: Cornell University Press, 1990.

Goldziher, Ignaz. *Muslim Studies*. 2 vols. London: Allen and Unwin, 1967–71.

Gordon, Matthew S. "The Breaking of a Thousand Swords: A History of the Turkish Community of Sāmarrā (218–264 A.H./833–877 C.E.)." Ph.D. diss., Columbia University, 1993.

Grabar, Oleg. "A Small Episode of Early 'Abbāsid Times and Some Consequences." *Eretz-Israel* 7 (1964): 44–47.

Gruber, E. A. *Verdienst und Rang. Die Faḍā'il als literarisches und gesellschaftliches Problem im Islam*. Islamkundliche Untersuchungen, b. 15. Freiburg im Breisgau: Klaus Schwarz, 1975.

Guérin, Alexandrine. "Terroirs, territoire et peuplement en Syrie méridionale à la période islamique (VIIe siècle-XVIe siècle)." Ph.D diss., Université Lumière, Lyon 2, 1998.

——. "Les territoires de la ville de Damas à la période abbasside." Unpublished paper presented at the "Table Ronde: Villes syriennes," Damascus, Institut Français des Études Arabes, 1999.

Haldon, John F., and Hugh Kennedy. "The Arab-Byzantine Frontier in the Eighth and Ninth Centuries: Military Organisation and Society in the Borderlands."In *Zbornik Radova Vizantoloskog Instituta XIX*, edited by Božidar Ferjančic, 79–116. Belgrade: Srpska Akademija Nauka i Umetnosti, 1980.

al-Ḥamārna, Ṣāliḥ. "Thawrat al-fallāḥīn fī filasṭīn wa-al-urdunn ayyām al-mu'taṣim sannat 227 h/842 m." In his *al-Nās wa-al-arḍ*, 129–47. Amman: Dār al-yanābī', 1991.

Hanagan, Michael P., et al., eds. *Challenging Authority: The Historical Study of Contentious Politics.* Minneapolis: University of Minnesota Press, 1998.

Hawting, G. R. *The First Dynasty of Islam.* Carbondale: Southern Illinois University Press, 1987.

Hilton, Rodney H. *Bond men made free; medieval peasant movements and the English rising of 1381.* New York: Viking Press, 1973.

Hitti, Phillip K. *History of the Arabs.* 3rd edition. London: Macmillan, 1943.

—. *History of Syria. Including Lebanon and Palestine.* New York: Macmillan, 1951.

al-Ḥiyārī, Muṣṭafā 'Alī, "Tawaṭṭūn al-qabā'il al-'arabiyya fī jund qinnasrīn ḥattā nihāyat al-qarn al-rābi' al-hijrī." In *Fī miḥrāb al-ma'rifah: Festschrift for Iḥsān 'Abbās,* edited by I. As-Sa'āfīn, 417–31. Beirut: Dār ṣādir, 1997.

Hobsbawm, E. J. *Primitive Rebels. Studies in Archaic Forms of Social Movement in the 19th and 20th Centuries.* New York: F. A. Praeger, 1959.

—. *Bandits.* New York: Delacorte Press, 1969.

—. "Peasants and Politics." *Journal of Peasant Studies* 1 (1973): 3–22.

Horsley, Richard A., and John S. Hanson. *Bandits, Prophets, and Messiahs. Popular Movements at the Time of Jesus.* San Francisco: Harper & Row, 1988.

Hourani, Albert. "Ottoman Reform and the Politics of Notables." *Beginnings of Modernization in the Middle East: The Nineteenth Century,* edited by W. R. Polk and R. L. Chambers, 41–68. Chicago:University of Chicago Press, 1968.

Humphreys, R. Stephen. *Islamic History. A Framework for Inquiry.* Rev. ed. Princeton: Princeton University Press, 1991.

Ḥusayn, Fāliḥ. *al-Ḥayāt al-zirā'iyya fī bilād al-shām fī al-'aṣr al-umawī.* Amman: al-Jāmi'a al-urdunniyya, 1978.

Ḥusaynī, Muḥammad Ṭāhir. *Maqātil al-umawiyyīn*. Beirut: Mu'assasat al-balāgha, 1990.

Jawda, Ṣādiq Aḥmad Dāwūd. *Madīnat al-ramla mundhu nashā'ihā ḥattā 'ām 492 H-1099 M*. Beirut: Dār 'ammār, 1986.

Johns, Jeremy, A. M. McQuitty, and R. Falkner. "The Fâris Project: Preliminary Report upon the 1986 and 1988 Seasons." *Levant* 21 (1989): 63–95.

Kaegi, Walter E. *Byzantine Military Unrest 471–843: An Interpretation*. Amsterdam: A. M. Hakkert, 1981.

Kennedy, Hugh. "Central Government and Provincial Élites in the Early 'Abbasid Caliphate." *BSOAS* 44 (1981): 26–38.

——. *The Early Abbasid Caliphate*. London and Sydney: Croom Helm, 1981.

——. *The Prophet and the Age of the Caliphates*. London and New York: Longman, 1986.

——. "Egypt as a province in the Islamic caliphate, 641–868." In *The Cambridge History of Egypt. Vol. II: Islamic Egypt, 640–1517*, edited by Carl F. Petry, 62–85. Cambridge and New York: Cambridge University Press, 1998.

Kister, M. J. "A Comment on the Antiquity of Traditions Praising Jerusalem." *The Jerusalem Cathedra* 1 (1981): 185–86.

Kurd 'Alī, Muḥammad. *Kitāb khiṭaṭ al-shām*. 6 vols. Damascus: Maṭba'at al-ḥadīth, 1925.

Lammens, Henri. *La Syrie. Précis historique*. 2 vols. Beirut: Imprimerie Catholique, 1921.

——. "Le «Sofiānī», héros national des Arabes syriens." In his *Études sur le siècle des Omayyades*, 391–408. Beirut: Imprimerie Catholique, 1930.

Lancaster, W., and F. Lancaster. "Land Use and Population in the Area North of Karak." *Levant* 27 (1995): 103–24.

Landau-Tasseron, Ella. "The Waning of the Umayyads: Notes on Ṭabarī's History Translated, vol. XXVI." *Der Islam* 59 (1992): 81–109.

Lassner, Jacob. *The Shaping of 'Abbāsid Rule*. Princeton: Princeton University Press, 1980.

——. *Islamic Revolution and Historical Memory: Abbasid Apologetics and the Art of Historical Writing*. New Haven: American Oriental Society, 1986.

Latron, André. *La vie rurale en Syrie et au Liban. Étude d'économie sociale*. Beirut: Institut Français de Damas, 1936.

Leder, Stefan. *Das Korpus al-Haiṭam ibn ʿAdī (st. 207/822). Herkunft, Überlieferung, Gestalt früher Texte der Ahbar Literatur.* Frankfurt am Main: Vittorio Klostermann, 1991.

LeStrange, Guy. *Palestine under the Moslems.* London: Palestine Exploration Fund, 1890.

MacAdam, Henry Innes. "Settlements and Settlement Patterns in Northern and Central Transjordania, *ca 550–ca 750.*" In *The Byzantine and Early Islamic Near East II: Land Use and Settlement Patterns,* edited by G. R. D. King and Averil Cameron, 49–94. Princeton: Darwin Press, 1994.

Madelung, Wilferd. "The Sufyānī between Tradition and History." *SI* 63 (1984): 5–48.

——. "Has the *Hijra* Come to an End?" *REI* 54 (1986): 225–37.

——. "Apocalyptic Prophecies in Ḥimṣ in the Umayyad Age." *Journal of Semitic Studies* 31 (1986): 141–85.

McQuitty, A. M., and R. Falkner. "The Fâris Project: Preliminary Report on the 1989, 1990 and 1991 Seasons." *Levant* 25 (1993): 37–62.

Morton, Alexander H. "Ḥisba and glass stamps in eighth and early ninth century Egypt." In *Documents de l'Islam Médiéval. Nouvelles Perspectives de Recherche,* edited by Y. Rāġib, 19–42. Cairo: Institut Français d'Archéologie Orientale, 1991.

Moscati, Sabatino. "Le massacre des Umayyades dans l'histoire et dans les fragments poétiques." *Archiv Orientální* 18 (1950): 88–115.

Mottahedeh, Roy. *Loyalty and Leadership in an Early Islamic Society.* Princeton: Princeton University Press, 1980.

al-Munajjid, Ṣalāḥ al-Dīn. *Madīnat dimashq ʿinda al-jughrāfiyīn wa-al-raḥḥālīn al-muslimīn.* Beirut: Dār al-kitāb al-jadīd, 1967.

——. *Muʿjam banī umayya.* Beirut: Dār al-kitāb al-jadīd, 1970.

Nagel, Tilman. *Untersuchungen zur Entstehung des abbasidischen Kalifates.* Bonner Orientalische Studien, N. S. 22. Bonn: Selbstverlag des Orientalischen Seminars der Universität, 1972.

——. *Rechtleitung und Kalifat. Versuch über eine Grundfrage der islamischen Geschichte. Studien zum Minderheitenproblem im Islam,* vol. 2. Bonner orientalistische Studien, n.s. 27. Bonn: Orientalische Seminar der Universität Bonn, 1975.

Omar, Farouk. *The Abbasid Caliphate, 132/750–170–786.* Baghdad: National Printing and Publishing Co., 1969.

——. *'Abbāsiyyāt. Studies in the History of the Early 'Abbāsids.* Baghdad: University of Baghdad, 1976.

Pellat, Charles. "Le culte de Mu'āwiya au IIIe siècle." *SI* 7 (1956): 53–66.

Prawer, Joshua. *Crusader Institutions.* Oxford: Clarendon Press, 1980.

al-Qāḍī, Wadad. "The Religious Foundation of Late Umayyad Ideology and Practice." In *Saber Religioso y Poder Político en el Islam. Actas del Simposio Internacional (Granada, 15–18 octubre 1991),* 231–73. Madrid: Agencia Española de Cooperación Internacional, 1994.

Reinink, G. J. "Pseudo-Methodius und die Legende vom römischen Endkaiser." In *The Use and Abuse of Eschatology in the Middle Ages,* edited by Werner Verbeke et al., 82–110. Leuven: Leuven University Press, 1988.

——. "Ps.-Methodius: A Concept of History in Response to the Rise of Islam." In *The Byzantine and Early Islamic Near East I: Problems in the Literary Source Material,* edited by A. Cameron and L. I. Conrad, 149–88. Princeton: Darwin Press, 1992.

Répertoire chronologique d'épigraphie arabe. Various editors. Cairo: Institut Français d'Archéologie Orientale, 1931–.

Robinson, Chase F. "The Early Islamic History of Mosul." Ph.D. diss., Harvard University, 1992.

Rudé, George. *Ideology and Popular Protest.* New York: Pantheon Books, 1980.

Sabari, Simha. *Mouvements populaires à Bagdad à l'époque 'abbasside, IXe-XIe siècles.* Paris: Librairie d'Amérique et d'Orient, 1981.

Salibi, Kamal S. *Syria Under Islam. Empire on Trial, 634–1097.* Delmar, NY: Caravan Books, 1977.

——. *A House of Many Mansions. The History of Lebanon Reconsidered.* Berkeley and Los Angeles: University of California Press, 1988.

Schick, Robert. *The Christian Communities of Palestine from Byzantine to Islamic Rule: A Historical and Archaeological Study.* Princeton: Darwin Press, 1995.

Sédillot, L. A. *Histoire générale des arabes.* 2d ed., 2 vols. Paris: Maisonneuve, 1877.

Shaban, M. A. *The 'Abbāsid Revolution.* Cambridge: Cambridge University Press, 1970.

——. *Islamic History. A New Interpretation.* 2 vols. Cambridge: Cambridge University Press, 1971.

Shahid, Irfan. *Byzantium and the Arabs in the Sixth Century*. 2 vols. Washington, DC: Dumbarton Oaks, 1995.

Sharon, Moshe. *Black Banners From the East*. Jerusalem: Magnes Press, 1983.

——. *Revolt. The Social and Military Aspects of the 'Abbāsid Revolution*. Jerusalem: Hebrew University, 1990.

Shoshan, Boaz. "The 'Politics of Notables' in Medieval Islam." *Asian and African Studies* 20 (1986): 179–215.

Sourdel, Dominique. *Le vizirat abbaside de 749 à 936 (132 à 324 de l'Hégire)*. 2 vols. Damascus: Institut Français de Damas, 1960.

——. "La Syrie au Temps des Premiers Califes Abbassides (132/750–264/878)." *Revue des Études Islamiques* 48 (1980): 155–75.

Spies, Otto. "Über die Kreuzigung im Islam." In *Religion und Religionen. Festschrift für Gustav Mensching zu seinem 65. Geburtstag*, 143–56. Bonn: Ludwig Röhrscheid, 1967.

Sylloge Numorum Arabicorum Tübingen. Palästina IV (Bilād aš-Šām I). Edited by Lutz Ilisch. Berlin: Ernst Wasmuth, 1993.

Tilly, Charles. *The Contentious French*. Cambridge, MA: Harvard University Press, 1986.

——. *From Mobilization to Revolution*. Reading, MA: Addison-Wesley, 1978.

——. *Popular Contention in Great Britain, 1758–1834*. Cambridge, MA: Harvard University Press, 1995.

Tuqan, Fawwaz Ahmad. "'Abdallāh Ibn 'Alī: A Rebellious Uncle of Al-Manṣūr." *Studies in Islam* 6 (1969): 1–26.

van Ess, Josef. "Les Qadarites et la Ġailānīya de Yazīd III." *SI* 41 (1970): 269–86.

van Vloten, Gerlof. "Recherches sur la domination arabe, le chiitisme, et les croyances messianiques sous le Khalifat des Omayades." *Verhandelingen der Koninlijke Akademie van wetenschappen te Amsterdam; Afdeeling Letterkunde*. Deel I: 3. Amsterdam: J. Muller, 1894.

Villeneuve, François. "L'économie rurale et la vie des campagnes dans le Hauran antique (Ier siécle avant J.-C.-VIe siécle aprés J.-C." In *Hauran I. Recherches archéologiques sur la Syrie du sud a l'époque hellénistique et romaine, deuxième partie*, edited by J.-M. Dentzer, 63–136. Bibliothèque Archéologique et Historique, v. 124. Paris: Paul Geuthner, 1986.

von Sievers, Peter. "Military, Merchants and Nomads: The Social Evolution of the Syrian Cities and Countryside During the Classical Period, 780–969/164–358." *Der Islam* 56 (1979): 212–44.

Walmsley, Alan G. "The Administrative Structure and Urban Geography of the Jund of Filastin and the Jund of al-Urdunn." Ph.D. diss., University of Sydney, 1987.

Wellhausen, Julius. *The Arab Kingdom and Its Fall*. Translated by M. G. Weir. Calcutta: University of Calcutta, 1927.

Weulersse, Jacques. *Paysans de Syrie et du Proche-Orient*. 6th ed. Paris: Gallimard, 1946.

Whitcomb, Donald S. "Archaeology of the 'Abbāsid Period: The Example of Jordan." *Archéologie islamique* 1 (1990): 75–85.

Wirth, Eugen. *Syrien. Eine geographische Landeskunde*. Darmstadt: Wissenschaftlische Buchgesellschaft, 1971.

Wolf, Eric R. *Peasants*. Englewood Cliffs: Prentice-Hall, 1966.

Zakeri, Mohsen. *Sāsānid Soldiers in Early Muslim Society*. Wiesbaden: Harrassowitz, 1995.

Zayyāt, Ḥabīb. "al-Tashayyu' li-mu'āwiya fī 'ahd al-'abbāsiyyīn." *Al-Mašriq* 26 (1928): 410–15.

General Index

Prosopographical Index